Sociology for a New Day

THOMAS FORD HOULT
Arizona State University

Sociology for a New Day

Random House **New York**

First Edition

9876543

Copyright © 1974 by Random House, Inc.

All rights reserved under International and Pan-American Copyright Conventions.
No part of this book may be reproduced in any form or by any means,
electronic or mechanical, including photocopying, without permission in writing
from the publisher. All inquiries should be addressed to Random House, Inc., 201
East 50th Street, New York, N.Y. 10022. Published in the United States by
Random House, Inc., and simultaneously in Canada by Random House of Canada
Limited, Toronto.

Library of Congress Cataloging in Publication Data

Hoult, Thomas Ford.
    Sociology for a new day.

Includes bibliographies.
    1. Sociology. I. Title. [DNLM: 1. Sociology. HM51 H838s 1974]
HM51.H67   301   73-17390
ISBN 0-394-31736-X

Manufactured in the United States of America.

Cover:

"The Sower" (June 1888) by Vincent van Gogh, courtesy Kröller-Müller
Stichting; typography by Gloria Gentile.

Photo credits:

P. 8: Allan L. Price/Rapho Guillumette

P. 36: Philip Teuscher

P. 58: Charles Gatewood

P. 80: Philip Teuscher

P. 96: Philip Teuscher

P. 120: Philip Teuscher

P. 146: Ray Ellis/Rapho Guillumette

P. 170: Bonnie Freer

P. 190: Bonnie Freer

P. 220: Bonnie Freer

P. 264: Bob Combs/Rapho Guillumette

P. 288: Bonnie Freer

Photo Editor: R. Lynn Goldberg

To Kit and Robin,

for whom the humanistic faith
has become a way of life.

...for ourselves and for humanity, comrades, we must turn over a new leaf, we must work out new concepts, and try to set afoot a new man.

Franz Fanon
— his last written words before dying of leukemia at age 36

Preface

My aim in preparing this book has been to provide a humanistically oriented introduction to the principles of sociology. But in writing such a work, one is immediately faced with a basic decision: Of the two aspects—humanistic perspective or sociological principles—which should receive prime emphasis? My decision was that since the book is meant as an introduction to a *principles* course, it should concentrate on those principles, adding humanistic insights where reasonably possible. Therefore, each chapter opens with a discussion of relevant principles and generally closes with a humanistic commentary.

Among the several interpretations of humanism, the emphasis I prefer is described in my introduction; the essence of my approach to humanism is the idea that the good life for all is most likely to be achieved when chances for individual self-development are realistically maximized. But adoption of this version of humanism does not imply a covert attempt to put down other interpretations that are more literary, psychological, or spiritual. Surely there is room for all types of workers in the humanistic vineyard.

Lest any unwarranted conclusions be drawn from the foregoing, I hasten to add two additional observations. The first is that my positive orientation to humanism does not mean that I therefore reject, out of hand—as do some humanists—such phenomena as the scientific method, behaviorism, or mathematical models. The cause of humanism is too important to risk rejecting any potential ally—scientific method especially, when properly understood and controlled, can be just such an ally.

The second additional observation is that the individualism emphasis in my humanistic stance does not lead me to an anarchist, libertarian ideological position. To me, it is utterly clear that the only really practical way to provide and protect opportunity for the many is through collective action; in contrast, so-called libertarianism benefits the privileged few alone. Therefore, I have arrived at an ideological stance that the late Arnold Kaufman termed *radical-liberal,* in many respects the polar opposite of libertarianism. Radical-liberalism is a political-economic orientation that is left-of-center activist, height-of-industry democratic-socialist, integrationist, and internationalist; it puts a heavy emphasis on the principle of the free marketplace of ideas, and therefore stresses civil liberties, rational analysis, openness to change, and the importance of liberal (that is, dogma-undermining) education.

With such an orientation, it will come as no surprise that my "humanistic commentary," where it appears, is often bitingly critical of many aspects of modern society. But the commentary does not add up to a muckraking attack on all that constitutes the present sociocultural order. To engage in such an attack would be to indulge in the extremism I find so repugnant when manifested by others—repugnant because its consequences, in social science and politics, are antithetical to rational analysis and humanitarian standards. As someone once remarked, heaven protect us from mindless true believers. We also need protection from the uncommitted who defer to anyone having power. Thus, as Max Weber indicated, what is imperative in both science and the political arena is people in whom are blended "a warm passion and a cool sense of proportion."

December 1973   T.F.H.

Contents

Introduction   **3**
   References   6

1. The Individual and the Group   **9**

   The Isolate   *10*
   Feral Children   *11*
   Sociology and Biology   *12*
   Intelligence   *14*
   Twin Studies   *18*
   Talent   *19*
   The Genetic Interpretation of I. Q.   *25*

   Summary   29
   References and Further Sources   30

2. Sex, Society, and Related Matters   **37**

   Mongoloid Children   *37*
   A Sociological Interpretation of Sexual
      Orientation   *40*

*Deviance and Conformity—a Learning
  Theory*   42
Reactions to Deviance   44
The Self   45

Determinism and Humanism   47
Summary   52
References and Further Sources   53

3. *The Sociological Point of View*   **59**

What Is Sociology?   59
The Historical Development of Sociology   61
Law of Three Stages   62

Comparative Disciplines   64

*Sociology and the Disciplines of Political Science
  and Economics*   64
Sociology and the Discipline of History   65
Sociology and the Discipline of Anthropology   66
Sociology and the Discipline of Psychology   67
Sociology and the Discipline of Social Work   69
Sociology as Pure Science   69
The Structural-Functional Point of View   70
Challenges to the Value-Free Position   71

Humanistic Sociology   74
References and Further Sources   77

4. *Sociology and Science*   **81**

Scientific Method and Human Welfare   81
The Problem of Objectivity   84
Sociology and Scientific Method   87

Controlling Variables   88
Mistaken Control of Variables   89
Empiricism—Merits and Demerits   90

References and Further Sources 92

5. *The Sociocultural Order:*
   Basic Concepts 97

   The Social Order 97

   Social Interaction 97
   Groups, Communities, and Society 98
   Just and Unjust Societies 100
   Ideal Types 101
   Primary and Secondary Groups 102

   The Cultural Order 104

   Culture 104
   Cultural Relativism 104
   Subcultures 105
   Culture as a Complex of Values 105
   Values 106
   Norms as Values Regarding Behavior 107
   Kinds of Norms 107
   Values Regarding People 110

   The Sociocultural Order and Freedom 112
   Sociology and Revolution 112
   Sociology and Counterrevolution 113
   The Task of Humanistic Sociology 115

   References and Further Sources 116

6. *Social Differentiation* 121

   Introduction 121

   My Fair Lady Revisited 121
   Three Dimensions of Social Differentiation 122
   The Life and Death Aspects of Social
   Differentiation 124

Status and Role   **128**

Status   *128*
Ascribed and Achieved Statuses   *129*
Role   *131*
Bureaucracy   *132*

Social Stratification   **133**

General Observations   *133*
Caste Stratification   *134*
The Estate System of Stratification   *136*
The Class System of Stratification   *137*
Classless Society   *140*

References and Further Sources   **142**

7. *Social Stratification in the United States*   ***147***

Caste in the United States   **148**
Characteristics of Major Strata in the United States   **151**

The Lower Class   *151*
Middle America   *152*
The Privileged Middle Class   *154*
The Upper Class   *155*

Vertical Mobility in the United States   **157**
A Major Trend in Stratification   **160**
A Humanistic Comment on Social Stratification   **163**
References and Further Sources   **166**

8. *Institutionalization: Process and Consequence*   ***171***

Sumner's Approach   *171*
MacIver's Approach   *172*

A New Approach   173
Bureaucracy and Institutionalization   177
Institutional Variability   178
The Institutionalization Process   181
Satirizing Institutions   183
Institutionalization and Humanistic Values   185

References and Further Sources   187

9. Three Major Institutions: Religion,
    Marriage and the Family, Education   191

Religion   192
Marriage and the Family   201

    Types of Marriage   201
    Types of Families   202

Education   205
References and Further Sources   214

10. Political-Economic Institutions   221

Introduction   221

    Two Theories of Political-Economic Power   222
    Power, Legitimacy, and Disorder   223
    The Spectrum of Political-Economic Systems   225

Political-Economic Élites   230
Keeping the Peace   232

    The American Empire   232
    National Security   233
    Law and Order   236
    Role of the Court System   238
    American Jails and Prisons   239

Constitutional Government   **239**

  Ideal vs. Real   239
  Civil Liberties   240

Western Economics   **244**

  Free Enterprise   244
  Keynesian Economics and Beyond   247
  Distribution of Income   250

Summary and Commentary   **254**
References and Further Sources   **257**

**11. *Ecology, Demography, and Humanity's
    Home***   ***265***

  The Radicalism of Modern Ecology   266
  The Population Problem   270
  The Problem of Technology   273
  The Limits to Growth   276
  Critics of Zero Growth   278
  Two Scenarios   280
  Our Ecological Future   282
  References and Further Sources   285

**12. *Collective Behavior and Sociocultural
    Change***   ***289***

  I. Collective Behavior   **289**

  Two Forms of Collective Behavior   290
  Elementary Collective Behavior   290
  Elementary Collective Groups   292
  Social Movements   295
  The Importance of Collective Behavior   298

II. Sociocultural Change   **299**

  Theories of Change   *299*
  Induced Change   *301*

  References and Further Sources   **308**

Glossary   *311*
Index   *325*

Sociology for a New Day

Introduction

The guiding theme of this book's approach to the principles of sociology is the following three-part proposition:

- Sociology is worthy of support only to the degree that it serves humanitarian ends.
- Such ends are best served when the sociologist assumes a role analogous to that of a skilled medical diagnostician who, though often describing wholesome situations, for therapeutic reasons concentrates on a complete portrayal of pathological conditions.
- In the same way, the sociologist who wishes to be relevant to the needs of the age will, without necessarily neglecting general descriptions of society, put a heavy emphasis on penetrating analyses of the seriously unjust, hurtful, and repressive aspects of human social life, boldly describing such aspects in the hopes that effective remedial action will be generated and facilitated.

The type of sociology indicated is often termed "humanistic" or "radical," depending upon the particular propensities of given observers. I prefer the term *humanistic* (or humanitarian), reserving the term radical—meaning deep, fundamental, going to the root of the matter—to designate the depth of analysis or action that is usually required to achieve humanistic goals.

As used here, the term *humanistic* means belief that every person has potential worth and should have the opportunity to develop to the greatest extent possible consistent with the development of others.*

---

* This is not a full definition of humanism, according to Paul Kurtz (1969:9–11); he says it is merely one among several basic principles that many humanists agree are essential to a meaningful definition of their philosophy. It is, nevertheless, the aspect of humanism that I wish to emphasize in the present context.

Corollary to this belief is the conviction that this philosophy can be implemented only in a society where equalitarianism and justice are basic values, and where truly democratic controls, due process, free inquiry, and free speech and press are meaningfully supported. A humanistic sociology, therefore, is one that helps a society to develop these characteristics. This means that humanistic sociology is and must be value-committed, in contrast to the value-free emphasis of the past; and its practitioners, to be effective, must typically engage in radical analysis and action. But opting for such analysis and action does not imply that sentimentalism should replace science; it does not suggest that the humanistic perspective requires one to be soft-headed; it does not take ". . . the distrust of reason as its model" (Bendix, 1970:741).* As will be indicated in due time, properly controlled science can be an invaluable aid in reaching humanistic goals.

It is obvious that humanism is a sheer faith; that is, it cannot be proven in any empirical sense. It, therefore, has no more scientific basis than does traditional religion. But to its adherents, it is an utterly pragmatic philosophy; it is a version of enlightened self-interest, springing from a conviction that alternatives to it contribute to a social order doomed to degradation, if not total destruction. One of the most likely alternatives today is the technocratic state conducted by "experts" who have but one prime value—mechanical efficiency. Such experts are manipulative types who, for example, did medical experiments in Nazi death camps, permitted known black American syphilis victims to die untreated so that specialized autopsy knowledge might be increased, and who today, under sponsorship of the U.S. Department of Defense, do health- and life-threatening research on human beings without duly informed consent (Jacobs, 1972).

What can we do about the situation? Perhaps nothing, given the withdrawal tendencies and political indifference of some of today's youth, together with other depressing political, economic, and ecological conditions. But if anything practical can be done, then the humanistic answer is to build a new society where justice is the watchword and where all individuals have a maximum of freedom tempered by a sense of responsibility for the welfare of others. Humanistic sociology's part in building such a society lies primarily in providing analysis and measuring techniques that pinpoint sources of injustice so observers are inspired to respond enthusiastically to appropriate calls to action. But in providing information about social situations, humanistic sociologists are incon-

---

* Full citation information is contained in the alphabetical listing which follows each chapter and this introduction.

sistent if they do not remain constantly alert to the possibility that even the most humanistically intended studies can be used for demagogic purposes. Therefore, humanistic sociologists must insist that the only endeavors, including those that are research-oriented, worth supporting are those permeated with a humanitarian spirit.

REFERENCES

Bendix, Reinhard
　1970　"Sociology and the distrust of reason." American Sociological Review 35 (October): 831–843.

Jacobs, Paul
　1972　"The Cabinet of Dr. DOD." New York Review of Books 18 (March 9): 32–34.

Kurtz, Paul (ed.)
　1969　Moral Problems in Contemporary Society: Essays in Humanistic Ethics. Englewood Cliffs, New Jersey: Prentice-Hall.

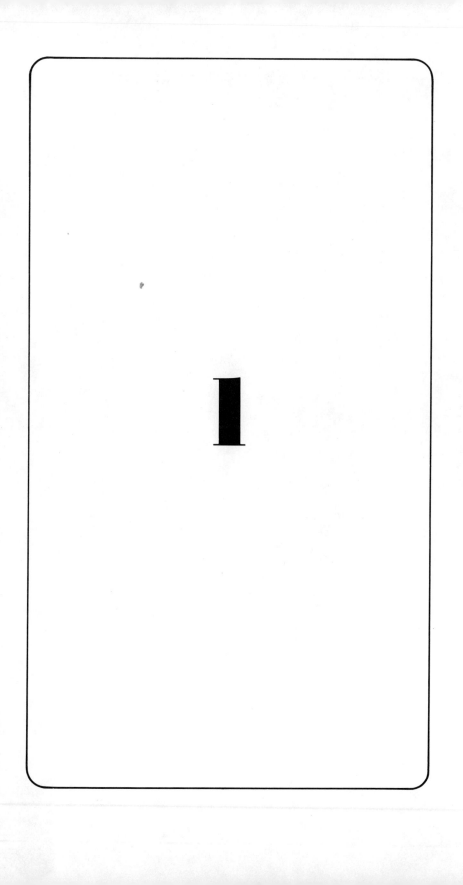

The Individual and
the Group

This and the following chapter will focus attention on personality development. Beginning an introductory sociology text with such material is unusual; almost all the basic texts begin with an abstract discussion of the history of sociology and methods of study. These matters, however, seem significant only to those who see the relevance of sociology to themselves personally. It is hoped that these two chapters will constitute a demonstration of such relevance; the intent is to show the reader that the most important aspect of one's life—his personality—is a product of the influences that sociology studies.

Sociology is concerned with all the *social* factors in human life. The importance of these factors is illustrated by the way that personality is affected by *society* (the group) and *culture* (the way of life of a group). A striking example is "Anna," the second illegitimate child of an illiterate farm girl. When Anna was born, her mother's father was outraged by his daughter's waywardness. Fearful of her stern parent, the daughter attempted to hide her child, first by giving her away and later by hiding her in an attic-like room. Anna remained in this room until she was six years of age.

During that time, she received practically no care whatsoever, aside from being given milk to drink. Apparently, that was her total food intake. Her mother, a sturdy woman who worked regularly in the fields, did nothing more for her daughter. Anna was not talked to, fondled, cleaned, picked up, handled, or in any way cared for. She simply lay in the room in the midst of her own filth.

9

The Isolate   In sociological terminology, Anna was an *isolate* who was deprived of normal *socialization*. An isolate is a child who has not been subjected to human social influences; socialization is the entire process whereby young people learn to behave in ways generally acceptable within their own sociocultural system.

When discovered, Anna could not walk, talk, smile, gesture, or even crawl. In short, she manifested none of the behavior that is uniquely human. However, four and a half years later—when she died as a result of disease—Anna could walk and run, play, dress, fit into a social situation, and talk. She learned these human behaviors even though, after being discovered, she was not placed into any environment where she could be given special compensatory socialization.

Kingsley Davis' descriptions of Anna's discovery and progress (1940; 1947) have become classics in sociological literature because her case so spectacularly illustrates a fundamental principle of sociology. The principle states: Only to the degree that infants are reared in human society can they learn to manifest the attributes that are generally regarded as the special mark of the human being.

This principle is further illustrated by another isolate described by Davis (1947). "Isabelle," as she was called, was the illegitimate daughter of an apparently retarded deaf mute who, along with the child, was placed in a darkened room apart from the regular household. For approximately six years, Isabelle was kept under inhumane conditions, isolated almost totally from normal society. When discovered, Isabelle could not talk at all—she also appeared to be deaf. She could not walk, but rather skittered about on her misshapen legs. The specialists who examined her said she was hopelessly uneducable. However, two clinical psychologists decided to see what could be done with Isabelle and saw to it that she was very carefully socialized. Two and a half years later, Professor Davis personally observed Isabelle. His conclusion was that she appeared to be a "very bright, cheerful, energetic little girl," close to being developmentally equal with her age mates.

Helen Keller is a well-known example of an isolate. Although she was not bodily isolated, until she was seven years old her blindness and deafness totally cut her off from beneficial social interaction. She was a " 'living nullity,' aware only of tactile sensations, vibrations and scents, dwelling in a world . . . that was a 'no-world' " (Brooks, 1956:6). As she later described it, she was in a state of anarchy:

> All she knew was that she was impelled to seek food and warmth, helpless and alone as she was in a deep dark pit. She was to compare herself in these hopeless silent years with a ship groping its way in a dense fog at sea, only she, with beating heart, waiting for something to happen, had no way of knowing that harbours existed (Brooks, 1956:7).

When first observed by her teacher, Anne Macy Sullivan, young Helen acted like a totally ungovernable wild animal although she was almost seven. But, with infinite patience, Miss Sullivan began teaching her charge a special version of the manual method of communication commonly used by the deaf.

The description of Helen's first known excursion into abstract thought is a thrilling episode (Keller, 1954:35–37; 253; 256–257). Miss Sullivan had been struggling for weeks to increase Helen's meager vocabulary. The difficulty was that though the child could spell out the names of a variety of objects, it was clear she had no understanding of what she was doing. Her confusion and limitations were especially apparent when it came to related terms such as "mug," "milk," and "drink." Thus, training was stymied until, one morning while washing, she wanted to know the name for "water." Miss Sullivan described the sequel:

> When she wants to know the name of anything, she points to it and pats my hand. I spelled "w-a-t-e-r" and thought no more about it until after breakfast. Then it occurred to me that with the help of this new word I might succeed in straightening out the "mug–milk" difficulty. We went out to the pump-house, and I made Helen hold her mug under the spout while I pumped. As the cold water gushed forth, filling the mug, I spelled "w-a-t-e-r" in Helen's free hand. The word coming so close upon the sensation of cold water rushing over her hand seemed to startle her. She dropped the mug and stood as one transfixed. A new light came into her face. She spelled "water" several times. Then she dropped on the ground and asked for its name and pointed to the pump and the trellis, and suddenly turning round she asked for my name. I spelled "Teacher" (Keller, 1954:256–257).

Then, greatly excited, Helen led her teacher around the farmyard and through the house, asking for the names of numerous items. Within a few hours, the child added fully thirty words to her vocabulary. But, far more important, she had grasped the abstract idea that everything has a name. The ability to understand an abstraction is uniquely associated with humans. Other animals can learn to identify a vast array of objects; however, as far as we know, only humans can think abstractly in any complex way. Thus, in effect, Miss Sullivan watched the birth of a human being when she stood with Helen in the pumphouse. Miss Sullivan was the appropriate midwife since it was her social interaction with Helen that changed the child from a "nullity" to a full-fledged human.

Feral Children   Occasionally there are news accounts about a special type of isolate technically termed a *feral*. These are children who have allegedly been reared by animals other than humans. But it should be noted that evidence for the existence of true ferals is most unsatisfactory. The best known case is that of Amala and Kamala, often termed the "wolf-children of India."

During the 1920s, a Christian missionary announced that he had found two girls, about eighteen months and three years old respectively, in a wolf den, and that the children's behavior suggested they had been reared by wolves almost from the time of birth (Singh and Zingg, 1942). Despite elaborate descriptions of the girls, pictures of their subsequent development at different stages, and widespread acceptance of the authenticity of their existence, sociologist W. F. Ogburn was not satisfied with available information. During the 1950s, he decided, upon retirement, to investigate for himself and, to that end, went to India. While there, he researched the Amala–Kamala case in lengthy detail, publishing the results in a monograph, *On the Trail of the Wolf-Children* (1959). He also studied *The Wolf Boy of Agra* (Ogburn et al., 1959). The essence of Professor Ogburn's findings was that there is not a trace of respectable evidence for the existence of feral children. In the case of both the Agra boy and Amala–Kamala, the popular reports were an amalgam of misinterpretation, unwarranted supposition, and press exaggeration, all interspersed with copious amounts of wishful thinking and superstition, not to speak of possible fraud.

In one sense, Ogburn's research is disappointing, for certainly feral children would be particularly convincing evidence of human adaptability. There is, however, plenty of other evidence for that adaptability; one need not resort to myths to substantiate it.

Sociology and Biology   Over the years, building on a great variety of evidence including that on isolates, the sociological view of the nature of human nature has been developed. At first, this sociological view was highly tinged with biological presumptions. One sociological pioneer, F. H. Giddings, reportedly even adhered to the theory that such behavior patterns as prostitution and pauperism are instinctive (Adams, 1955:13), with *instinct* being defined as a biologically inherited predisposition to react to particular stimuli in a particular way. However, as more and more evidence was accumulated, it gradually became apparent that humans have evolved to a stage where their central trait is plasticity. It is this characteristic that, in one form or another, is heavily stressed in the now long prevailing sociological interpretation of human nature. In Charles Bolton's words:

> If there is anything that is clear about the nature of human nature, it is the enormous flexibility and plasticity of human development (1967:100).

Thus, the modern sociologist agrees with his professional forebears—that humans are a product of their biological heritage. But the sociologist today stresses that what people normally inherit is not specific traits or instincts—such as "natural aggression" claimed for humankind by playwrights-turned-amateur-anthropologists who write flamboyantly about "naked apes" and an alleged "innate longing to touch"—but, rather, a potential for learning to become what we call human. As Charles Horton Cooley put it long ago, ". . . human nature is not something existing separately in the individual. . . . Man does not have it at birth; he cannot acquire it except through fellowship, and it decays in isolation" (1909:29–30). Robert E. Park stated the point thus:

Man is not *born* human (Park and Burgess, 1921:76; italics added).

Thus, the essence of the sociological view of human nature is that it is socially learned behavior manifested by an organism whose most important characteristic is a great capacity for adaptability. A logical deduction is that all human beings born with biological equipment falling in the broad range of "normal" can be trained to manifest almost an infinite variety of attributes. The sociologist, therefore, typically pays little attention to biological characteristics; he sees the biological state of the human as a given.

It is important to understand what it means, and what it does not mean, to say that the sociological view sees the biological state of man as a given. It *means* that sociologists concentrate on social factors, leaving the study of other factors to specialists; it does *not* mean that sociologists deny the importance of biological matters. It is, after all, biological heritage that constitutes the base of human potential. Thus, despite sociological emphasis on social aspects of environment, no responsible sociologist would claim that a child whose brain has been badly damaged before birth or by a grossly inadequate diet could, even with special training and care, be turned into a normally functioning human being.

But, of course, most people are born with physical equipment that falls within a normal range and are thus potential subjects for social influences that can turn them into the proverbial silk purses or sow's ears. This principle is illustrated by the following two-part discussion—intelligence, twins, talent, and genes which we will discuss in this chapter, and mongolism, sociological interpretation of sexual orientation, learning theory, deviance and conformity, the self, and determinism presented in Chapter 2. The discussion will concentrate on the impact society and culture have on personality development. However, this deliberate stress on just one direction of the two-directional relationship between individuals and society should not be interpreted to mean that individuals are only tools of society as such. Individuals can also be prime movers, as is indicated in the sociological specialty called *social psychology*. Social psychologists concentrate on a systematic and searching study of the relationships between individuals and the sociocultural order. Such relationships are the concern of this chapter and the next; therefore, taken together, they are actually an essay in social psychology. The presentation, though seemingly extensive, is limited by space to an indication of just some of the major directions and dimensions of the many aspects of social psychology.

Intelligence   One of the principles of sociology has long been that what we measure and call human intelligence is a broad coping ability, including the capacity to adapt to new situations, to perceive and understand relationships, and to acquire new, without losing grasp of old, knowledge. Some aspects of such coping ability can, it seems clear, be measured roughly by scales known as I.Q. tests. The limited applicability of these tests will be discussed later.

The idea that intelligence is essentially learned, hence, varies significantly with environment, contrasts sharply with the belief, on the part of some, that 80 percent of intelligence is biological, physically inherited through the medium of *genes* (elements of the germ plasm that transmits hereditary characteristics). This genetic view of intelligence has had little widespread professional support since the first decade of the twentieth century, but defenders of the view appear from time to time and cause excitement. Two defenders received wide publicity in the late 1960s and early 1970s—Arthur Jensen, a psychologist at the College of Education, University of California, Berkeley, and William Shockley, a Stanford University physicist. These two men will pass from the scene, but they are representative of their type; hence, it is convenient to speak of the "Jensen–Shockley" thesis. It is important to note that this thesis is not unique to Jensen and Shockley. In essence, the thesis is now accepted by all who put stress on the alleged physical aspects of intelligence (for example, Herrnstein, 1971; Eysenck, 1971).

The Jensen–Shockley genetic interpretation of human intelligence claims that the average 15-point I.Q. differential between black and white Americans is largely immutable because it is basically inborn. This is why, Jensen said, "Compensatory education has been tried and it apparently has failed" (Jensen 1969:2). Shockley asked the National Academy of Sciences to sponsor a test of the hypothesis that intelligence differences among racial groups are biologic in nature. His request was denied by the members of the NAS, prompting a nationally syndicated columnist, Jenken Lloyd Jones, to ask a question that was probably asked by numerous others:

Dr. Shockley doesn't ask that his views be accepted. He asks that they be tested.

What's unreasonable about that?

The answer to the question appeared in the form of a letter-to-the-editor written by a sociologist. He said that what was unreasonable about Shockley's desire for a test of his views could best be suggested by an analogy:

> . . . Let us imagine that I, as an outsider to physics, propose that physicists seriously test a proposition based on Newtonian principles. Physicists across the land would simply laugh at my naïveté. They would point out that Newtonian physics went out with the Victorian age. . . .
>
> This is exactly the way that sophisticated behavioral scientists regard the proposal to give a serious test to the heredity versus environment idea. Since 1910 we have accumulated a mountain of data to show that people with normal biological equipment are almost infinitely malleable.
>
> The data have become increasingly impressive as the years have rolled by. Therefore, we find it difficult to take seriously those few who, getting far out of their depth, want to test once again the ancient and largely outmoded instinct theories. It is as if someone were to propose that medical research should revert to the miasma theory of disease which prevailed before Pasteur developed germ theory . . . (*Arizona Republic*, August 6, 1971).

The "mountain of data" mentioned in the quoted letter includes studies varying greatly in nature and in scientific exactitude. One of the studies, conducted by Professor Jane R. Mercer (1971), is a recent representation of responsible research efforts. Professor Mercer's study was based on findings of another project that concentrated on distribution of mental retardation in Riverside, California. Concern arose because so many more black and Chicano children, compared to Anglo, were retarded. The question was: Are ordinary diagnostic procedures biased and therefore misleading?

Using a carefully drawn sample to represent all the people living in Riverside, and with specially developed scales to compare with the findings of standard I.Q. tests, the researchers reached several major conclusions. One was

> . . . the I.Q. tests now being used by psychologists are Anglocentric. They tend to measure the extent to which an individual's background is similar to that of the modal, cultural configuration of American society (p. 12).

As a result of this conclusion, Mercer decided to study two different samples of persons to determine amount of variance in I.Q. scores that could be explained *solely* by obvious sociocultural factors. Her findings in this part of the study were that known sociocultural variables alone account for between 25 and 32 percent of I.Q. score variation; undetected sociocultural variables may, of course, account for still more variance. A related finding was that Chicano school children with higher I.Q. test scores tend to come from less crowded homes and have mothers who want their children to have some higher education. This is also true of the black children with higher I.Q.s.

> Thus the more the family is like the modal sociocultural configuration of the community, the higher the I.Q.s of the Black and Chicano children on the [given I.Q. test] . . . (p. 16).

Even more significant: "When social background was held constant there was no difference between the measure of intelligence of Chicano and Anglo children" (p. 17). The situation was just as dramatic for the black children who were studied. ". . . Black children who came from family backgrounds comparable to the modal patterns for the community, did just as well on the Wechsler Intelligence Scale for Children as the children on whom the norms were based" (p. 12).

In short, the Mercer study found that when sociocultural differences were held constant, there were no measurable intelligence differences between racial groups.

The practical consequences of the Mercer study became evident when it prompted a rediagnosis of 268 children in the study area; they were in classes for the educable mentally retarded in two school districts. It was concluded that approximately 75 *percent* of the children would not have been placed in special education if their adaptive behavior and sociocultural backgrounds had been sufficiently considered when they were originally assessed.

> When they were taken into account the proportion of children diagnosed as mentally retarded from each ethnic group was approximately the same as the proportion of children from that ethnic group in the total public school population (Mercer 1971:23).

The same general results have been suggested by a multitude of other studies. In 1909 Alfred Binet, the French psychologist who created the first useful intelligence test which, revised as the Stanford–Binet, remains the standard instrument, wrote:

> Some recent philosophers appear to have given their moral support to the deplorable verdict that the intelligence of an individual is a fixed quantity, a quantity that cannot be augmented. We must protest and act against this brutal pessimism. We shall endeavor to show it has no foundation whatsoever.

He added, in connection with a discussion of his experimental teaching of retarded children:

> A child's mind is like a field for which an expert farmer has advised a change

in the method of cultivating, with the result that in place of desert land, we now have a harvest. It is in this particular sense, the only one which is significant, that we say that the intelligence of children may be increased. One increases that which constitutes the capacity to learn, to improve with instruction (Skeels, 1940:281–282).

The first extensive evidence regarding the possible importance of learned aspects of intelligence appeared after World War I. All the American soldiers participating in that conflict were given an intelligence test and classified as either alpha (literate) or beta (illiterate). Observers were not surprised to find that in this classification blacks, in general, scored significantly lower than whites; such a finding was in keeping with the popular stereotype. Later, however, it was found that some *northern* blacks, considered as a group, scored higher than some groups of *southern* whites. Still later, anthropologist Otto Klineberg published the details of his finding that black school children in northern cities had I.Q. scores directly proportional to the length of time their families had lived away from the South (Klineberg, 1935). As a result, the I.Q. test became questionable as the only valid indicator of intelligence.

This question prompted many studies; one, done by Speer, reported (1940) that when children of feeble-minded mothers are tested for intelligence, the older they are when tested, the lower their I.Q. will be, suggesting that at least certain forms and aspects of lower intelligence are *acquired*, not *inborn*. Related findings were reported by Marie Skodak and Harold Skeels in a study published in 1949. They described the fourth and final follow-up examination of a group of children adopted before they were six months of age. The investigators found that the "true" mothers of the children had an average I.Q. of 85.7, whereas the average I.Q. of their offspring, measured at 13 and one-half years of age, was somewhere between 107 and 117 (the range being due to different results obtained on two forms of the Stanford–Binet test). The children's I.Q.s were comparable to that of their adoptive parents, judging by educational and occupational level of the parents. Skodak and Skeels concluded:

> The intellectual level of the children has remained consistently higher than would have been predicted from the intellectual, educational, or socioeconomic level of the true parents, and is equal to or surpasses the mental level of own children in environments similar to those which have been provided by the foster parents (pp. 116–117).

A similar result was found in Milwaukee, Wisconsin by Professor Rick Heber. In 1967, he and other specialists began working with a group of children living with their nearly illiterate parents in a slum having the dubious distinction of a much higher mental retardation rate than any other area in the city. A "total saturation" technique was used—"The specialists intervened very early and with a variety of devices that reached both children and parents" (Welsh, 1971:1)—since other research has shown that dealing with the children alone, by just enriching the schools for example, does not make a significant difference for most children (see James S. Coleman, et al.—Equality of Educational Opportunity, 1966:21–22). After 42 months, children in Heber's "active stimulating" group averaged 33 I.Q. points higher than children of a like group not specially handled. It remains to be seen if such gains are permanent. Other projects of a similar nature (although with intervention beginning later and not so extensive or intense) have shown that early gains are not maintained when children are returned to an environment that has limited opportunity and stimulation (Welsh, 1971:2).

Twin Studies   Some observers, convinced that biological conditions are the most important bases of personality, are fond of referring to the results of certain twin studies. These studies indicate that people have similar I.Q.s to the degree that they are biologically related to one another (Erlenmeyer–Kimling and Jarvik, 1963). The studies show that I.Q.s of identical twins are characteristically very similar; there is less similarity when fraternal twins are compared, and still less among ordinary siblings. Also, the similarity decreases as regularly as the relationship becomes more distant. This correlation indicates—according to those who have what might be termed a biological orientation—the genetic basis of what is measured by I.Q. tests.

However, a socioculturally oriented person can point to the same studies and assert that the closer the physical relationship of people, the more they are likely to be exposed to a similar environment. Therefore, it should be expected (given the learned nature of what is measured by intelligence tests) that identical twins would have highly similar I.Q.s. With reference to the studies showing that even separated identical twins have like I.Q.s, the sociological suggestion is that, given their genetic sameness and, therefore, similar appearance, identical twins tend to evoke like interaction responses, even in different settings, thus often developing roughly similar personality traits. Further, when twins are separated, adoption is usually part of the picture; and adoption agencies, at least until recently, attempted to put children in homes socially similar to those of the biological parents. It is therefore not surprising that separated twins are so often quite alike.

The point is that test results that are correlated with a biological relationship do not *prove* anything about the *cause* of the correlation. On the contrary, we know from adoption studies and others that measurements of I.Q. can vary tremendously depending on social factors.

This was demonstrated in a classic study of identical twins (Newman, 1940:Chap. 15). The results of this study by Horatio Newman and his colleagues were particularly significant, for the investigators were biologists. They found that separated identical twins had I.Q. differences as high as 24 points, depending upon the degree of difference of environment. This is a large difference indeed considering that there is only a 20 point difference between normal I.Q. and that which is usually interpreted as indicative of mental retardation.

Talent   It has long been accepted by many people that talent such as artistic ability is largely inborn. For example, in a widely sold introductory psychology text, by E. R. Hilgard, a full page is devoted to a graphical depiction of five generations of the Bach family, showing that approximately 60 percent of the male members of that family earned their living primarily from music (Hilgard, 1962:433). The caption reads, "The unusually high percentage of musicians in the Bach family seems to point to the inheritance of musical talent. . . ." However, the prevalence of a given occupation in a family proves little about inborn abilities—would anyone, observing that 60 percent of the male members of a given family are teachers, assert that teaching is somehow genetically inherited?

The sociological interpretation of talent, like that of human behavior in general, prompts sociologists to set genetic questions aside because previous answers to most of those questions indicated they were hardly relevant to people with normal physical attributes. Instead, the sociological approach is, in effect, to ask and answer these two queries: 1) What social conditions, if any, are highly correlated with a particular talent? and 2) Are the correlations, when found, such that the relevant social conditions appear to be a sufficient causal explanation for the talent? If the talent in question is music, then it may be significant that children reared in families where music is very much emphasized tend to become musically oriented, at the least, and often talented. Is this due to environment or heredity? The question could be answered conclusively by ascertaining the musical talent of a representative sample of musicians' infants who are given up for adoption. At the same time, the sociological hypothesis is that such children would be no more musical, on the average, than children in general. Predicting such a finding would be prompted by theoretical considerations and by the knowledge (already in hand) that musical essentials such as hearing pitches can be cultivated by training in interval recognition (tone differences).

The sociological view of artistic talent does not apply just to family situations. The point has been illustrated by the experience of Shinichi Suzuki, a famous Japanese teacher of music (Kendall, 1966). Shortly after World War II, Suzuki decided to put to the test his conviction that musical ability is purely a function of learning. He, therefore, chose a large number of children without regard to musical inclination, and, with a special technique he had developed, trained every one of them— *without exception*—to be excellent string musicians. Such consistent success would be hard to explain if musical talent is largely inborn.

Suzuki received widespread acclaim when he began to sponsor a yearly Spring Festival during which up to 1,800 students, ranging from age 5 to 13, simultaneously and in perfect unison, without any joint practice and largely playing solely by ear, expertly performed such numbers as Bach's difficult Double Violin Concerto. This very impressive result is achieved with a teaching method called "listen and play," which involves training parents along with their children. It stresses the fun aspects of musical performance, subordinating the study of theory until children are so experienced that they are psychologically committed to the art of music. They are "hooked," so to speak, before they are expected to learn basic techniques that are boring and, thus, unrewarding to those without some established basis for interest. "Consider Wolfgang Mozart, Jascha Heifetz, and others we call prodigies," string instruments Professor Clifford A. Cook has written. "Their parents followed exactly these procedures!" (Quoted in prospectus for Suzuki's "1966 Talent Education Tour.")

Another example of the relationship between learning and talent is provided by numerous children whose parents decide in advance to make their offspring geniuses and use special training procedures to accomplish this purpose. Philosopher—economist John Stuart Mill (1806–1873) was an outstanding result of such training. His father, historian James Mill, was philosophically committed to the "tabula rasa" principle— since man is born as a blank tablet, any normal, healthy child ·can be made a genius or a moron depending on how the child is socialized. James Mill decided he wanted a genius in the family and, therefore, isolated his son John for this purpose. Isolation was essential, in James Mill's mind, because he felt that, in order to succeed, he would have to make study the be-all and end-all of existence for the boy— which would not be the case if John Stuart Mill discovered there were other things in life than Latin declensions and algebraic formulae. Young Mill was kept from any interaction with his peers until he was about fourteen years old. His days consisted solely of reading, writing, and study, supplemented by discussions with his father and his father's gifted friends.

Mill later attributed all his intellectual gifts to his father's teaching methods:

> If I had been by nature extremely quick of apprehension, or had possessed a very accurate and retentive memory, or were of a remarkably active and energetic character, the trial would not be conclusive; but in all these natural

gifts I am rather below than above par; what I could do, could assuredly be done by any boy or girl of average capacity and healthy physical constitution; and if I have accomplished anything, I owe it, among other fortunate circumstances, to the fact that through the early training bestowed on me by my father, I started, I may fairly say, with an advantage of a quarter of a century over my contemporaries (Mill, 1946:34–35).

There are a number of other examples of prodigies produced with the methods adopted by James Mill—such as Francis Galton, Karl Witte, J. W. Goethe, Gottfried Leibnitz, Blaise Pascal, Thomas Macaulay, Hugo Grotius, Samuel Butler, Adolf A. Berle, and Roger Sessions. A more recent case was widely reported in the daily press (AP dispatch, May 30, 1968). "Through college at 15," the headline read. The story related, "In the academic world, Edith finished grammar school in four years, skipped high school altogether. She begins a teaching fellowship at Michigan State University, hopes for her doctorate before she is 18." Her father, the story said, ". . . created in his home a total teaching environment; reading, mathematics, classical music, discussion and debate, chess, whatever he could glean from the world's literature and experience. Edith's days, from the time she cast aside her dolls, were filled with learning."

A more famous case was described by Norbert Weiner in the autobiography of his early years (1953). Professor Weiner first achieved fame as a child prodigy, having entered Tufts College at eleven years of age. When he was eighteen, he completed work for his Harvard Ph.D. in philosophy. Later, he became a prime mover in the development of computers and the entirely new field of cybernetics (the study of phenomena, ranging from the human brain to electromechanical devices, that are self-correcting by means of "feedback"). Weiner describes how his parents, who were linguists, decided in advance of the birth of their first child to handle the child so that it would become a genius. Later, Weiner's father stressed his conviction that his son ". . . was essentially an average boy who had had the advantage of superlative training" (Weiner, 1953:119). Such training was quite compatible with the life-style of the Weiners; their home, like that of the Mills, was an intellectual center. Weiner observed:

> I was brought up in a house of learning. My father was the author of several books, and ever since I can remember, the sound of the typewriter and the smell of the paste pot have been familiar to me. . . . I had full liberty to roam in what was the very catholic and miscellaneous library of my father. At one period or other the scientific interests of my father had covered most of the imaginable subjects of study (1953:62–63).

Professor Weiner's childhood experiences constitute a rather clear demonstration of the practical meaning of two key experimental psychology concepts, *positive reinforcement* and *negative reinforcement*. Positive reinforcement, relative to a given behavior, is anything which, *when it occurs,* is followed by an increase in the behavior; *negative reinforcement* is anything which, *when it is removed,* is followed by an increase in the behavior (Keller and Schoenfeld, 1950:61). The terms *positive reinforcement* and *negative reinforcement* are analogous to reward and punishment which, in formal sociological terminology, are referred to as *sanctions,* positive or negative respectively. Because of this similarity, the terms reinforcement and sanction, positive or negative, are used interchangeably in the present context (although the terms are not adequate substitutes for one another in work that involves precise measurement).

Reinforcement in the Weiner household, as in the Mill home, was associated with the child's extreme emotional dependence on his parents. "The very tone of my father's voice," Weiner observed, "was calculated to bring me to a high pitch of emotion, and when this was combined with irony and sarcasm, it became a knout with many lashes" (p. 68). A typical example of negative reinforcement is described by Weiner:

> . . . My father's way of teaching . . . was scarcely conducive to peace of mind. Every mistake had to be corrected as it was made. He would begin the discussion in an easy, conversational tone. This lasted exactly until I made the first . . . mistake. Then the gentle and loving father was replaced by the avenger of the blood. The first warning he gave me of my unconscious delinquency was a very sharp and aspirated "What!" and if I did not follow this by coming to heel at once, he would admonish me, "Now do this again!" By this time I was weeping and terrified (1953:67).

Despite such treatment, the father's knowledge and values were such that he seemed to his son ". . . a noble and uplifting figure, a poet at heart, amid the frigid and repressed figures of an uninspiring and decadent Boston" (Weiner, 1953:74). Therefore, Weiner wrote, "My taskmaster was at the same time my hero." With such an attitude, the father did not have to do anything elaborate for positive reinforcement— " 'All right,' or 'Very good, you can go and play now' " were sufficient (Weiner, 1953:94).

A New York observer, Leta Hollingworth, professor of education at Columbia University, sought more information on genius. By chance, she was introduced to an eight-year-old boy who tested 187 on the Stanford–Binet I.Q. test. The boy's clarity of thinking so impressed Professor Hollingworth that she spent the next twenty-three years looking for more youngsters with extremely high I.Q.s, and finally located twelve. Putting these cases together with nineteen previously reported, she wrote the beginnings of a volume entitled *Children Above 180 IQ Stanford–Binet, Origin and Development* (1942). She died before she could complete her analysis, but fortunately her husband, who was also a scholar, finished the study.

The Hollingworth book is written in a case study fashion, one example after another described in detail. The major message that one gleans from the accumulation of data is that all these children with very high I.Q.s, in addition to special talents, were associated with parents (or parental substitutes) who were, consistently, very intellectual and possessed of incredible drive—one facet of which became expressed in their creative domination over their offspring. Very often, the parent was saying, in effect, "I didn't rise to the top, but I will do it with my child substituting for me." It was typical of the parents to devise, as had James Mill and the elder Weiner, a total learning situation. The children characteristically had little free time to play; if they played at all, it was something like: "Today you may have an hour to play at four o'clock. You will play chess with Johnny. He is fifteen and will be a challenge to you. At five o'clock you will cease playing."

It would probably not be too difficult to do a Hollingworth-type study of what might be termed "athletic genius." We have all heard stories about great athletes who appear to be the product of special handling. The famous baseball star Mickey Mantle (1967) is a classic example. Both his father and grandfather had dreamed of being big league players; both were frustrated. But, in young Mickey they had somebody to sub for them. As soon as Mickey could stand he was supplied with a glove and taught to throw, catch, and bat. As he describes it in his own story, his father

> . . . was almost comic in his determination to make a baseball player out of his little boy. When I was still in the cradle, I had a knitted baseball cap; and a pair of his old baseball pants were whittled down to fit me before I was in kindergarten. I believe too that he put a baseball and a glove in my crib when I was still too new to do much more then chew at them (Mantle, 1967:11).

The reward and punishment system of the Mantle family motivated Mickey to practice prodigiously so he might increase his positive results and decrease the negative ones:

> No boy, I think, ever loved his father more than I did. . . . he worked hard to help me improve and he gave me good advice to follow and played with me when he had the chance. It wasn't the thought of riches and fame that drove me. . . . What did keep me driving hard, from the time I was ten, to hit the ball better and farther was first of all my own love for the game and then my love for my father (Mantle, 1967:11–12).

No doubt there are other individual examples such as the Mickey Mantle story.

There are also group examples. One is the prevalence of top-notch tennis players from Australia; another is the prowess of black Americans in basketball, baseball, and football; Indiana basketball players are still another; we also could cite hockey champions from Canada, long-distance runners from Finland, women athletes from the Soviet Union, soccer champions from Brazil, and so on. However, would anyone assert that perhaps Australians have a tennis gene, or that Canadians have special genes for hockey, and Brazilians for soccer? Is there anyone willing to assign black Americans a baseball–football–basketball gene, while asserting that they lack skiing, bowling, and golf genes, since blacks excel so exceptionally in the former sports and not in the latter? But even if we cannot say anything very meaningful about the possibility of such specialized genetic inheritance, we *can* say something positive about the unique rewards and facilities that are offered to hockey players in Canada, soccer players in Brazil, and track runners in Finland. And we *can* say something believable about the prejudice that long held back black Americans, except in selected athletic and artistic fields, thus channeling their hopes and energies with the result of uneven visibility.

The tennis situation in Australia is representative of what can be done to cultivate a given talent. In Australia, all school systems are set up in such a way that tennis playing is maximized, and the facilities for tennis and for developing oneself in tennis are available everywhere. *The Christian Science Monitor* (April 25, 1968) reported that for 30 cents each, in Sydney, Australia, youngsters can receive morning-long instruction at the finest tennis schools employing top professionals for coaching staffs. Accompanying this report was a picture reminiscent of those showing thousands of Chinese engaged in group calisthenics; it depicted a mass of tennis courts sprinkled with dozens upon dozens of youngsters clad in tennis outfits and stroking their racquets to improve their style.

In short, athletic talent rates seem to be highly correlated with particular social arrangements. However, anecdotal evidence such as that presented does not constitute scientific proof that social factors alone are sufficient to account for the distribution of various forms of talent. One of the important missing links is information about what may be termed the "non-cases." That is, we can come up with many examples of parents who decided to produce a skating champion, let us say, and who adopted successful measures as evidenced by the later wins of their child. But what about the parents who wanted to produce a champion and tried but failed? These cases do not become news, and there may be many of them; this we cannot measure. Therefore, all we can say for certain, at the moment, is that there seems to be a very strong association between the producing of geniuses of various kinds, on the one hand, and unique sociocultural pressures and opportunities, on the other. Whether or not these unique arrangements inevitably work is another question; the final answer to that may have to include a genetic component.

The Genetic Interpretation of I.Q.   In view of the foregoing discussion, it is perhaps now apparent why the so-called Jensen–Shockley thesis seems so gratuitous from a sociological point of view (with the "Jensen–Shockley thesis" being used simply as a convenient way to designate all those who believe that ordinary I.Q. differences are basically genetic). But gratuitous or not, the genetic interpretation of I.Q. has great appeal for many who believe in the established distribution of power and privilege; the idea seems to be that, if it can be proved people are essentially born what they become, then there is a biological rationale for a distributive system that results in sharp differences between haves and have-nots. Such an idea has vital implications for a host of education and welfare policies. Therefore, it is important to note that the genetic explanation of I.Q. differences among normal people is not just theoretically weak; it is at the present time not logically defensible. This point is well illustrated by the work of Arthur Jensen; his publications are representative of the biological view.

In support of his point of view, Jensen has collected and summarized a vast number of studies relating to his central idea (Jensen, 1972). He has done this work in a responsible and scientific way, in contrast to some of his critics who have gone so far as to demand that Jensen be silenced. Jensen's presentation of the accumulated evidence on I.Q. is enough to shake certain details of confidence of even the most dedicated "environmentalist," whom Jensen describes as the individual who holds out for the primacy of environmental factors "no matter what." But admiration for Jensen's professionalism and remarkable productivity does not eliminate two basic weaknesses I see in his work. The weaknesses in Jensenian data need particular attention because they are typical of the shortcomings characterizing almost all studies that make extravagant claims for the biological factors in I.Q.

The first aspect of weakness is methodological. The difficulty is that the entire structure of such work is dependent upon the general applicability of intelligence tests. *But they are not generally applicable* because they are culturally biased—an observation that has no pejorative intent. To speak of the "bias" of I.Q. tests is simply a way of referring to the fact that such tests reflect selected aspects of the sociocultural order. The selective bias of I.Q. tests is clearly indicated by items included in the two most widely used tests, the Stanford–Binet (1960 revision) and the three major forms of the Wechsler (preschool, child, and adult). This point cannot be adequately documented here since full-scale public analysis of the tests may undermine their validity. However, it is possible to describe a few random details of the tests, enough so that the general rationale is understood.

The Stanford–Binet and other I.Q. tests measure intelligence by asking those being tested to respond as correctly and appropriately as possible to a number of questions involving mathematical reasoning, the use of analogies, history, literature, and so forth. When eight- and nine-year-olds are tested, they achieve points by knowing the meaning of such words as Shetland, influenza, and foolish. Twelve-year-olds receive plus marks for knowing who Abraham Lincoln and Christopher Columbus were, for knowing what the Gulf Stream is, and for knowing the meaning of such words as grief, pity, and jealousy. Other positive responses for children are the correct use of words or concepts like sewer, maple leaf, paring knife, stucco, loquacious, proverb, and harmonious. Those who would indicate at least a modest I.Q. must also know the meaning of such words as Mars, brunette, and disproportionate. Still higher scores are achieved by knowing the meaning of mosaic, bewail, piscatorial, limpet, ambergris, achromatic, casuistry, homunculus, sudorific, parterre, and others. On the preschool Wechsler test, plus marks are given for knowing what cows are for, what shines at night, what is the color of rubies, what is the meaning of snap, castle, hero, nuisance, and missing. Test instructions are better understood if the child is familiar with the concept of blind alley or blocked path. Zero points are awarded if, in response to the question, "Why should you go to the toilet before going to bed?" a child answers "You've got to go." On the Wechsler test for children between the ages of 6 and 15, it is handy to know who Genghis Khan, Leif Ericson, and Roald Amundsen were, and to know who wrote *Romeo and Juliet*. A child also increases the test score if he or she can distinguish between liberty and justice and knows the meaning of hieroglyphic, lien, dilatory, traduce, aseptic, shilling, spangle, and mantis.

Knowledge about such little-known phenomena is no doubt handy for certain purposes and predictive of certain limited classes of behavior. But one is led to wonder how any logical person could possibly claim that a poor slum child, housed with a nonreading family, has low intelligence potential as evidenced by lack of acquaintance with these phenomena.

It is a fundamental methodological principle that any test is meaningfully applied only to populations similar to that in terms of which the test is worked out. Thus one cannot devise a social rank scale based on the furnishings of American living rooms and expect the scale to provide useful information about differences among Greek peasants. Yet this is precisely analogous to what Jensen–Shockley-type theorists do. They take measures of coping ability developed in terms of what is more-or-less standard for relatively privileged whites, and apply the measures to blacks who by definition—given the traditional patterns of segregation and discrimination—are generally disprivileged. As Marsh has noted:

> It would be equally wrong (if morally just) for Bushmen to devise a test of intelligence that included the tracking of game over rock and the instant recall of complex genealogies and then announce that the derisory scores obtained by "carefully matched" samples of Europeans "might well be due to genetic inferiorities" (1971:73—74).

There have been two types of attempts to circumvent the problems associated with the limited applicability of I.Q. tests. One attempt centers on the creation of what have been called "culture-fair" tests (Jensen, 1968); the other concentrates on differentiating between the phenotypic (individual characteristics discernible by means other than genetic study) and genotypic (purely genetic) aspects of I.Q. Neither type of attempt has yielded impressive results. Studies of the alleged different aspects of I.Q. have depended, in part, on the use of the tests, which, as indicated above, are culture-biased. Beyond this, it seems reasonable to assert that directly measuring genetic factors in I.Q., uncontaminated by environment, would necessitate giving the test at the instant of conception.

Meaningful culture-fair tests have not yet been produced and are not likely to be in the near future. Testing *in itself* is a culture-loaded idea, and testing always involves elements of interaction, manipulation, language, values, and attitudes, all of which are the very essence of culture. The naiveté of some proposals for culture-free tests is mystifying in the extreme. The latest example is a machine called a "neural efficiency analyzer." By indicating the speed of the brain's response to a flashing light, the machine supposedly indicates a subject's physical (inborn) ability to learn. A moment's contemplation, however, would bring to mind the elementary point that physical aspects of the body are highly influenced by thought processes ultimately grounded in the sociocultural order; therefore, there is no presently reasonable basis for believing that a brain's reaction speed is, alone among the bodily processes, unaffected by psychological and cultural factors. Furthermore, as admitted by John Ertl, developer of the neural efficiency analyzer, establishing standards for the analyzer's findings necessitates using correlation studies involving the I.Q. test—"At the moment, we can't get away from relating to the I.Q. test system" (Kappan Interview, 1972:91) —which brings one full circle.

Not all is lost, however! It is appropriate to use culture-biased tests under certain conditions. For example, if a particular I.Q. test has been developed among representative, white, middle-class Americans, then usually the test can be applied to such Americans in general. Stated more formally, it is scientifically defensible to use relevant culture-biased tests in any given investigation, including the study of I.Q., if those being tested are socially similar to those who were studied in connection with development of the test. But Jensen, for example, objects to this requirement on two grounds; first, he asserts that *social* similarity implies *gene* similarity and thus undermines any attempt to find the behavioral consequences of gene difference; and second, he says I.Q. tests are, in effect, color-blind—that is, not affected by the biological race of those being tested (Jensen, 1970b:424–430). Such objections to the similarity requirement suggest lack of awareness of the elementary point that the very heart of scientific method is elimination of all but known factors so that when comparisons are made one need not speculate about which factors are related to a particular effect.

There are other methodological shortcomings in Jensen's interpretations. For example, in answer to the criticism that black children, in comparison to white children, are reared in such a way that they are less motivated to respond to paper and pencil tests, Jensen asserted (when lecturing to a group of students at Arizona State University) that on an incentive test blacks get higher scores than whites and therefore, it is not a lack of *incentive* that causes the relatively poor performance of blacks on I.Q. tests. *However*, any incentive test that produces differential results by race must itself be culturally loaded.

Another example: Jensen points to the high I.Q. scores of American-born Jews as evidence of their *genetic* uniqueness (1969:70). But, he ignores the conflicting fact that the immediate genetic forebears of these Jews—their foreign-born parents—scored *below average* on the Stanford–Binet and other often-used I.Q. tests (Hirsch, 1926:290). It seems unlikely—to my mind—that there could be such a genetic alteration in one generation. On the other hand, it seems quite plausible that high achievement by *native*-born Jews, in contrast to *foreign*-born, is associated with the American environment that gives relatively free rein to the Western Jew's admiration for learning and accomplishment.

The second major difficulty with the Jensen–Shockley type of research is *psychological*. The problem is this: both Jensen and Shockley seem remarkably insensitive to some realities of the modern world. For example, they speak constantly of "Negroes" rather than of "blacks," and differentiate between "Mexicans" and "whites." They write about "dysgenic" (detrimental) birth rates among blacks, and Jensen asserts that the desire to equalize children's school performance is like attempting to "transmute base metals into gold" (Jensen, 1970a:20). Such expressions are what one would expect of those in the grip of negative stereotypes. This impression is further suggested by Jensen's favorable reaction to the proposal that if lighter-skinned blacks, in comparison with darker-skinned, have higher I.Q.s, then ". . . the hypothesis of a racial genetic difference in intelligence would be supported" (Jensen, 1972:191). This hypothesis is naïve when examined on both biological and sociological grounds in that it ignores the fact that minority group members, to the degree that they are integrated into the majority group, tend to share the outlook of the members of that group; and it presumes that races are purely biological entities whereas, in truth, as Marsh has put it, " 'Races' then are contrived *social* categories that bear scant scientific relation to those genetic traits they are supposed to possess" (1971:72).

SUMMARY

The study of isolates and of talent, especially the intellectual variety, prompts the sociologist to stress the adaptability of humans rather than their biological characteristics. Humans apparently learn to be what they become; their nature is thus not inborn, although of course the potential for becoming human has a genetic base. The importance of the adaptability principle becomes even more evident when one considers such questions as sex, education, deviance and conformity, and the self, all of which are discussed in the following chapter.

REFERENCES AND FURTHER SOURCES

Adams, Charles Hopkins
1955   "The Juke myth." Saturday Review 38 (April 2): 13, 48–49.

Bolton, Charles D.
1967   "Is sociology a behavioral science?" Pp. 95–108 in Jerome G. Manis
and Bernard N. Meltzer (eds.), Symbolic Interaction: A Reader in
Social Psychology. Boston: Allyn and Bacon.

Brooks, Van Wyck
1956   Helen Keller: Sketch for a Portrait. New York: Dutton.

**Coleman, James S., Ernest Q. Campbell, Carol J. Hobson, James
McPartland, Alexander M. Mood, Frederic D. Weinfeld, and
Robert L. York**
1966   Equality of Educational Opportunity. Washington, D. C.: Government
Printing Office.

Cooley, Charles Horton
1909   Social Organization: A Study of the Larger Mind. New York: Charles
Scribner's Sons.

Davis, Kingsley
1940   "Extreme social isolation of a child." American Journal of Sociology
45 (January): 554–565.

1947   "Final note on a case of extreme isolation." American Journal of
Sociology 52 (March): 432–437.

Erlenmeyer-Kimling, L. and Lissy F. Jarvik
1963   "Genetics and intelligence: a review." Science 142 (December): 1477–
1479.

Eysenck, Hans Jurgen
1971   The IQ Argument: Race, Intelligence and Education. New York:
Library Press.

Herrnstein, Richard
1971   "I.Q." The Atlantic 228 (September): 43–64.

Hilgard, Ernest R.
1962   Introduction to Psychology. New York: Harcourt, Brace and World.
Third Edition.

Hirsch, N.D.M.
1926   "A study of natio-racial mental differences." Genetic Psychology
Monographs 1: 231–406.

Hollingworth, Leta S.
    1942   Children Above 180 IQ Stanford-Binet: Origin and Development. New
            York: World Book.

Jensen, Arthur R.
    1968   "Another look at culture-fair tests." Pp. 50–104 in Western Regional
            Conference on Testing Problems, Proceedings 1968, Measurement for
            Educational Planning. Berkeley, California: Educational Testing
            Service.

    1969   "How much can we boost IQ and scholastic achievement?" Harvard
            Educational Review 39 (Winter): 1–123.

    1970a   "Race and the genetics of intelligence: a reply to Lewontin." Bulletin
            of the Atomic Scientists 26 (May): 17–23.

    1970b   "Selection of minority students in higher education." Toledo Law
            Review (Spring–Summer): 403–457.

    1972   Educability and Group Differences. London: Methuen. (Note: pp.
            references are to the earlier mimeographed version titled Genetics,
            Educability, and Subpopulation Differences.)

Kappan Interview
    1972   "Goodbye IQ, hello EI (ERTL index)." Phi Delta Kappan 64 (Octo-
            ber): 89–94.

Keller, Fred S. and William N. Schoenfeld
    1950   Principles of Psychology: A Systematic Text in the Science of
            Behavior. New York: Appleton-Century-Crofts.

Keller, Helen
    1954   The Story of My Life. Garden City, New York: Doubleday.

Kendall, John D.
    1966   What the American Music Educator Should Know About Shinichi
            Suzuki. Washington, D.C.: Music Educators National Conference.

Klineberg, Otto
    1935   Negro Intelligence and Selective Migration. New York: Columbia
            University Press.

Lewontin, Richard C.
    1970a   "Further remarks on race and the genetics of intelligence." Bulletin of
            the Atomic Scientists 26 (May): 23–25.

    1970b   "Race and intelligence." Bulletin of the Atomic Scientists 26 (March):
            2–8.

Mantle, Mickey
    1967   The Education of a Baseball Player. New York: Simon and Schuster.

Marsh, Alan
    1971   "Race, heredity and I.Q." New Community 1 (October): 71–74.

Mercer, Jane R.
    1971   "Pluralistic diagnosis in the evaluation of black and chicano children:

a procedure for taking sociocultural variables into account in clinical assessment." Paper presented to the meetings of the American Psychological Association, Washington, D.C., September 3–7.

Mill, John Stuart
1946　"Unwasted years: James Mill." Pp. 15–39 in Houston Peterson (ed.), Great Teachers. New York: Vintage.

Newman, Horatio H.
1940　Multiple Human Births. Garden City, New York: Doubleday.

Ogburn, William Fielding
1959　"The wolf boy of Agra." American Journal of Sociology 64 (March): 449–454.

Ogburn, William Fielding and Nirma K. Bose, with the assistance of Joyoti R. Moyee Sarma
1959　"On the trail of the wolf-children." Genetic Psychology Monographs 60 (August): 117–193.

Park, Robert E. and Ernest W. Burgess
1921　Introduction to the Science of Sociology. Chicago: University of Chicago Press.

Pines, Maya
1971　"A child's mind is shaped before age 2." Life 71 (December 17): 63, 67–68, 71, 90.

Singh, J. A. L. and Robert M. Zingg
1942　Wolf Children and Feral Man. New York: Harper and Brothers.

Skeels, Harold M.
1940　"Some Iowa Studies of the mental growth of children in relation to differentials of the environment: a summary." Pp. 281–308 in Thirty-Ninth Yearbook of the National Society for the Study of Education, Part II—Intelligence: Its Nature and Nurture. Bloomington, Illinois: Public School Publishing.

Skodak, Marie and Harold M. Skeels
1949　"A final follow-up study of one hundred adopted children." Journal of Genetic Psychology 75 (September, 1st half): 85–125.

Speer, G. S.
1940　"The mental development of children of normal and feebleminded mothers." Pp. 309–314 in Thirty-Ninth Yearbook of the National Society for the Study of Education, Part II—Intelligence: Its Nature and Nurture. Bloomington, Illinois: Public School Publishing.

Terman, Lewis M., Melita H. Oden, et al.
1947　Genetic Studies of Genius. Vol. 4: The Gifted Child Grows Up: Twenty-five Years Follow-Up of a Superior Group. Edited by L. M. Terman. Stanford, California: Stanford University Press.

Weiner, Norbert
1953   Ex-Prodigy: My Childhood and Youth. New York: Simon and Schuster.

Welsh, James
1971   "D.C. perspectives: mental health research." Educational Researcher 22 (December): 1–2.

2

Sex, Society, and Related Matters

Mongoloid Children The critical importance of the socialization process for the appearance of human behavior is well illustrated by the variety of results obtained in the handling of children who are the victims of Down's syndrome, more commonly known as *mongolism*. Mongoloid children are very obviously abnormal in a biological sense since they have an aberrant number of chromosomes (Turkel, 1971:7). Consequently, they generally suffer from various metabolic imbalances affecting their appearance and causing certain degrees of brain damage. The traditional conclusion has been that such damaged children are uneducable and, therefore, should be confined to mental hospitals. Clemens Benda, M.D., has written:

> The treatment of children with mongolism has met with much opposition and has been the subject of often highly emotional controversy. It is the opinion of a number of leading physicians that such treatment is not only useless but even wrong from a theoretical point of view (1960:237).

This attitude has become so pervasive an influence that it has led to a form of acceptable murder. "Mongoloid Infant Consigned to Death from Intestinal Defect," read a headline in *The Denver Post* dated October 17, 1971. The Associated Press dispatch from Baltimore included the following on the same story:

> Because the infant was mongoloid, the parents refused permission for intestinal surgery and let the child starve, says Dr. William Bartholome. "It took 15 days for the baby to become dehydrated enough to die," said

37

Bartholome, senior assistant resident in pediatrics at Johns Hopkins Hospital.

"That was an awful long time. It was a long agonizing wait. I tried not to look at the baby and when I did, I didn't want to touch it. . . .

"The father would call and ask, 'How are things?'—meaning did the baby die yet?" Bartholome related.

He said the baby could have been saved by a simple operation to remove an intestinal blockage. . . .

The doctor said this was the fourth time in five years he had seen parents refuse minor surgery in order to let a mongoloid child die. . . .

In institutional settings, Down's syndrome children are typically regarded as purely custodial problems not worth teaching, since it is predetermined they cannot learn. Another rationale for neglect is that their disability characteristically causes them to die young; hence, it is not sensible to invest time and effort in treatment. One can easily predict the result—rooms full of children and young adults who are useless to themselves and to society.

Thus, traditionally handled, mongoloid victims constitute an illustration of the *Thomas theorem:* "If men define situations as real, they are real in their consequences." This statement by W. I. Thomas has been evaluated by Robert K. Merton as "a theorem basic to the social sciences." Merton explains:

> Though it lacks the sweep and precision of a Newtonian theorem, it possesses the same gift of relevance, being instructively applicable to many, if indeed not most, social processes (1968:475).

As one example of the relevance of this theorem, Merton describes a *self-fulfilling prophecy,* which is a prediction based on false premises but which, when considered accurate by a number of people, evokes behavior that causes the prediction to come true. "If men *define* situations as real, they are real in their consequences." As in Merton's classic example, if enough depositors believe the false rumor that their highly solvent bank is about to fail, the resulting run on the bank will render the rumor a "fact" (1968:476–477).

Rosenthal and Jacobson (1968) describe how a self-fulfilling prophecy can have profound effects on an educational endeavor; these effects can be benign or destructive depending on the nature of the prophecy in a given case. The central hypothesis of the Rosenthal–Jacobson study is that one person's expectations about another's behavior can, even if the expectations are unrealistic, generate conditions that produce the behavior. A specialized version of the hypothesis was tested in a public elementary school in an underprivileged community.

At the beginning of a particular school year, eighteen teachers in six different grades were given the names of children in their classrooms who could be expected to show dramatic intellectual growth. The predictions were allegedly based on careful testing. Actually, the names had been chosen on the basis of a table of random numbers. Hence the difference between the potential achievers and the other children was solely in the minds of the teachers. The results of the study were complex and varied, but essentially it was found that there was greater progress in the children for whom special achievement had been predicted:

> Expectancy advantage was defined by the degree to which I.Q. gains by the "special" children exceeded gains by the control-group children. After the first year of the experiment a significant expectancy advantage was found . . . (Rosenthal and Jacobson, 1968:176).

It should be noted, however, that the Rosenthal–Jacobson study is methodologically weak and has been sharply criticized. Nevertheless, on theoretical grounds one would be justified in predicting results similar to those reported by Rosenthal and Jacobson and confirmed by others cited by them. A teacher expecting a pupil to improve may anxiously watch for signs of betterment, ignoring possible indicators of inadequacy. And, if something is observed suggesting improvement, a quick reward may follow, a *positive reinforcement* for effort. This, in turn, may enhance interest and inspire the particular child to exert even greater efforts.

In light of the above, it is not difficult to see why mongoloid children are so often severely handicapped. They not only suffer from the physical effects of their disease; they suffer from a social system that assumes mongoloids cannot achieve and, therefore, no one should bother helping them. Thus we have a classic vicious circle. Much the same result would be obtained with normal children if the same attitudes prevailed. *Of course*, the Down's syndrome child who is not trained will not develop skills!

The converse of this principle is illustrated by the success achieved with mongoloid children handled by people whose expectations are high. The work of Henry Turkel, M.D., is especially notable. First, he refused to accept the medical dictum that mongolism, being inborn, is untreatable. He agreed the *cause* is untreatable at the present time, but he also believed the resulting chemical imbalances could be minimized by proper treatment. He has published numerous studies showing the results of his treatment process. In addition, he and others have described the dramatic behavioral changes that occur when a mongoloid child is given special attention and training (Turkel, 1971:27–30; Benda, 1960:*passim*). A representative description of such a child appears in a report by Mrs. Gladys O. Kjose, a South Dakota school superintendent:

Her entire body has changed in appearance. . . . The facial expression has especially improved. Mentally, she has made a decided growth. When she first started to attend our public school we were told that she was not educable, and the teacher was advised not to waste any time trying to teach her. Now, however, she is able to work at the third grade level. She can add and subtract simple arithmetic problems and she nearly always makes 100 in spelling ("A Treatment for Mongolism," 1970:66).

The progress reported for Mrs. Kjose's pupil is not surprising to those who adopt the sociological idea that the most essential aspect of human nature is its extreme plasticity. To the degree that this principle is in accordance with reality, to that degree it is logical to *expect* success in socializing practically all human infants, including many of the seriously handicapped. Skeptics should be referred to Chapter 1 and its description of isolates such as Anna and Isabelle.

A Sociological Interpretation of Sexual Orientation   The tremendously varied sexual preferences of people constitute a rather compelling example of the present adaptability of humankind. In sexual behavior we have what seems to be something biological. But this biological phenomenon is so overlaid with cultural factors and special learning that its genetic basis is almost lost in the shuffle. This point can be illustrated rather handily by describing the "sex education" experienced by many middle-class youths, especially in past generations.

In the preceding sentence, the term *sex education* is shown with quotation marks around it because, for middle-class Americans, education in sexual matters has not traditionally derived from formal learning. It has, rather, been an amalgam of parental expressions of distaste, fear, and embarrassment, together with a variety of personal experiences and the misinformation obtained from peers. For example, parents warned their children about the evils of masturbation; and boys especially speculated about the possibility that masturbation causes insanity or pimples. Nevertheless, almost all young people masturbated regularly; they still do, pending other forms of sexual expression. They do so because, despite widespread uncertainty about the practice, for most it is pleasurable and relieves sexual tension. It is therefore an example of positive reinforcement; when a given practice is rewarding to people, they are encouraged to try it again, and perhaps again and again, so long as they are positively reinforced.

But young people also receive negative reinforcement. Sometimes they are overwhelmed with irrational guilt when they reject parental advice that masturbation is "evil." Every time they feel the inclination to stimulate themselves—and they do quite naturally feel the inclination—they get such negative reinforcement from their guilt feelings that they are less inclined to try again.

The same principles apply when young people have shared sexual experiences. If a young man and girl find pleasure in their first attempt at intercourse, they will be inclined to say, as they might about a delectable dessert: "That was delicious. Let's have another." But sometimes that first "nibble" is not pleasant—perhaps because of interruption or guilt feelings. When this happens, no harm is done if there are subsequent favorable experiences. Unfortunately, however, some young people have several unpleasant intercourse experiences and therefore develop negative feelings about it. In formal terminology, the behavior in question is less likely to be manifested because it is not positively reinforced. Let us imagine a young man who has had some such experience, and let us imagine a subsequent event. Another youth, who perhaps has also had adverse experiences, says to the first youth, in effect, "Why don't you and I try something together, since we didn't enjoy girls?"

For most youngsters, such a homosexual experience would not be pleasant because they have heard repeatedly that homosexuality is unnatural or immoral:

> American parents go in dread of rearing children whom their neighbors will regard as aberrations, and pay particular attention to securing a son from any accusation of being a "sissy." Clothes, games, and toys are chosen from the earliest feasible moment, and frequently before, to distinguish the sexes and encourage them in their different roles . . . . Children are thus led to act out their sexual identities before they know what sex is about, and it is scarcely surprising that so many of them remain sexual actors all their lives. The anxiety of parents cannot fail to transmit itself to the children . . . (Segal, 1968:52).

Despite such anxiety and training, some people of the same sex do get together sexually. This kind of experience, where youths are concerned, has no necessary permanent significance, with three possible exceptions. One possibility is that a person may become so traumatized by guilt as to reject all kinds of sexual expression. Another possibility is that a person may develop the usually inconvenient tendency to be what is sometimes termed AC/DC—that is, sexually attracted to others regardless of their sex. The third possibility is more significant because it is so much more likely: that is a homosexual experimenter who, while receiving positive reinforcement for his or her sexual behavior, *also* labels himself or herself as more-or-less exclusively inclined toward that type of behavior. Such a person is unlikely to seek any contrary experiences. This orientation is formed by a positive reinforcement and labeling process that is sometimes associated with nothing more elaborate than unchallenged repetition; the process is more often associated with psychological problems motivating given individuals to view favorably what repels multitudes of others.

Whatever the basis of the positive reinforcement in any particular case, if there is enough of it the result will be an individual who is technically termed a *deviant* (and the behavior *deviance* or *deviancy*). In the broadest sense, a deviant is one who engages in behavior that is noticeably different from the average; deviance therefore includes approved behavior such as successful invention and artistic genius. However, the concept usually denotes the person who engages in disapproved behavior that goes beyond community tolerance limits; the sexual deviant is a conspicuous example.

Deviance and Conformity—a Learning Theory   The major point to be gained from the discussion of sexual behavior is that *all* significant human behavior is learned—or heavily influenced by learning—whether the behavior is "normal" or "deviant." Thus the "sociological interpretation of human sexual orientation" set forth above is actually a learning theory. It could have been phrased more broadly—called a "sociological theory of behavior in general"—but the same principle would apply. This principle is that behavior is a function of the differential learning that occurs in association with sanctions. That is, if any given behavior is positively reinforced, the learning is "Repeat for further reward." If it is negatively reinforced, the learning is "Avoid it if you want to escape punishment."

This process of learning in association with positive and negative sanctions is most fully developed as a theoretical point of view in the works of psychologist B. F. Skinner (1953; 1971).[*] The process has also been explicated in a number of recent sociological publications; those by Burgess and Akers (1966) and Kunkel (1970) are representative of some of the data. The entire process and its implications have been described succinctly by sociologist Harry Bredemeier in his discussion of the tragic killing of several dozen people during a riot at Attica prison:

> If we want someone—guards or prisoners—to act in certain ways rather than others, *two* things are necessary. One is to make sure that things they value are available to them contingent on their behaving that way. The second is to make sure that those things are *not* available to them *unless* they behave that way (Bredemeier, 1971:2).

Thus, the process of generating conforming and/or deviant behavior appears to be quite simple. However, there are complications in the process that are not made clear to students studying and training animals in psychology laboratories. The most important complication is that

---

[*] The indicated acceptance of the Skinnerian view of learning—a view I regard as important, yet sometimes oversimplified and, therefore, misleading—does not imply agreement with the authoritarian ideology often associated with Skinner's work, or the notion that human behavior is essentially the same as that manifested by other organisms.

behavioristic principles established by studying *nonhuman* organisms are generally useless for interpreting *human* behavior. Almost all significant examples of human behavior are affected by language-based meanings, as indicated by a number of sociological behaviorists (Singelmann, 1972:416–417); hence humans almost never judge pleasure and pain on strictly rational grounds. Another complication is that responses to reinforcement (positive or negative) are tendencies, not inevitabilities. In any event, the learned basis of behavior means that the psychiatric notion that deviant behavior is necessarily "sick" is just that—a notion. Such behavior can be inconvenient, widely disapproved, or disliked; it still arises in the same general way as does approved behavior.

Whatever the genesis of deviant behavior, most societies attempt to insure that disapproved varieties will be as rare as possible. *Norm* observation is generally desired. The concept of norms is discussed in detail in Chapter 5; here, it is sufficient to indicate that the *norms* in any given society are the behaviors expected in particular situations. Such expected behavior is cultivated in two major ways: first, the only behavior receiving regular and certain positive reinforcement is that in accordance with the norms; norm-violating behavior, or deviance, is usually negatively reinforced; second, educational facilities, frequently elaborate ones, are developed to supplement informal socialization processes—the basic aim of such education is to train people so they will approximate a norm-observing, deviance-avoiding model. As John Stuart Mill phrased it:

> A general state education is a . . . contrivance for molding people to be exactly like one another; and . . . the mold in which it casts them is that which pleases the predominant power . . . (Arons, 1972:54).

When norm observation is so stressed, it is not surprising that a majority of people learn to be conformists in most aspects of their lives. They are not just knuckling under; the typical socialization process includes techniques and sanctions motivating most people to readily and gladly *internalize* the norms—that is, to adopt, as their personal value orientation, the norm system of their society. In anthropologist Margaret Mead's phraseology:

> The average man in any society looks into his heart and finds there a reflection of the world about him. The delicate educational process that has made him into an adult has assured him this spiritual membership in his own society (1950:197).

One of the evidences for (and consequences of) the learned basis of most deviant behavior is that its prevalence among humankind is not in accordance with any known physical law including that governing random distribution. If such deviancies were a function of inborn characteristics, they would be distributed like hereditary traits; they are not. Their distribution is strictly in accordance with the cultural values and special learning situations in each society. For example, homosexuality was very prevalent among male American Indians who once lived on the western plains. Apparently the performance demands on young males were so intense that many of them could not make the grade (M. Mead, 1950:199). When they did not, they were regarded as having female interests, including sexual ones. They tended to act accordingly, expressing thus the tendency of the deviant to "hold the same beliefs about identity" that the majority do (Goffman, 1963:7). This happened so regularly that there was a special category for them. They were called *berdache* (men who adopt the dress and social role of a woman) and were expected to do women's work since they could not behave like men.

Margaret Mead (1950:199) found that homosexuality was all but unknown among the mountain Arapesh of New Guinea. The apparent reason was that Arapesh values are that males and females are treated very similarly and are expected to behave accordingly. Thus, when an Arapesh deviates—and there are deviates among the Arapesh as among all groups—no one can ever say, "That girl acts like a boy" or "That boy acts like a girl," thus raising questions about sexual orientation.

> In societies without sex-dichotomy of temperament, one aspect, one very basic aspect, of the child's sense of its position in the universe is left unchallenged—the genuineness of its membership in its own sex (M. Mead, 1950:201).

Reactions to Deviance   The differential degree that Arapesh and plains Indians have been considered homosexual thus is basically *social* in nature. This is also true of a vast variety of deviancies, ranging from alcoholism to xenophobia. On the other hand, it is obvious that fundamentally organic deviancies, such as mongolism (see pp. 37–40), occur irrespective of sociocultural conditioning. But *reactions* to such deviancies are sociocultural phenomena, and these reactions are often more significant than the deviancy itself. This is illustrated by the stigma attached to dwarfism and other such organic conditions (Goffman, 1963:1–8; Viscardi, 1952). In itself, dwarfism is mainly a physical disadvantage for little people who live in a world dominated by bigger people. But if the relevant prevailing value says "It is bad to be small and good to be big," then dwarfism becomes much more than a purely organic disability.

The same principle applies to some learned deviancies. The applicable social definitions and related legal provisions are frequently the only real problems; they are, in addition, often the true source of the psychological difficulties so commonly associated with deviance.

The Self   In sociology, the concept *self* is defined as the attitudes that an individual has toward his own person; that is all that is meant by *self*. We do not, as in some social sciences, mean the *real person* or the *inner person* or the *true self*. We mean nothing other than the attitudes an individual has relative to his character. These attitudes, being subjective, are not directly observable; rather, they are inferred from external behaviors that are generally agreed to signify particular states of mind.

Given the sociological concept of self, it is logical to ask how feelings about one's person are acquired. The answer is that such feelings arise in social interaction; thus, the self is a product of society. As far as we know, an isolate would have no self, in a sociological sense, because the true isolate would have no basis for thinking about self. But, quite obviously, the vast majority of people do grow up in social situations and do learn to think abstractly; and, through the medium of such thoughts, they draw certain conclusions about themselves. Therefore, sociologically, almost every human has a self.

"So what?" a skeptic may respond. "Why should anyone care what the self is?" The answer is that the self is the very core of *personality*, defined as the organized totality of personal traits that are unique to an individual. As the core of personality, the self deeply affects, if not totally governs, the individual's confidence in dealing with others and in undertaking tasks. Confidence, in turn, is a vital element of ability. The ineptness of a person who, even though highly trained and intelligent, lacks belief in his own competence is something familiar to us all. Also familiar are those very different people who, though untrained, are able to make it through, sometimes with dash, because they "know" they can.

Given the importance of the self, a number of scholars have written extensively about the concept. The two best known treatments are those by George Herbert Mead (1934:142ff) and Charles Horton Cooley. Cooley's description is summed up in what has been termed "a happy phrase": *the looking-glass self*. As Cooley described it, the self arises as the result of a three-part process:

1. an individual observes others' reaction to his person;
2. the individual draws conclusions about the meaning of the reactions; and,
3. the individual has a resulting feeling about what he is like (Cooley, 1964:183ff).

In effect, Cooley said, the self is built out of assumptions about the meaning of the reactions of others to one's own person. Of course, such assumptions are often erroneous; the self may be built on shifting sand at best. It is not unusual to meet a pretty girl who thinks of herself as unattractive; when other people laud her beauty, she decides they are just covering up their scorn for her, or some further excuse. On the other hand, one can consider a very plain child who is the delight of her parents and grandparents; they all exclaim, "Oh, you darling baby. Oh, you cute thing," and as the child develops, she builds the notion that she is rather grand. If this conclusion is not challenged seriously by other-than-family experiences, even the plainest child can well be very self-accepting.

G. H. Mead's description of the growth of self was more complex. As he put it, the self arises only as a given individual mentally takes another's role and looks back on his own person. We will discuss details about the meaning of *role* in Chapter 6. At the moment, it is sufficient to define role as the relative position one holds in a group. A mother is one role; a father another; a student another. Using role in this sense, Mead asserted that self arises only as a given individual mentally assumes another's role and, using the other's presumed values, looks back on his own person and comes to negative or positive conclusions. Mead called this process *taking the role of the other.*

It was central to Mead's theory of the development of self that the process of taking another's role is purely *symbolic interaction,* done mentally, using words as symbols for action, and, therefore, cannot occur until some understanding of language is achieved. This is because complex thought is, in effect, sub-vocal language. Therefore, a dog cannot have a self because it has none of the tools needed for engaging in abstract thought and thus cannot conceive of what it might be like. Humans alone appear to have this ability, potential or realized, but babies have nothing but the potential until they develop a useful knowledge about relevant words. This knowledge is very crude on first appearance, children typically understanding some words before they can vocalize them and vocalizing others before they understand; but when their language knowledge is sufficient to permit a measure of abstract thinking, whether or not they can vocalize meaningfully, children are able to take another's role (mentally speaking, of course), and then have the possibility for developing a self.

Now, said Mead, as people grow older and develop greater language ability and more subtlety of thought, they are able to take the role of several others at once, and thus conceive of themselves from the viewpoint of a number of others. Mead calls this *taking the role of the generalized other.* This is the basis for the self of a developed adult. This adult mentally assumes the role of numerous others and, looking back on himself, makes judgments about that person from a variety of stand-points. Doing this, there may be a misinterpretation of views of many of those whose role is taken, leading to development of a self not in accordance with reality. If the reality distortion is severe enough, the person may be defined as mentally sick.

Incidentally, Mead felt that "mind" arises in much the same way—through symbolic interaction. He defined an individual's mind, as distinguished from an organic brain, as the constellation of abstract ideas known to the individual. His thought on the matter is summed up in the following statement made by one of his disciples:

> . . . mind and . . . self are, without remainder, generated in a social process . . . (G. H. Mead, 1934:xv).

In short, the mind and the self are totally social products; without human society, there is no mind and no self.

DETERMINISM AND HUMANISM

The philosophically inclined will already have recognized that in their thinking about personality, most sociologists are determinists rather than indeterminists. *Determinism* is a causal philosophy; it is the belief that any given event is best explained in terms of the conditions that apparently are necessary for the event to occur. *Indeterminism* is the belief that some events are not necessarily the result of antecedent conditions. Relative to human behavior, indeterminism is called "free will"; this is the idea that humans are capable of making choices that are not necessitated by antecedent factors.

I feel positive about the sociological commitment to determinism because I see humanism and most aspects of sociological determinism as complementary. In contrast, some of my fellow humanists have not been happy about the seeming rigidity of determinism. John Glass has written:

> Both a humanistic psychology and sociology essentially take a similar view about the nature of man, as a choosing, existential being, only partly determined by his culture, and reject the mechanistic-behaviorist view of man so prominent now in both fields (Glass, 1970:2).

Despite such reservations, the following discussion will indicate that determinism and humanism are related to one another in such a basic way that it can be considered legitimate to sometimes think of the two views as one.

It should be noted that although determinism is a causal philosophy, one cannot meaningfully speak about "final" or "true" cause; it is impossible to ascertain such since almost everything is ultimately related to everything else. But even with nothing more than relatively immediate factors in mind, it is logical to conclude that any phenomenon at any given moment must be as it is at that moment because it could not exist *as is* without sufficient cause and could not fail to exist *as is* if those causes are sufficient. This conclusion, applied to human behavior, implies that all human action results from internal or external forces and, therefore, there is no "free will."

A purported example of free will is the individual prompted by every conceivable circumstance to punch someone in the nose but deciding at the last minute not to do so. A determinist would respond to such an example by saying that, as far as we know, nothing happens without adequate cause. Therefore, it seems logical to assert that *something* led to the last-minute change of mind—a fleeting thought, the appearance of the victim, and so forth—and that "something" is the determining factor (or factors).

The point that disturbs indeterminists most is the belief that determinism undermines moral choice. The indeterminist view has been phrased thus:

> If determinism is true, then my will also is always determined by my character and my motives. Hence I do not make free choices and should not be held responsible for my acts, since I can do nothing about my decisions and cannot help doing what I do. If the determinist is right, I have not chosen either my motives or my character; my motives come to me from both external and internal causes and my character is the necessary product of the influences which have been effective during my lifetime. Thus determinism and moral responsibility are incompatible. Moral responsibility pre-supposes freedom, that is, exemption from causality (Gruenbaum, 1952:669–670).

The deterministic answer is that even a committed determinist accepts ordinary obligations. The determinist does not, for example, insult people and then say, "I couldn't help it; it was determined." Generally, the determinist does what most everyone else does—acts in accordance with the socialization process experienced, and that process is generally compatible with the expectations of the sociocultural system. Therefore, where choice, moral or otherwise, can be exercised, the determinist makes choices just as does the indeterminist. There is *one* difference; the determinist is aware that choice itself is determined. This does not mean that determinism per se forces people to do something against their will. In Western society, at least, one generally does what one prefers—as it were, what one "will." *But our will is determined.* If, for example, you decide to reject the philosophy of determinism, you are not forced to do so. You have decided to reject it because you are convinced against it;

but, your rejection of this philosophy is caused, *determined*, by elements of complex factors that make you what you are.

It should be noted that the implicit determinism of the sociological view of personality development is neither a hopeless fatalism nor the simplistic notion of classical physics that asserts every event has a specific and inevitable consequence. Fatalism is the belief that "what will be, will be"; hence human choice is not effective. In contrast, sociological determinism asserts that choice matters greatly since ends are always a product of means, and this is true even though any given choice process is almost always affected by sociocultural influences.

This does not imply a mechanical determinism inexorably creating simple-minded robots, thus making it impossible to achieve the humanistic goal of maximizing individual freedom in the real world. First, it is unrealistic to think of the relationship between society and the individual as a one-way process, with the individual simply reacting. The individual also "determines," that is, has his impact on the environment. Therefore, as Platt has put it: ". . . self and environment form an indissoluble complex with no sharp boundary." Platt goes on:

> My voice fills the room; the wave of my hand or the blink of my eye changes all the holograms throughout the space to the distant hills. And if this environment reacts back on me and redetermines my new behaviors, it is self-determination in this larger and truer sense. I—which means I-and-the-environment—have done something and learned something, together (1972:46).

Hence, Platt concludes, "The humanists and the environmental determinists are simply emphasizing opposite sides of the same interacting subject."

Secondly, the deterministic process can contribute to a form of personal autonomy. This occurs because socialization in particular cases includes factors that give people enough insight into their own background and current situation that they become psychologically free of the irrational notions controlling the lives of many. These freer people are the "autonomous" personalities described by sociologist David Riesman and his associates; they are ". . . those who on the whole are capable of conforming to the behavioral norms of their society . . . but are free to choose whether to conform or not" (1956:276). Thus the seeming iron law of determinism can, in some cases, become the instrument of its own undoing, at least from a psychological point of view. As sociologist Robert Friedrichs put it:

> When the genesis of a particular social compulsion, cognitive or behavioral, has been carefully and accurately described—and understood as such—the

conditions necessary to transcend it are at hand. One then becomes capable of "standing outside" the internalized norm, the prescribed role, the cultural expectation, or the structural niche for a shorter or longer period (1970:310).

Another sociologist, Peter Berger, stated the point succinctly:

Unlike . . . puppets, we have the possibility of stopping in our movements, looking up and perceiving the machinery by which we have been moved. In this act lies the first step toward freedom (1963:176).

A further humanistic goal is that every person should, as far as possible, be treated as an individual totality and not simply as a cog in a process. The hope for achieving this goal—like that of increasing individual freedom to make choices that are unhampered by irrational ideas or political/economic injustices—is enhanced by deterministic philosophy. This can best be seen in connection with the concept of responsibility. Indeterminists may often say: "If everything is determined, then you have no basis for punishment. I could kill everyone in this room because, after all, it was determined by my background and the way my father beat me, or something, and, therefore, I am not responsible, so you can't punish me." It is true that from the deterministic point of view no person is ultimately responsible for personal behavior; but, it is also true that no organized society could continue to exist if, as in a jungle, anything is permissible as long as the perpetrator has sufficient power. Therefore, *human* society presupposes holding people accountable for given acts.

Which people should be accountable for what? In the short run—in isolated instances of important norm violation—the norm violator must be held accountable, if anyone is. This is not because of individual *responsibility*, but because the individual alone is the culmination and focus of long term personal and impersonal forces that lead to disapproved behavior. Such an answer, however obvious, is superficial on two grounds. First, it leaves untouched the processes that produce unwanted norm violators; hence, it is a superficial type of therapy. Second, it is one of those blame-the-victim answers that are so popular with people who are powerful and privileged. This, by the way, is another reason why the genetic explanation of the black–white I.Q. differential is so inadequate. Following centuries of maltreatment that would have had a serious deleterious effect on a race of Einstein-Samsons, black I.Q.s average—at worst and with biased tests—15 points less than those of whites. The basic reason for this, say those who prefer a genetic interpretation, lies in the black people; it is black *genes* that are at fault! They thus shift the spotlight from the racism that is logically the fundamental proximate cause of the entire situation, focusing instead on a superficial consequence.

Similarly, the indeterminist shifts attention from cause to consequence. In the case of an alcoholic whose neurotic parents and sociocultural situation led him to drink, the indeterminist cites *weak will* rather than the causes of such will. But the indeterminist cannot logically say, having explained an action on the basis of free will: "I am going to punish you so your will can be strengthened." Such a statement makes sense only in terms of the deterministic orientation. Therefore, revenge is the sole logical justification for punishment administered by an indeterminist, and punishment based on revenge is widely recognized as ineffective in producing meaningful change. The classic example of free will approach to deviation and punishment is the now discarded idea that the insane are responsible for their madness.

In contrast, the determinist, having discarded the idea of personal responsibility, is relatively free of the temptation to take revenge on even the most blatant norm violator. He too is a product of his past, usually more victim than victimizer. If this is the case, what can be done about deviancy that victimizes others? The answer is the same from both humanists and determinists, indicating the blend between the two schools of thought: Any sociocultural system has precisely the amount of crime and other destructive deviance that it "deserves"—i.e., that is produced by the prevailing sociocultural processes. Hence, those genuinely desiring a decline in the deviance rate have no alternative to changing the basic system producing that rate. Among the elements that must be changed is the traditional punishment system; it is well known that harsh penalties and prisons are not only totally ineffective methods of bringing about progressive change. They actually, by consuming energy and giving the illusion that *at least something is being done,* play a large part in insuring that injustice, faulty socialization procedures, and other determining factors that produce deleterious deviance are permitted a continued free rein (see Menninger, 1968; Clark, 1970; and Jackson, 1971).

But, of course, the consistent humanist will not want to confine his or her socialization-affecting efforts to a relatively negative concern with deviance, together with its antecedents and consequences. Humanists also, says Glass, want to

> . . . ask which institutions and social arrangements, supported by which values and norms, promote the capacity and ability of groups and individuals to make free and responsible choices in light of their needs, to grow, to explore new possibilities, and to do more than simply survive (Glass, 1971:179).

SUMMARY

The sociological approach to personality development has been illustrated by describing a variety of things: isolates, ferals, prodigies, I.Q., talent, athletes, sex education, deviance, the self, and determinism. These phenomena have been discussed so that the sharp and important contrast between the sociological and the genetic view of personality would become evident. The sociological view is that almost all important human behavior is totally a product of social and cultural influences; those who emphasize the genetic view assert that behavior is basically due to physical heritage. Sociology does not deny the obvious importance of biology; the discipline simply stresses the learned aspects of human behavior since it has been shown repeatedly that physically normal offspring of humans behave in a human way only insofar as they are taught to do so. The teaching that produces humans, behaviorally speaking, is a function of complex social and cultural conditions that constitute the focus of attention in most of the chapters that follow.

REFERENCES AND FURTHER SOURCES

Arons, Stephen
1972   "The plain people resist." Saturday Review 55 (January 15): 52–57.

Benda, Clemens E.
1960   The Child With Mongolism (Congenital Acromicria). New York and London: Grune and Stratton.

Berger, Peter L.
1963   Invitation to Sociology: A Humanistic Perspective. Garden City, New York: Anchor.

Bredemeier, Harry C.
1971   "On Attica and Related Matters." Unpublished.

Burgess, Robert L. and Ronald L. Akers
1966   "A differential association-reinforcement theory of criminal behavior." Social Problems 14 (Fall): 128–147.

Clark, Ramsey
1970   Crime in America: Observations on its Nature, Causes, Prevention and Control. New York: Simon and Schuster.

Cooley, Charles Horton
1964   Human Nature and the Social Order. New York: Schocken.

Friedrichs, Robert W.
1970   A Sociology of Sociology. New York: Free Press.

Glass, John F.
1970   "Toward a humanistic sociology." Association for Humanistic Psychology Newsletter 6 (April): 1–2.
1971   "The humanistic challenge to sociology." Journal of Humanistic Psychology 11 (Fall): 170–183.

Goffman, Erving
1963   Stigma: Notes on the Management of Spoiled Identity. Englewood Cliffs, New Jersey: Prentice-Hall.

Grunbaum, Adolf
1952   "Causality and the science of human behavior." American Scientist 40 (October): 665–676, 689.

Hoult, Thomas Ford
1966   "Determinism and mental health." Insight 4 (Spring): 25–29.

Jackson, Bruce
1971   "Beyond Attica." Transaction 9 (November/December): 4, 6–7, 10.

Kunkel, John H.
1970   Society and Economic Growth: A Behavioral Perspective of Social Change. New York: Oxford University Press.

Mead, George H.
1934   Mind, Self and Society: From the Standpoint of a Social Behaviorist. Chicago: University of Chicago Press.

Mead, Margaret
1950   Sex and Temperament in Three Primitive Societies. New York: Mentor Books.

Menninger, Karl, M.D.
1968   The Crime of Punishment. New York: Viking Press.

Merton, Robert K.
1968   Social Theory and Social Structure. New York: Free Press. Enlarged edition.

Platt, John
1972   "Beyond freedom and dignity: a revolutionary manifesto." The Center Magazine 5 (March/April): 34–52.

Riesman, David, Nathan Glazer, and Reuel Denney
1956   The Lonely Crowd: A Study of the Changing American Character. Garden City, N.Y.: Anchor.

Rokeach, Milton
1964   Three Christs of Ypsilanti: A Psychological Study. New York: Knopf.

Rosenthal, Robert and Lenore Jacobson
1968   Pygmalion in the Classroom: Teacher Expectation and Pupils' Intellectual Development. New York: Holt, Rinehart and Winston.

Segal, Ronald
1968   The Americans: A Conflict of Creed and Reality. New York: Viking Press.

Singelmann, Peter
1972   "Exchange as symbolic interaction: convergences between two theoretical perspectives." American Sociological Review 37 (August): 414–424.

Skinner, B. F.
1953   Science and Human Behavior. New York: Macmillan.

1971   Beyond Freedom and Dignity. New York: Knopf.

"A treatment for mongolism—stymied by FDA."
1970   Prevention (March): 61–69.

Turkel, Henry, M.D.
  1971   Medical Amelioration of Cytogenetic Anomalies. New York: Copen Press.

Viscardi, Henry, Jr.
  1952   A Man's Stature. New York: John Day.

3

The Sociological
Point of View

What Is Sociology?   The foregoing discussion of society's impact on
personality development illustrates one of the practical implications of
the sociological point of view. We should now turn to the more formal
concern embodied in this question: What is sociology? Some editorial
writers often answer this question by saying that sociology is "a subject
which describes what everyone knows in words that no one can
understand." Other evaluations are more positive: "Sociology progresses; the infant mortality rate among Negroes goes down," an essayist
recently observed (Hoagland, 1970:14).

Ideas about sociology include the belief that it is synonymous with
socialism or social work. For example, professional sociologists are
accustomed to having their untutored relatives say something like this:
"You ought to know how to help that old lady. After all, you're a
sociologist." Friedrichs has noted:

> Indeed, the public image is a curious one. Sociologists are regarded as
> rebellious adolescents, kicking over the facts and fables laid down by the
> hard-headed adults of this world . . . . Laymen typically conceive of
> sociologists as institutionalized muckrakers. . .(1970:57).

There is some truth in these lay ideas, especially where humanistic or
radical sociology is concerned. But sociologists generally, including the
humanistically oriented, prefer a descriptive appellation conveying an
idea of the breadth of sociological study as well as its scientific
aspirations. Therefore, when brevity is called for, sociologists prefer the
following type of definition: *Sociology* is the academic discipline

concerned with the systematic study of human social relationships in the most general sense.

"What does *that* mean?" one might ask. The question can be answered by the use of an analogy, although it should be kept in mind that analogies are, at best, accurate in broad outline only.

Let us imagine that an academic discipline is organized to study the social life of termites. The practitioners in the discipline would then concentrate on studying the relationship between termites. They would, therefore, give no *primary* attention to the "psyche" of the individual termite, or the biology of the termite, or their history or "economy." All of these matters might be significant, but it is only as they impinge on the social relationships of termites that the practitioners of the new discipline would become interested.

In short, the termitologist would concentrate on a sheer abstraction— namely, the relationship of termites to one another. These relationships are abstract in the sense that usually they are not, in themselves, physical; they are, nevertheless, quite observable.

As the termitologists develop their discipline, they would find that one of the major aspects of termites' relationships to each other is the formation of *groups*. That is, it might well be discovered that the termites having a particular relationship to one another could be thought of as an economic grouping. It would also be discovered that the essence of the relationship between particular termites is that some are workers protected by warriors, and some are exploiters who do practically nothing while the majority slave. Further, it would be discovered that some of the termites are related to one another because they belong to the same family group, or the same swarming group, and so on.

Now, like the hypothetical termitologists, sociologists concentrate on *social relationships*—among humans of course. These social relationships have a multitude of ramifications. For example, they result in the formation of groupings which, on the basis of one or more special characteristics, are set apart from other groups. Many of these relationships are based on the fact that some humans are *subordinate* and some *superordinate*. The relationships are affected by the presumed inner feelings that are often termed *attitudes*. And the relationships are products of long-term historical developments, both resulting from and having an impact on economic, religious, familial, and educational conditions.

In short, sociologists are concerned with all kinds of human social relationships and with the antecedents and consequences of such relationships. On the other hand, sociologists are not basically concerned, as sociologists, with the biological nature of man, with the psyche of the individual, or with human history as such. These aspects of life are obviously important, but they are the special concern of other disciplines. The relationship of these disciplines to sociology will be discussed later in this chapter.

The concentration of sociology on human social relationships is an irritation and a puzzle to many. These feelings arise because it is hard to think about something as seemingly elusive as "relationships" being the focus of a developed discipline. Nevertheless, social relationships—or, in sociological language, social *interactions*—are the essence of sociology. For example, a sociologist could point out two men, Mr. A and Mr. B, and say, "Now, as a sociologist I am not primarily interested in either Mr. A or Mr. B. But I am interested in the relationship between the two men and with the effects of that relationship; the latter interest may arouse a secondary concern with the men themselves. But the central focus of my interest is their relationship. I am concerned with the material or non-material effect that Mr. A has on Mr. B, and vice versa— in short, with their interaction. This and similar phenomena, along with their consequences, is the subject matter of sociology."

The Historical Development of Sociology   Man's concern with human relationships is as old as recorded history. In some of the most ancient biblical texts, one can read speculations about the social factors in human life. But interest in such social interaction was not systematically developed until the nineteenth century. Until that time most people, when they had a question about human society, were content to consult Aristotle or to depend on religious literature and leaders. The more credulous gleaned their "knowledge" from soothsayers, or from the readings of bones, palms, and head bumps.

Such methods of attaining insight on why people relate as they do were satisfactory only so long as it was believed that humans were special creatures of God and therefore relatively unaffected by natural history. However, during the seventeenth and eighteenth centuries, some scholars began to assert that humans too are products of nature and hence "unnatural" or supernatural methods of studying them are unsatisfactory.

Nothing much was done to systematize the study of human action, however, until the French philosopher Auguste Comte (1798–1857) became interested. Comte's concern was aroused because, observing the chaos that followed the French Revolution and the fall of Napoleon (roughly 1790 to 1815), he sought knowledge that would prove useful in re-establishing order.

But when Comte asked, in effect, "How does one study human society?" he had few guidelines. All he knew was that nothing practical could be achieved by studying religious literature that was the product of individual prejudice; nor was anything useful to be gotten from those whose knowledge was basically "intuitive."

On the other hand, it was evident to Comte that the then developed sciences—physics, chemistry, astronomy—possessed reasonably firm knowledge about some important aspects of life. How was such knowledge obtained? To answer this question, Comte set himself to a task that had not been accomplished since Aristotle during the fourth century B.C. He decided to become a firsthand expert in every known branch of developed knowledge. Thus, in effect, he became a physicist, economist, astronomer, biologist, chemist, and so forth.

Law of Three Stages When he finished his study of the various disciplines, Comte wrote his basic work, *The Positive Philosophy*. This four-volume publication described the knowledge-obtaining methods in the various disciplines and indicated the implications of such methods for the study of the numerous aspects of human society. The most important implication was drawn from Comte's basic finding that all of the systematized intellectual disciplines have gone through three major development periods. This process was termed "The Law of Three Stages."* The stages were referred to as the *theological*, the *metaphysical*, and the *positive*. By the positive, Comte meant an up-to-date synthesis of knowledge, a process and result that we now generally refer to as *scientific*.

Although Comte's law is not now taken seriously by many, in its day it played a significant part in making credible the scientific method of obtaining information that he saw as more reliable than the traditional methods. Comte used physics as a prime example of how a branch of knowledge progresses toward the more scientific. He said that physical knowledge was in its most primitive state when people generally believed that material occurrences are ultimately caused by erratic non-natural forces. A rock tumbles down a mountain side and observers say, "God's will moved the rock."

But as man became more sophisticated, he began to see there was a certain regularity in nature, and, therefore, the notion that important events were effected by the will of forces that were, by definition, capricious made little sense. If such forces were indeed in control of events, then the observed regularities would not exist. And so, as people became more knowledgeable, they began to conceive of physical events as being controlled by abstract principles that were not random. When they absorbed this point of view rather thoroughly, they had reached the stage that Comte referred to as metaphysical.

---

* This idea was first suggested by Comte's early associate, Henri de Saint-Simon. Sometimes Comte used the phrase "Law of the three states."

Gradually, it became clear to the more observant that no certain knowledge could be achieved on the basis of an assumption that physical events were caused by *any* factors external to the world of nature, be they the will of gods or abstract principles. Finally, the most sophisticated observers began to assume that *all* events are products of natural forces inherent in the events or impinging on them. Comte asserted that to the degree people make this type of assumption, they have a basis for making sensory observations about which there can be general agreement and, therefore, about which one can feel "positive" in more than a purely subjective sense. It is such observations that the most developed sciences rely on almost exclusively; hence the positive stage of knowledge is the scientific stage.

Comte found that all the advanced sciences had gone through a similar evolutionary process. He asserted that the lesson to be learned was this: Only insofar as a scientist assumes that any phenomena studied develop in accordance with their "nature," and not because of forces unrelated to them, can reliable knowledge be assembled. Thus in chemistry no meaningful information could be produced so long as people tried to ascertain the chemical nature of things by, for example, studying the stars. It was only when those interested turned to the substances themselves that they were able to assemble the principles of chemistry.

Comte's own words, summarizing this point of view, are still impressive:

> . . . each branch of knowledge in its development is necessarily obliged to pass through three different theoretical states: the Theological or fictitious state; the Metaphysical or abstract state; lastly the Scientific or positive state.
>
> In the first state supernatural ideas serve to bind the small number of isolated observations which then constitute science. . . .
>
> The second state is simply destined to serve as a means of transition from the first to the third. It has a mongrel nature, connecting facts by ideas which are no longer entirely supernatural and have not yet become completely natural. . . .
>
> The third is the definitive state of all knowledge whatsoever; the two first having been destined to prepare it gradually. Then facts become connected by general ideas or laws . . . suggested or confirmed by the very facts. . . .
>
> Men familiar with the progress of the sciences can easily verify the truth of this general historical *résumé* in reference to the four fundamental sciences already rendered positive, Astronomy, Physics, Chemistry and Physiology, as well as their dependent sciences. . . .
>
> Considering Politics as a science and applying to it the preceding remarks, we find that it has already passed through the first states and is now on the point of reaching the third.
>
> The doctrine of Kings represents the theological state of politics. In the last result, this is in truth based on theological ideas. It exhibits social relations as resting on the supernatural idea of Divine Right. It explains the successive political changes of the human race by immediate supernatural guidance . . . (1877:547–548).

Comte's final conclusion was that knowledge about human social relationships, like that of physical events, would remain unreliable until the relationships were studied as purely natural phenomena controlled by their own laws, so to speak. Hence, one must make the assumption that gods and other such forces have no physical impact on human society. Based on an assumption of this type, social research would be analogous to research in physics and chemistry, Comte said. He suggested that a suitable name for the new systematic study of society might be *sociology*. Thus, he became known as the father of sociology, both because he named the discipline and because he stated the basic conditions necessary for it to flourish.

Comte's conclusions were further expounded by others—about the same time by Herbert Spencer and John Stuart Mill in England, and several decades later by William Graham Sumner and Lester Frank Ward in America. All these pioneers in sociology called for an objective study of human society, and all of them met with considerable opposition. Theologians decried the notion that human beings should be regarded as purely natural phenomena. This theory, given immense impetus by Charles Darwin's *Origin of Species*, was seen as undercutting the idea of humankind as the special creation of God and that, therefore, the study of humans is more properly a theological question. The established academic disciplines were also antagonistic to the introduction of sociology, seeing it as an alien approach to the study of man.

Despite opposition, sociology as a social science gradually became established, especially in the United States. Indeed, development of the discipline in the states has been so intensive that sociology is sometimes referred to as The American Science.

COMPARATIVE DISCIPLINES

Sociology and the Disciplines of Political Science and Economics

All of the social sciences are, by definition, interested in the *social* aspects of human life, that is, in human interaction. Therefore, if strict logic prevailed, there would be only one all-encompassing social science. But tradition prevails in academia as in most other realms of life, and one of the traditions is that social science shall be subdivided into specialties. And surely there is need for at least some specialization since the subject matter is so vast. As Kenneth Boulding remarked, in calling for the establishment of social data banks that would be somewhat analogous to weather stations:

> The sociosphere, that is, the total sphere of man and his social organizations and relationships, is even more complicated than the atmosphere. It has more

severe storms and disturbances, it is more heterogeneous, it has more significant variables probably by several orders of magnitude (1967:5).

But what, if any, should be the dividing lines between anthropology, political science, economics, psychology, history, and sociology? Some anthropologists ignore the question, imperialistically defining their subject as "the science of man," leaving little territory, if any, for the other disciplines. It may seem equally grandiose to indicate that sociology's subject matter is social relationships in general.

Economist Boulding, seconded by sociologist Talcott Parsons, solves certain aspects of the problem by asserting that exchange relationships constitute the special field of economics, leaving integrative relationships for sociology and threat relationships for political science (Boulding, 1967; Parsons, 1967). However, this logical division does not do much for anthropology or history.

The historical fact is that—imperialistic or not—sociologists have studied, and continue to study, interaction in general. As George Simpson has phrased it,

> For much as we may tactfully explain to disciplines like economics, history, and political science that we are a special science with a circumscribed sphere of reference which does not intrude on their imperial domains, we know well in the dim silences of the night that we are a general science (1953:44).

This general coverage is so broad that it leads some sociologists to widen their perspective and specialize, for example, in the study of political life or economic conditions. But even these specialists are usually glad to defer to the expertise of their professional colleagues in political science and economics when it comes to the question of highly technical in-depth studies of government and monetary exchange.

Sociology and the Discipline of History   Although history is usually termed a social *science*, it is not regarded as such by many professionals in the other disciplines. Rather, they think of history as having the same relationship to the social sciences as mathematics does to science in general. That is, history is viewed as a fundamental tool, but not as a science in itself; it is not seen as a science because its data and methods allegedly do not lend themselves to the systematic control that is the essence of scientific method. *New history* advocates vigorously disagree; as early as the 1920s, they attempted to make historical studies more scientific, speaking disparagingly of the traditional *narrative history*. Historian Crane Brinton wrote,

> Historians to-day seem pretty much agreed to leave kings and courtiers, statesmen and generals to the more graceful talents of the new biographers.

History, as one of the social sciences, can no more than biology make the study of exceptional individuals an end in itself . . . . For the historian, too, aspires to the discovery of uniformities, or laws, which will enable him to arrange the chaotic past in an order not merely chronological (1930:1).

Brinton added, "Our new social history must . . . never lose sight of its ultimate goal, the discovery of scientific laws" (p. 2).

Despite the long-term development of "new history," many traditional historians still concentrate on descriptions of unique sequences of events. Sociologists, in contrast, characteristically attempt to find the common elements in seemingly dissimilar happenings. Thus, it has been typical for sociologists to write about revolutions and conventional historians to describe a *particular* revolution. But sometimes a sociologist concentrates on a unique event—perhaps a race riot—and thus acts as a narrative historian; and a historian may use a variety of events as a base for discussing the general aspects of kingship, thus becoming a sociologist for all practical purposes. The suggested breakdown of barriers between the two disciplines has recently been given added impetus by *new, new history* (that is, neo-Marxian) and *new sociology* advocates who are all but indistinguishable in their use of data and critical analyses of modern society.

Even if there were no close links between up-to-date history and sociology, it would still be true that the data of history are vitally significant to all the social sciences. As sociologists Gerth and Landau have argued, it would be impossible to have a meaningful sociology devoid of historical perspective. They write, "Historiography offers a great storehouse of facts and ideas to the sociologist in quest of insight into total social structures, their phases of growth, decline and destruction" (1959:14).

Sociology and the Discipline of Anthropology   Sociology is not the only academic discipline concerned with human social relationships in general. This is also the basic concern of sociocultural anthropology.* Why then, one might ask, are there two separate disciplines? The reason is that during the last century, each of the various scholars who became interested in developing the systematic study of the social factors in human life tended to specialize in one of two broad fields. One consisted of the study of relatively less complex, isolated societies, such as American Indian tribes. The other was the study of more complex and generally Western societies. Those specializing in the smaller societies became known as social or cultural anthropologists; and those specializ-

---

* There are a number of kinds of anthropology—archaeology, physical anthropology, linguistics, and so on—but that branch of anthropology known as "cultural" or "social" has the same general subject matter as does sociology.

ing in the complex societies took, or were given, the title of sociologists.

Because of this division of labor, the two disciplines attracted different kinds of people. Sociocultural anthropology drew those who thought that knowledge about social relationships is best achieved by observing whole societies at work, and then describing the observations in sensitive interpretations that are in some respects a form of art. This kind of observation-reporting could not be readily accomplished in complex settings. So those who wanted to engage in such procedures usually concentrated on seemingly simple social situations, such as isolated tribal life.

Sociologists, on the other hand, generally could not readily encompass all they were interested in; therefore, they had to develop expertise in sampling and other techniques for observing part of a complex phenomenon and extrapolating the results to the whole. Thus, sociology tended to attract the more mechanical or mathematical, rather than the intuitive.

As the years have passed, the division of labor between sociocultural anthropology and sociology has diminished. At present, a number of sociocultural anthropologists are studying complex Western societies; some sociologists have studied smaller societies. Furthermore, some of the recently developed methods for sociological research resemble the classical methods used in anthropology. Under a variety of names— ethnomethodology and phenomenological sociology, together with the longer-established symbolic interactionism and participant observation (all of which will be defined in Chapter 4)—a number of sociologists are studying social situations in ways that are quite compatible with the sociocultural anthropologist, whose primary research technique is to live and work with a group while sympathetically studying it. Such approaches to research take as a point of departure

> . . . the world as the individual or group studied sees it and constructs it, rather than how the researchers themselves predefine or categorize it. They recognize that man is a thinking, feeling, experiencing intentional being, and that he should not be studied as an object, thing, or subject detached from the researcher who gathers "information" about him (Glass, 1971:175).

Sociology and the Discipline of Psychology   The major difference between sociology and psychology is the varying amount of emphasis the practitioners of these disciplines have traditionally placed on groups or individuals as the prime source of human behavior. In general, sociologists explain behavior, individual and group, as due to collective influence; psychologists stress individual tendencies, psyches, orientations, abilities, and so forth, as the most important factors in all forms of human behavior.

It is true that some psychologists have been *social* psychologists. As far back as the mid-1930s, Muzafer Sheriff said it was artificial to conceive of individual psychology in opposition to social psychology:

> The psychology of the individual is valid social psychology, and social psychology is valid individual psychology. There are not two psychologies, but one (1936:4).

In practice, however, psychologists have generally placed little emphasis on social aspects of behavior. Indeed, most social psychologists, specializing in studying the relationships between individuals and groups, receive their fundamental training in sociology, not psychology; or, as culture-and-personality specialists, are trained in anthropology.

In addition to the varying emphasis they place on social and individual behavior, sociologists and psychologists part company when the question of biological aspects of human life comes into play. Psychologists are usually much more concerned with the biological; notable exceptions include humanistic psychologists such as the late Abraham Maslow, many clinical psychologists, and a number of psychologically trained social psychologists such as Gardner Murphy. The physical orientation of psychology in general is symbolized by Sigmund Freud's famous saying, "Anatomy is destiny." A more recent example is provided by Berkeley psychologist Arthur Jensen (1969), who, as described in Chapter 1, claims that genes account for most of the I.Q. variance between racial groups. The laboratory research use of rats, pigeons, and so forth, by many psychologists is still another indication of the tendency of psychologists to stress biological factors. Believing that all behavior, human and nonhuman, is basically physical, most experimental psychologists conclude that it is useful to study the actions of readily available organisms other than humans. Sociologists generally reject such studies on the grounds that the behavior of cultureless organisms indicates practically nothing significant in relation to humans, whose behavior is almost totally cultural in nature, or at least heavily affected by culture.

The differences between sociology and experimental psychology (not *social* psychology) are well illustrated by their respective approaches to leadership. The psychologist typically concentrates on particular leaders, stressing their unique characteristics in the belief that such phenomena sufficiently account for leadership. A typical sociological study of leadership avoids focus on any given leader (except insofar as the example might be used for illustrative purposes). Instead, attention is given to the social factors associated with leadership in general. And, it would be asked, what are the *social* conditions that apparently motivate people to follow certain leaders? For example, what were the social variables (not psychological, biological, or otherwise) that seemingly caused 100,000 Frenchmen to move on Moscow when just one man, Napoleon Bonaparte, said "March!"?

Sociology and the Discipline of Social Work   One of the most common misconceptions is that sociology and social work are synonymous. In reality, they have been almost totally separate fields of interest. Traditionally, the emphasis of social work has been on helping individuals in trouble to make suitable adjustments; this remains a major element in social work. In contrast, the emphasis in sociology has been on research. Even modern, humanistic sociologists, who stress the importance of action, are usually more inclined to do research on fundamental causes of injustice than to do, as social workers, therapeutic work with victims of injustice.

Thus, a suitable analogy for describing what has been the relationship of sociology to social work is that the former has been to the latter as medical research is to medical practice. Furthermore, social work training, in contrast to sociological training, emphasizes psychological knowledge, especially Freudian conceptions. Despite these differences, the dichotomy between sociology and social work is less clearcut than it once was. Social work as a discipline has become more and more concerned with fundamental analyses that may help to prevent the need for therapy; and a number of sociologists have become involved in therapeutic work—counseling, encounter-group direction, industrial relations, and similar activities.

Sociology as Pure Science   Although the discipline of sociology began with the reformist ideas of Auguste Comte and others, the major thrust in the discipline has been, until very recently, to make it a pure rather than an applied science. The prevailing voices asserted that just as physics is to engineering, so should sociology be to social action. In the words of one pioneer sociologist, Franklin Henry Giddings:

> We need men . . . who will get busy with the adding machine and the logarithms, and give us *exact studies,* such as we get from the psychological laboratories . . . . *Sociology can be made an exact, quantitative science* if we can get *industrious* men interested in it (Bernard, 1909:196).

The view expressed by Giddings became so dominant that, by the 1930s, sociologists who spoke about helping others were commonly scorned as simplistic do-gooders motivated by a social worker mentality. "In a graduate seminar led by a neo-Darwinian professor in the 1920s," Eldridge Sibley recalled, "an adult student aroused only amused condescension when he asked, 'What has sociology done to make folks more kindly disposed toward one another?' " (1971:14).

Rather than a "helping discipline," sociology was regarded as "ethi-
cally neutral" or "value-free" in relation to ideological questions of the
day. The practical implications of this view were given expression by
the late George Lundberg in a widely quoted passage:

> The services of *real* social scientists would be as indispensable to Fascists as
> to Communists and Democrats, just as are the services of physicists and
> physicians (1961:57).

Therefore, Lundberg concluded, the true social scientist need not be
concerned with the nature of any given political regime; even a fascist
government will let an apolitical technician alone, over the long run,
because "No regime can get along without this technology" (pp. 57–58).
So, the proper political behavior for "*real* social scientists" is to be
useful to the existing power structure even if it is despotic because after
all "science has gone forward under a great variety of forms of
government."

> I have emphasized that physical scientists are indispensable to any political
> regime. Social scientists might well work toward a corresponding status
> (Lundberg, 1961:57).

The Structural–Functional Point of View   The value-free approach to social data has been an important aspect of the work of many
who adopted the structural–functional viewpoint. This view was especially dominant in the sociology of the 1940s and 1950s. Some regarded
it as a theory in its own right; others asserted it was nothing more than a
new name for an approach that was as old as sociology (Davis, 1959). In
any case, functionalists—as structural–functionalists are usually called—
place a heavy emphasis on the *functions* of various aspects of a social
system. That is, they concentrate on the negative or positive contributions of any social entity to the system of which it is a part. Thus,
functionalists have usually avoided making moral judgments about, for
example, political events. Instead, they have tried to ascertain the ways
in which political regimes accomplish their manifest (obvious) and latent
(hidden or unintended) purposes.

It should be noted, however, that some functionalists *have* cast
judgment on the status quo. Karl Marx, for example, made a functional
analysis of the economy and concluded that it "works," despite its
manifest injustices, only because laborers are misled by a "false
consciousness." Therefore, the functional view does not force its users to
be value-free or to support the established order (Merton, 1968:91–96).
But many functionalists have used it to that end.

Status quo functionalists have become enthusiastic about the concept *system*—any set of interrelated elements that may be regarded as a single entity. Popularity of the concept was insured when it was found that only within the framework of such a conceptual idea could electronic analyzing devices be utilized adequately. *System*, thus, gave an aura of "real science" to a discipline that was often unsystematic. In the words of Robert Friedrichs, " 'System' had an obviously attractive ring . . ." for sociologists who wanted to be known as scientists. The concept

> . . . anointed their work with the clarity of logic, [and] blessed it with a conceptual rigor that they associated with the more firmly established sciences (1970:16).

System was admirably suited to the inclinations of value-free advocates because the concept generally connotes a set of nested subunits interacting in dynamic equilibrium (subunits interacting and changing yet remaining in balance). If society is thus perceived, then continuity and stability are regarded as normal, and change and challenge as deviant. This being the case, there is ample justification for not making critical judgments about society. Instead, value-free system analysts asserted that the central problem for a truly objective social science is, first, to specify the *needs* (in systems language, *functional prerequisites*) of societies and, second, to indicate how to avoid upsetting an on-going process.

Challenges to the Value-Free Position   Politically neutral sociology has been challenged from time to time. Perhaps the most significant and relevant challenger for present purposes was Robert S. Lynd (1939). In the late 1930s, speaking far before any significant number would listen, Lynd asserted in his *Knowledge for What?* that when it comes to anything that counts in human affairs, there is no such thing as a truly value-free position. When considered in terms of its consequences—and what matters other than consequences? Lynd asked—it is clear that a value-free stance gives support to the existing order and is thus a commitment, a value stand. An Adolf Hitler can function with impunity if the intellectuals of his society tender him nothing but "benign neglect." With such "neutrality" he has little need for storm troopers and secret police. Or, to bring the point closer to home, an American government can, with relative ease, commit the nation to an inhumane, exploitative war just so long as those who are most knowledgeable will say, "I take no stand on the war; I am a scientist, and scientists do not indulge in value judgments regarding their subject matter."

One reviewer, an historian, termed Lynd's book a "portrait in acids." Said the reviewer:

His colleagues won't like what he bids them see. They will refuse to face the fairly patent fact that the "detachment" and "objectivity" that they have exacted of themselves have been excuses for keeping quiet, dodges to avoid thinking, devices for saving their skins (Lerner, 1939:257).

In 1953, George Simpson published a monograph dealing with "Science as Morality." The morality of science—the moral order to which scientists give their highest loyalty—is the rational society, the society based on reason. Thus:

The sociologist is reason in action, and he cannot rest content where non-rationality holds sway in our society, whether in the local community or the State. Moreover, social science needs certain conditions for its survival: freedom of speech, of the press, of assembly; equality of opportunity so that it may tap resources throughout society; tolerance; and a political apparatus through which it can work for the application of its findings. The idea that as professional people we have no political role to play . . . is sheer nonsense. When freedom is under attack even in our own country—and when is it not?—this is the road to the extinction of the sociologist (1953:45).

Criticism of ethical neutrality reached a new high in the late 1950s with the work of C. Wright Mills, a Columbia University sociologist. He expressed his own evaluations in searing analyses of "white collar" workers, "the power elite," "the causes of World War Three," "the new men of power," and sociologists lacking in meaningful "sociological imagination" (all titles of his work).

The revolutionary events of the 1960s—the black power movement, campus revolts, the Vietnam war, government spying on civilians, inflation, urban riots, to name a few—gave unparalleled impetus to a new sociology, one that evaluates and criticizes. One of the most notable new sociology papers was "Anti-Minotaur: The Myth of a Value-Free Sociology," published by Washington University sociologist Alvin Gouldner in 1962. Gouldner's paper seemed to open a floodgate, symbolized by the appearance in 1965 of The New Sociology, edited by well-known sociologist Irving Louis Horowitz. By the end of the decade in 1970, Gouldner had produced The Coming Crisis of Western Sociology; its central thesis is that sociology is at a turning point because the functionalist view that has prevailed—whether "value-free" or as a partner of the totalitarian-leaning warfare-welfare state—cannot do what a sociology worth having ought to do. Therefore, Gouldner called for the development of a radical sociology whose practitioners are self-under-standing and self-controlled (that is, reflexive) to such a degree that they can adequately help liberate humanity by combining needed social action with vital social analysis.

A remarkably similar conclusion was reached quite independently by Robert W. Friedrichs in his A Sociology of Sociology (1970), published

within a month of Gouldner's *Crisis*. In 1971, signaling the pervasive-
ness of the trend toward a new sociology, the American Sociological
Association gave one of its most important awards to Friedrichs for his
contribution to sociological theory. In the work that was the focus of the
award, Friedrichs wrote:

> . . . the old scientist's tale that indifference to application is to be justified
> by the value-free nature of science is sheer rubbish—but rubbish packaged so
> attractively and distributed so widely from so many admirable retail outlets
> that the scientist himself has become a "true believer." He is even less aware
> of its role as a disguise cloaking his self-interest than is the general public
> . . . . It would appear, then, that sociologists cannot even in principle claim
> the value-free label, that they must move beyond the priestly posture of
> neutrality and accept responsibility for value-laden action that is essentially
> prophetic in nature (1970:163, 197).

Also significant is the recent revival of one of the two major schools of
thought in social science. The two basic views are usually termed the
conflict school and the *structural-functional* (or *consensus*) school. It is
the former which, for a number of decades, has been neglected. As
implied in William Chambliss' persuasive account (1973:1–34), one of
the reasons conflict theory fell out of favor was because it is politically
inconvenient to those in power. It is such because it shows so clearly
that the ruling elements of all societies have special power and privilege
primarily because they control the major means of coercion and not
because of general agreement that they are especially deserving or
meritorious. In contrast, functionalist theorists often stress that those
who control society do so because there is consensus that they should;
corollary to this view is the idea that the state is a prime instrument for
promoting the common good. With such views, many functionalists
readily become "establishment sociologists";* because they generally
confine their studies to abstract discussions of how a society's various
parts contribute to the whole, they do not raise critical questions about
who particularly benefits from given social arrangements. "Whether
they are studying war, social class, or deviant behavior, latter-day
functionalists typically ask what functions it serves; the conflict approach adds: *for whom* is it functional?" (Chambliss, 1973:5; italics
added). The latter question frequently has the effect of laying bare the
myths used by those in power to help maintain their special privileges
and control over the masses; hence conflict theory is inherently critical

---

* "Lackeys for the ruling class" is what they typically become, according to one radical
analysis by Martin Nicolaus; they often call for an "end to ideology" as a cover for their
abandonment of radically liberal social criticism in favor of a politically safer and
personally more lucrative technocratic corporate–statism (see Kleinberg, 1973:10-12).

of the status quo, unlike functionalism as it has been commonly used in recent decades.

HUMANISTIC SOCIOLOGY

As implied by the ASA award to Robert Friedrichs, today there is a sizable number of sociologists whose major interest is the establishment of a sociology that is variously referred to as new, reflexive, radical, existential, evaluative; perhaps the most general all-inclusive designation is *humanistic*. The designation is not particularly important; the function is. The fundamental role of the new, humanistic sociology is to help implement the humanistic values described in my foregoing Introduction. As indicated, humanism is the conviction that all humans have potential worth and should have the opportunity to develop themselves to the fullest possible extent consistent with the development of others.

The individual development goal of humanism appears to run counter to the modern trend toward collectivism. As Teilhard de Chardin phrased the point:

> Whether we wish it or not, Mankind is becoming collectivised, totalised . . . . Out of this has arisen, in the heart of every man, the present-day conflict between the individual, ever more conscious of his individual worth, and social affiliations which become ever more demanding (1969:201).

But, Teilhard observes, the conflict is only apparent. Because of the basic nature of humans, it is only in *appropriate* association with one's fellows that the individual can even hope to reach full personal development: ". . . we do not become completely 'reflective' (that is to say, 'men') except by being reflected in each other" (Teilhard de Chardin, 1969:202). Therefore, "Collectivisation and individualisation (in the sense of personality, not of social autonomy) are . . . not opposed principles"—they are interrelated and mean that we must develop social structures such that

> . . . the inevitable totalisation of Mankind may be effected, not only without impairing but so as to enhance . . . the incommunicable singularity of being which each of us possesses.

Teilhard goes on:

> We must no longer seek to organize the world in favour of, and in terms of, the isolated individual; we must try to combine all things for the perfection ("personalization") of the individual by his well-ordered integration with the unified group in which Mankind must eventually culminate, both organically and spiritually.

These observations lead to three principles that Teilhard offers as a basis for a new Declaration of the Rights of Man. The principles are an appropriate orientation for those who would create a meaningfully humanistic sociology:

a. The individual in a human society in process of collective organization has not the right to remain inactive, that is to say, not to seek to develop himself to his fullest extent: because upon his individual perfection depends the perfection of all his fellows.

b. Society, embracing the individuals which comprise it, must in its own interest be so constituted that it *tends* to create the most favourable environment for the full development (physical and spiritual) of what is special to each of them . . . .

c. Whatever measures may be adopted to this end, there is one major principle which must be affirmed and always upheld: in no circumstances, and for no reason, must the forces of collectivity compel the individual to deform or falsify himself . . . (Teilhard de Chardin, 1969:202–203).

How, it may be asked, can a humanistic social science help establish principles such as those outlined by Teilhard? The question can be answered in various ways; one answer is embodied in this text. A less complex answer is to suggest that social scientists give more attention to real situations and less to abstract ones. One cannot abandon abstractions altogether; they are the essence of scientific method. But the social scientist who constantly speaks in abstract terms instead of getting down to basic problems, helps to perpetuate the status quo with all its injustices. How militarists must treasure social scientists who carefully avoid speaking about "bombing hell out of a small country," choosing instead to describe "the parameters of political action"! Scientists who speak in this manner are described by establishment authority as "certified realists," "hard research personnel" (Roszak, 1969:143). Such personnel, whether they intend it or not, obviously provide a gloss of respectability for some of the uglier aspects of power politics.

In contrast, when the self-consciously humanistic social scientist is confronted with a manure shovel; he or she calls it that or something more pungent. Similarly, when reality prompts, the humanistic social scientist graphically describes threats to kill and burn hundreds of thousands of people; there is no making-do with misleading vocabulary such as "free fire zones" or "water-borne guard posts"; "search and destroy" is not sanitized to "search and clear," nor is bombing termed "reconnaissance in force." There is no use of "personnel management" to cover employer subversion of worker attempts to improve their lot. There is no "operation this" or "operation that" to disguise the possibility of megadeaths from hideous new weaponry. In short, the humanistic scholar *actively* declines to help make science a craven handmaiden for the politics of exploitation; instead, science is used to depict accurately what is really going on in the world, in contrast to the myths and misinformation that so many of those in power would like one to believe. Thus, the humanistic social scientist *is* a scientist in desiring to view events systematically and accurately—but if truly humanistic, is also possessed by an overwhelming desire to have science used solely for the betterment of humankind in general.

REFERENCES AND FURTHER SOURCES

Bernard, L. L.
  1909   "The teaching of sociology in the United States." American Journal of
         Sociology 15 (September): 164–213.

Boulding, Kenneth E.
  1967   "An economist looks at the future of sociology." et al. 1 (Winter): 1–6.

Brinton, Clarence Crane
  1930   The Jacobins: An Essay in the New History. New York: Macmillan.

Chambliss, William J.
  1973   Sociological Readings in the Conflict Perspective. Reading, Massachu-
         setts: Addison-Wesley.

Comte, Auguste
  1877   System of Positive Polity. Vol. 1 of four volumes. London: Longmans,
         Green. Reprint of translated first edition published in 1854.

Davis, Kingsley
  1959   "The myth of functional analysis as a special method in sociology and
         anthropology." American Sociological Review 24 (December): 757–
         772.

Friedrichs, Robert W.
  1970   A Sociology of Sociology. New York: Free Press.

Gerth, Hans and Saul Landau
  1959   "The relevance of history to the sociological ethos." Studies on the
         Left 1 (Fall): 6–14.

Glass, John F.
  1971   "The humanistic challenge to sociology." Journal of Humanistic
         Psychology 11 (Fall): 170–183.

Gouldner, Alvin
  1962   "Anti-minotaur: the myth of a value-free sociology." Social Problems
         9 (Winter): 199–213.

  1970   The Coming Crisis of Western Sociology. New York: Basic Books.

Hoagland, Edward
  1970   The Courage of Turtles. New York: Random House.

Horowitz, Irving Louis
  1965   The New Sociology: Essays in Social Science and Social Theory in
         Honor of C. Wright Mills. New York: Oxford University Press.

Jensen, Arthur R.
  1969   "How much can we boost IQ and scholastic achievement?" Harvard
         Educational Review 39 (Winter): 1–123.

Kleinberg, Benjamin S.
1973   American Society in the Postindustrial Age: Technocracy, Power, and the End of Ideology. Columbus, Ohio: Charles E. Merrill.

Lerner, Max
1939   "The revolt against quietism." The New Republic 91 (July 5): 257–258.

Lundberg, George A.
1961   Can Science Save Us? New York: McKay. Second edition.

Lynd, Robert S.
1939   Knowledge for What? The Place of Social Science in American Culture. Princeton: Princeton University Press.

Merton, Robert K.
1968   Social Theory and Social Structure. New York: Free Press. Enlarged edition.

Parsons, Talcott
1967   "Comment to Kenneth Boulding." et al. 1 (Winter): 6–7.

Roszak, Theodore
1969   The Making of a Counter Culture: Reflections on the Technocratic Society and Its Youthful Opposition. Garden City, N. Y.: Anchor.

Sheriff, Muzafer
1936   The Psychology of Social Norms. New York: Harper and Brothers.

Sibley, Eldridge
1971   "Scientific sociology at bay?" The American Sociologist, supplementary issue, Sociological Research and Public Policy 6 (June): 13–17.

Simpson, George
1953   Science as Morality. Yellow Springs, Ohio: Humanist Press.

Teilhard de Chardin, Pierre
1969   The Future of Man. Translated from the French by Norman Denny. New York: Harper Torchbooks.

Wallace, John
1971   Psychology: A Social Science. Philadelphia: Saunders.

4

Sociology and Science

Scientific Method and Human Welfare As indicated in the preceding chapters, this text is written from a humanistic standpoint and is, therefore, not value-free. At the same time, it is maintained here that sociology is and ought to be at least relatively scientific.

However, according to some social scientists it is not possible to serve scientific and humanistic ends simultaneously. A typical statement to this effect was recently made by Eldridge Sibley, a widely respected elder statesman of sociology. He wrote, in an article titled "Scientific Sociology at Bay?" that humanistic trends in the discipline are in many cases the equivalent of a renunciation of "objective scientific sociology." One must choose, he declared, ". . . between the ideal of objectivity and intellectual anarchy" (1971:16, quoting Robert Nisbet).

Sibley is most certainly correct to the degree that he refers to those who claim that conclusions based on "inner light," as compared with those drawn from systematic research, are inherently superior. It is true that "echoes from within are sometimes revelations from God." But they are equally likely to be "rumblings of a sour stomach" (Erikson, 1972:436). Still, the thorough scientist does not, a priori, rule out any potential source of evidence or insight, including the often misleading feeling of intuition.

Sibley is also accurate insofar as he denotes two other types: 1) extremists who, in the United States during the 1960s and in Germany of the early 1930s (Berger, in Berger and Neuhaus, 1970:44), rejected value-free social science *solely* because it does not help out-of-power demagogues to become dominant; and 2) true believers who are so single-mindedly committed to a value stand that, consciously or otherwise, they engage in biased observation and reporting. However, not all value-committed people are extremist; true humanists cannot be such. It would be contradictory to claim a belief in the potential independence and dignity of all, yet approve the coercive and sometimes underhanded procedures so commonly associated with extremism and delusion.

Furthermore, it seems rather obvious that scientific method, properly applied, enhances the possibility that certain humanistic ends can be achieved. For example, because science enshrines rational thought, it ". . . is the sworn enemy of human prejudice, intolerance, superstition, and all other methods alternative to the discovery of truth" (Simpson, 1953:36). A case in point is the development by scientists of measuring devices that, effectively described and utilized, have a potential for widespread acceptance in contrast to the limited appeal of guess estimates based on prejudice. Cuzzort has expressed the point very well:

> A measuring instrument is not . . . something that takes the spring out of spring and the life out of living. Indeed, it is something of a paradox that humanists who shout most loudly for better communication between men can, at the same time, deride a certain kind of communication—the scientific measuring instrument (1969:108).

Even certain aspects of behaviorism can be used to help achieve humanistic goals. Behaviorism, in all of the sciences, is a research–action orientation in which every type of phenomenon—organic or inorganic, human and nonhuman—is viewed as *nothing more* than the end product of past and present conditions. So, to the complete behaviorist, the human species is not perceived as unique and, therefore, the question of manipulating individuals as one would a "thing" is viewed as merely a technical problem that can be solved rather readily. Thus, many observers have feared what might occur if behaviorists obtained political power; the prospect conjures up visions of Aldous Huxley's *Brave New World* or George Orwell's description of Big Brother in *1984*. Such fears were given new impetus by psychologist B. F. Skinner's recent *Beyond Freedom and Dignity* (1971) in which he argues that we can no longer afford the luxury of permitting individuals to be even relatively autonomous.

But, as Donald E. Tarter has pointed out (1971), we are shortsighted if we fail to consider the possibility that some features of the behavioristic perspective may be beneficial from a humanistic point of view. Even Abraham Maslow, a patron saint of humanistic science, has written, ". . . I am behavioristic and I am humanistic . . ." (1971:4). Further, as indicated by Noam Chomsky (1971:19), "Skinner's strictures do not define the practice of behavioral science." And, as Tarter says, almost any form of knowledge can harm humans if it is ill-used; many forms of knowledge that seem inherently bad may be used for good purposes. "Just as the harnessing of atomic energy has the potential for destructive as well as constructive purposes, so the harnessing of behavioral energy will have both peril and promise" (Tarter, 1971:28). In both cases, the key to obtaining desired ends is the development of adequate guidelines. In the case of behaviorism, it is critical to understand that to the degree that humans are regarded as not essentially different than nonhuman phenomena, then to that same degree it is likely that inhumane methods of dealing with people are generated.

Keeping in mind the ethical and political problems associated with behaviorism, Tarter lists a number of ways it can benefit humanity:

> Another humanistic implication emergent from the experimental analysis of behavior concerns the removal of blame for an organism's behavior from the organism to the environment. . . . To the environmentalist, hating a person for his deeds makes no more sense than to hate a soft drink dispenser for not giving you candy. . . . If you want more humane people, you engineer a more human environment.
>
> Finally, those who see the development of social engineering as a prelude to *1984* where behavior is controlled by fear and intimidation should take heart in the findings supported by massive evidence that punishment is the least efficient method of behavioral management (Tarter, 1971 p. 29).

To many observers, the chief virtue of scientific method is that it produces *verifiable* knowledge. That is, scientific study uses standardized knowledge gathering and analyzing techniques, including a detailed description of the specific procedures used, so that independent appraisals can be made of the study's findings. Therefore, to the extent that people are guided by scientific information, they are freed from dependence upon a soothsayer, for example, whose claims cannot be verified because they are based on methods of knowing that are unique to the claimer. These are the methods employed by witch doctors, fortune tellers, astrologers, and the like. They are methods, in short, of many of those who, through the ages, have tended to enslave humankind by playing on man's irrational fears or superstitions.

But we are not so gullible now, largely because of the relative dominance of the spirit of science, a spirit that says "Show me." This is the orientation that no doubt motivated the proverbial medieval monk who was asked by his colleagues, "How many angels do you think can dance on the point of a pin?" He answered, "Bring me a pin and some angels and we'll see." There is the scientific spirit! It says, "Show me adequate evidence and then, and only then, will I have a reasonable basis for knowing what conclusions, if any, are justified."

The scientific spirit has sometimes been termed a healthy skepticism.

It is healthy because, while it keeps one from jumping to unwarranted conclusions, it does not, as does cynicism, block out belief in anything. Therefore, the scientific attitude is a useful one for everyone, not just the scientist.

The usefulness of the scientific point of view for people in general becomes evident when one considers the unreliability of personal experience as a basis for making rational judgments. Jackson Toby (1961) tries to make this point with his students by indicating how readily people conclude, while waiting for a bus, that busses going where one wants to go are almost always outnumbered by busses going in the opposite direction. They come to this conclusion because their observation is biased. Of course, they get on the very first bus going their way; hence they always see only one going in that direction; but while waiting, they may often see several busses going in the other direction. Moral: casual observation is frequently, if not always, misleading. The only accurate way to see if an equal number of busses go in two directions is to do as scientists would have to do if they really want to know—keep a count of all pertinent busses over a truly representative period of time. This is obviously never done by passengers impatiently waiting for "their" bus.

The contrast between ordinary and scientific methods of observing busses or any other phenomena is well stated by Robert K. Merton:

> . . . the great difference between social science and social dilettantism resides in the systematic and *serious*, that is to say, the intellectually responsible and austere, pursuit of what is first entertained as an interesting idea (Merton, 1968:xiv).

The Problem of Objectivity   Many observers have noted that most people, not trained in scientific method, draw conclusions on the basis of prejudice and misinformation. Thus, one can say they are not "objective," objectivity being defined as the ability to describe the facts strictly in accordance with the way they "really are." Another common assertion is that the objectivity potential of most people is increased if they are trained in scientific method. This idea has some merit, as indicated above, but even the most carefully trained must still determine the answer to the question—*Whose* objectivity?

The phrase "Whose objectivity?" suggests still another common question. As the philosophically sophisticated have long noted, facts never speak for themselves. They always speak in terms of a theory and, thus, vary depending upon the point of view in terms of which they are observed.

A simple example will illustrate the control that a theoretical orientation exerts over observation. Let us imagine two people *equally trained* in scientific method; one of them is a Marxist, the other a "capitalist." They study a West European factory and see that each worker receives money in accordance with the number of hours worked. Now, what has really occurred? The capitalist terms money a wage, which he defines as the return a worker gets for selling his labor to management. The Marxist calls the money a pacifier that management uses to maintain the' illusion among workers that they are free agents in the bargaining process.

What has been observed? Is it a wage? Or is it a cover?

That depends on several factors. It depends on the individual observer's point of view, and it depends on the prevailing political regime. If, in a given social system, the ruling regime is "capitalist," then most participants in the system will be trained to see worker pay as an aspect of free exchange. If the regime is Marxist, then most system participants will speak of "wage slavery" when they talk about workers in non-Marxist countries.

One cannot escape the difficulty by saying, "Well, then, I'll just stick to pure empirical description." This would be handy if it led to anything, but the important question is always *meaning*, not simple data. If this were not true, then "umbrellaology" (systematic study of umbrella usage) would be as significant as Einstein's work on relativity theory (Somerville, 1941).

The above remarks are meant to suggest that there is no easy answer to the problem of objectivity. Perhaps we cannot do better than to note the ugly consequences so frequently resulting from observation that is unconsciously biased and thus doubly misleading. This suggests, in turn, that there was merit in Karl Mannheim's idea that the goal of objectivity is best served by simple honesty and openness. These characteristics encourage one to be self-correcting and, thus, reasonably able to counteract personal biases that tend to warp sense impressions. If such self-knowledge and control on the part of a researcher are not sufficient to make accurate observations possible, then there are no sound grounds for accepting any conclusions, including those arguing that objectivity is a sham.

A related approach to the objectivity problem has been suggested by Gunnar Myrdal, a well-known Swedish social scientist (1958). His advice is to assume that *all* people have biases; having such is the essence of being human. Therefore, it is useless to be concerned about the objectivity of a given investigator. One need not even worry about an observer who sets out to prove a given point. To Myrdal, the only important question in any investigation is this: Are the data and analysis adequate and fair, and do the conclusions of the study follow from the data and analysis? If the answer to this question is *yes*, then the study has at least some scientific merit. Environmentalist Barry Commoner makes a similar point when he writes,

The reason why the scientific enterprise has a well-deserved reputation for unearthing the truth about natural phenomena is not the "objectivity" of its practitioners, but the fact that they abide by a rule long established in science—open discussion and publication. Whatever his personal aims, values, and prejudices, when a scientist speaks and publishes openly—presenting facts, interpretations, and conclusions—he has done his service to the truth. For science gets at the truth not so much by avoiding mistakes or personal bias as by displaying them in public—where they can be corrected (1971:86–87).

Many humanistically inclined sociologists feel that honesty and precise data, though very important, do not sufficiently solve the problem of objectivity. Their point is that when human behavior is studied in the traditional scientific way, using as a model techniques employed in physics and chemistry, the typical results are superficial at best and dangerous at worst. The danger potential arises because the coldly objective physical science approach to data stresses manipulation and control, both of which, when applied to human society, are the very essence of totalitarianism. The superficiality obtained with many physical science techniques when applied to human society arises from the imposition of the predefined categories of the observer on the study objects. These problems are eliminated or minimized by points of view and research techniques that, as indicated in the previous chapter, are akin to those long used by sociocultural anthropologists. The names and definitions of these approaches to the study of social phenomena, together with relevant references, are:

reflexive sociology—commitment to the principle that sociology is a liberating discipline that ideally embodies both a critical analysis of society and an obligation to act on the basis of the results of the analysis (Gouldner, 1970; especially 489ff).

phenomenological sociology—attempts to ascertain the complete meaning of social phenomena, in contrast to the superficial knowledge achieved when readily perceivable actions alone are studied—hence, stresses the *intent* aspects of human action (Cicourel, 1964).

participant observation—research in which the researcher becomes part of the situation being studied—for example, the student of dance bands who, as an aspect of research, plays in such bands—thus hopefully achieving an empathic understanding (Bruyn, 1966).

ethnomethodology—primarily by means of participant observation, systematic study of the hidden formal phenomena underlying informal interaction patterns (Garfinkel, 1967).

symbolic interactionism—a theoretical–methodological perspective especially concerned with the subjective aspects of social interaction, particular emphasis being given to man's use of symbols—for example, language (Blumer, 1969).

unobtrusive measures—stresses research that retains as much as possible of the precision of traditional methods, yet avoids the contaminating effects of study subjects knowing they are objects of attention—hence, uses methods other than interviews and questionnaires (the *exclusive* use of which is rejected) while keeping conscious of a moral obligation not to manipulate people or invade their privacy (Webb, *et al.*, 1966).

It is evident that there is much overlapping in these various approaches to the study of social phenomena. One of the reasons is that there is a strong humanistic strain running through all of them. They are also methodologically allied because, although each has its own special emphasis, all use the viewpoint of their study objects as a basic guide, attempting to be ever conscious of the impact of the researcher on the researched:

> . . . the proper study of human behavior requires an intuition, an empathy, an awareness of the other as a person who places meanings on his behavior and who cannot really be understood without an awareness of the relationship between the researcher and the subject and selfawareness on the part of the researcher (Glass, 1971:175).

Sociology and Scientific Method   It seems logical to assert that any knowledge-gathering-and-analyzing enterprise is scientific to the degree that its relevant procedures and goals are those associated with science in general. This is as true of sociology as it is of any other academic discipline. The relevant procedures are those that tend to minimize undesired effects of individual idiosyncrasy in making observations. This minimization is achieved with greatest efficiency in a laboratory where one can control most *variables*—scientific parlance for potential influencing factors—and, thus, measure accurately the possible effects of any given variable.

But humans are not so readily placed in test tubes or spread on specimen slides. Even so, social scientists have devised a number of techniques whereby certain forms of relatively non-complex human behavior can be observed with at least some accuracy. An example is provided by a classic study described in *Experimental Design in Sociological Research* (Chapin, 1955:99–124).

In this study, the observer wanted to measure the relationship between amount of education and later economic adjustment (with such adjustment being regarded as an indicator of occupational success). The population studied had attended a particular high school system a varying number of years. The subjects were, therefore, divided into four groups: One consisted of those who had graduated after four years; the other three were made up of those who had completed one, two, or three years of the standard course.

The observer devised a measure of economic adjustment involving such variables as job shifts that led to a salary increase or decrease. However, the observer did not simply apply the economic adjustment measure to each of the four year-groups, something an unknowledgeable person might do. But a more informed investigator would say:

> If you apply an economic adjustment measure to four groups about which you know nothing except that each group is made up of people having a particular amount of education, you would have no worthwhile knowledge. To illustrate, let us assume you found that the group made up of people with the most education is the group whose members have the greatest economic adjustment. Such a finding proves nothing. For all you know, your high education group consists of people who are, on the average, significantly older than those with less education, and it may be maturity, not education, which is associated with monetary adjustment.

CONTROLLING VARIABLES

Hence, in the study described above, as in any study purporting to be scientific, relevant variables must be *controlled* (at least intellectually) before meaningful conclusions can be reached, even tentatively. *Control of variables* means that the possible effects of major potential influences must somehow be ruled out before one can reasonably claim to be measuring the effects of any particular influence. Control of this type was achieved in the education-economic study by a method known as *ex post facto* design. This is a technique that controls variables by equalizing experimental groups in terms of basic attributes such as age, religion, home neighborhood, grade average, and occupation of the family's major breadwinner. All these factors were controlled in the education-economic study; only education and economic adjustment were "allowed" to vary. Therefore, it could be said that the final comparison was made between four similar groups to which a diverse amount of a single "substance" was initially "applied." The substance in this case was education—one drop, so to speak, to one group, two drops to another, three to another, and four to another. And since the drops were applied to phenomena that were for all practical purposes equal, any subsequent differences among the phenomena might reasonably be ascribed to the varying number of drops.

The term *drop* has been used to underscore the idea that, with sufficient control over variables, human beings can be studied under conditions somewhat analogous to those in a chemical laboratory. In such a laboratory, one might imagine a well-trained chemist busily engaged in purifying the contents of four test tubes each of which contains the same amount of a given substance. The chemist might then place a varying number of drops of some new element in each of the tubes. And if the findings are a different reaction in each tube, the scientist will usually be justified in associating the difference with the new element introduced since that is the only one in the experiment that has been allowed to vary.

In a similar fashion, when the education-economic experimenter found, as she did, that the study population had economic adjustment in direct proportion to amount of education, she was justified in making a tentative claim that the association between the two phenomena was a significant one. She was justified because the method of study was such that the two major factors had been isolated and had been found to vary together, suggesting a relationship between them. Finding such a relationship does not constitute an *explanation* in any sophisticated theoretical sense, but it is a vital step toward explanation.

Another important aspect of the study described is that it is a very old one. It was chosen for description deliberately because it is old, to make the point that reasonably objective studies of some types of human behavior have long been practicable. Since the study described was published, we have devised many more sophisticated ways of controlling variables, a process that has been enhanced by computers and mathematical models. Thus it should be clear that it is now possible to develop some of the positive knowledge about which Comte could only dream.

"If such positive knowledge," some may be inclined to assert, "is typically as trivial as that developed in the education–economic study, then is is hardly worth gathering. Everyone knows that people with more education get better jobs." The appropriate answer to such an assertion is: Yes, it is useless to document the truly obvious. But frequently, what "everyone knows" turns out not to be so; everyone once knew that the world was flat. Further, careful research alone can pinpoint the exact dimensions of "the obvious" in ways that no amount of casual observation can ever do.

MISTAKEN CONTROL OF VARIABLES

A much more recent study made the point, among others, that accuracy is sacrificed if a researcher fails to be properly selective when deciding which variables should be controlled. In this research effort, Elton Jackson and his associates (1970) studied the relationship between particular religious preferences and occupational achievement. For data, they used the results of a national survey conducted by the University of Michigan Survey Research Center. The survey was a sample of 766 people chosen to represent the totality of white male Americans.

The basic question Jackson and his associates sought to answer was this: What differences, if any, exist between the occupational achievements of Protestants and Catholics whose fathers have roughly the same occupational status? In answering the question, the researchers decided to control the following characteristics of those involved in the sample: specific occupation of father, ethnic affiliation, region and size of community in which reared, age, and number of years from immigration. (Race was controlled, in effect, by studying only one racial group.) It was noted that:

> Certain variables, however, should *not* be introduced as controls in checking to see if the religion–achievement relationship is spurious. These variables include education, size of city of *current* residence, and region of *current* residence (Jackson, *et al.*, 1970:51).

Such variables should not be controlled because religious values may generate occupational achievement by motivating people to obtain more education and/or move away from areas having restricted work opportunities.

The research procedures described by Jackson and his associates— procedures only lightly touched on here—further illustrate the point that it is reasonable to claim that selected human behavior can be observed under conditions roughly approximating the most important aspects of laboratory study. By controlling the relevant variables and otherwise observing the canons of scientific method, Jackson and his associates were realistically confident in reporting that suspected relationships between occupational success and religious affiliation were not spurious (as some other observers have claimed).

EMPIRICISM—MERITS AND DEMERITS

The two studies described above would be characterized by most knowledgeable observers as examples of applying the purely empirical methods of physical science to the study of human behavior. *Empiricism* in science is the philosophical assumption that sense impressions alone are a reliable source of knowledge. Now, the question arises, is scientific method based on empiricism meritorious or not? Some representatives of the humanities (literature, art) and some humanistic social scientists assert it is not, claiming that when it comes to human affairs, physical science methods usually produce trivia that do nothing more than prove the obvious. In contrast, technically minded observers defend empiricism whether the study objects are humans or not; they claim that only to the degree that a researcher uses purely empirical data can unwarranted personal feelings be avoided.

It seems sensible to me to take a middle-ground position on this issue. On the one hand, it is clear that the empirical methods of science are an extremely important way to obtain knowledge because such methods tend to free us from uncertainty when we must decide the degree of credence to apply to particular claims. But on the other hand, from the humanist standpoint there are three major limitations to the argument that only empirical studies are worthwhile. First, as indicated above in the discussion of objectivity, the strictly empirical approach to research, when applied to human affairs, has a high superficiality and danger potential. Second, since the classical empirical study is rigidly external (based solely on what can be observed in a physical sense), it tells us almost nothing significant about the inner life that is the most distinctive feature of the human species. This inner life consists primarily of our *consciousness* of values, meaning, and science itself; and it is the essence of such consciousness that it is subtle, elusive, non-material, so that empirical description can no more do it justice than can technical sound analysis convey the beauty of a great symphony.

The third major limitation of the argument for pure empiricism is that it rules out the guidance one might get from studies that are not empirical in the strict sense of the term. Conspicuous examples are provided by the work of such men as Karl Marx with his celebrated class analysis of society, Alexis de Tocqueville with his description of the young American democracy, and Thorstein Veblen with his ironic *Theory of the Leisure Class.* Surely, the work of these men amply testifies to the proposition that observations of perceptive social scientists can often provide a reasonably firm basis for drawing particular conclusions even if the observations are concerned with complex situations and do not involve formal field studies. As Cameron put it so concisely:

> . . . not everything that can be counted counts, and not everything that counts can be counted (1963:13).

REFERENCES AND FURTHER SOURCES

Berger, Peter L. and Richard John Neuhaus
    1970   Movement and Revolution. Garden City, N. Y.: Doubleday.

Blumer, Herbert
    1969   Symbolic Interactionism: Perspective and Method. Englewood Cliffs,
            New Jersey: Prentice-Hall.

Bruyn, Severyn T.
    1966   The Human Perspective in Sociology: The Methodology of Participant
            Observation. Englewood Cliffs, New Jersey: Prentice-Hall.

Cameron, William Bruce
    1963   Informal Sociology: A Casual Introduction to Sociological Thinking.
            New York: Random House.

Chapin, F. Stuart
    1955   Experimental Designs in Sociological Research. New York: Harper
            and Brothers. Revised edition.

Chomsky, Noam
    1971   "The case against B. F. Skinner." New York Review of Books 17
            (December 30): 18–24.

Cicourel, Aaron V.
    1964   Method and Measurement in Sociology. New York: Free Press.

Commoner, Barry
    1971   The Closing Circle: Nature, Man, and Technology. New York: Knopf.

Cuzzort, R. P.
    1969   Humanity and Modern Sociological Thought. New York: Holt,
            Rinehart and Winston.

Erikson, Kai T.
    1972   "Sociology: that awkward age." Social Problems 19 (Spring): 431–436.

Garfinkel, Harold
    1967   Studies in Ethnomethodology. Englewood Cliffs, New Jersey: Pren-
            tice-Hall.

Glass, John F.
    1971   "The humanistic challenge to sociology." Journal of Humanistic
            Psychology 11 (Fall): 170–183.

Gouldner, Alvin W.
    1970   The Coming Crisis of Western Sociology. New York: Basic Books.

Jackson, Elton F., William S. Fox, and Harry J. Crokett, Jr.
    1970   "Religion and occupational achievement." American Sociological
            Review 35 (February): 48–63.

Manis, Jerome G. and Bernard N. Meltzer
1972   Symbolic Interaction: A Reader in Social Psychology. Boston: Allyn and Bacon. Second edition.

Maslow, Abraham H.
1971   The Farther Reaches of Human Nature. New York: Viking Press.

Merton, Robert K.
1968   Social Theory and Social Structure. New York: Free Press. Enlarged edition.

Myrdal, Gunnar
1958   Value in Social Theory: A Selection of Essays on Methodology. New York: Harper and Brothers.

Sibley, Eldridge
1971   "Scientific sociology at bay?" The American Sociologist, supplementary issue, Sociological Research and Public Policy 6 (June): 13–17.

Simpson, George
1953   Science as Morality. Yellow Springs, Ohio: Humanist Press.

Skinner, B. F.
1971   Beyond Freedom and Dignity. New York: Knopf.

Somerville, John
1941   "Umbrellaology, or methodology in social science." Philosophy of Science 8 (October): 557–566.

Szymanski, Al
1973   "Marxism and science." The Insurgent Sociologist 3 (Spring): 25–38.

Tarter, Donald E.
1971   "Pragmatic sociology: sociology and the behavior modification movement." LSU Journal of Sociology 1 (March): 20–37.

Toby, Jackson
1955   "Undermining the student's faith in the validity of personal experience." American Sociological Review 20 (December): 717–718.

1961   "Further comments on the limitations of personal experience." American Sociological Review 26 (April): 279–380.

Webb, Eugene J., Donald T. Campbell, Richard D. Schwartz, and Lee Sechrest
1966   Unobtrusive Measures: Nonreactive Research in the Social Sciences. Chicago: Rand McNally.

5

The Sociocultural Order: Basic Concepts

Every learned discipline has its own technical vocabulary. In the social sciences this vocabulary includes coined words and ordinary words used in a special way; such words are usually called *concepts*. These are frequently referred to outside the discipline as "jargon." But to the expert, a technical vocabulary summarizes a vast amount of experience; it is a kind of shorthand that obviates the need for extended and often imprecise verbiage.

Therefore, to those in the know, expertise in any given discipline consists to a large degree of an intelligent grasp of its special terminology. The clear implication for present purposes is that those who wish to claim at least minimal knowledge of sociology, humanistically oriented or otherwise, must learn its terminology. Some of this terminology has already been used informally, but the full dimensions of many terms do not become apparent until they are discussed and defined. It is no doubt better to engage in such discussion in appropriate contexts; however, some terms are general and will be used throughout the following material. Hence, let us define them now.

THE SOCIAL ORDER

Social Interaction   One of the basic terms in sociology, *social interaction*, has already been introduced. As indicated, social interaction in the most general sense denotes relationships between organisms—that is, the effects, and the consequences of the effects, that one organism has on another. It is the human variety of such relationships that constitutes the core of sociology.

In the early days of the development of sociology in the United States, much attention was given to various forms of interaction. These forms were collectively termed *social processes*. Any given social process was defined as a mode of interaction. Five such modes were identified as covering the entire spectrum of interaction; these were *accommodation, assimilation, conflict, cooperation*, and *competition*. According to early observers, all types of interaction could be classified as falling into one or another of the five forms of interaction.

Although we do not now put so much stress on the classification of types of interaction, it is still handy to have at least some knowledge about their meaning.

1. Conflict—two or more persons or groups seeking consciously to block one another in reaching a goal, or to injure, defeat, or even annihilate one another.
2. Competition—two or more people or groups making a regulated and mutual attempt to achieve a goal which is such that goal achievement by one of those involved precludes full goal achievement by the others.
3. Cooperation—two or more individuals or groups deliberately working together to achieve a shared goal.
4. Accommodation—any of a number of means (such as arbitration, armistice, compromise, truce) used to reduce conflict between groups or individuals.
5. Assimilation—in the most general sense, a fusion process whereby members of divergent groups become similar; more specifically, the disappearance of the visibility of immigrants in their new social setting.

Sometimes the totality of interaction and its consequences, in a given group or among people in general, is denoted by three terms that are used synonymously. These are *social order, social organization*, and *social system*. All three terms, when used conceptually, are meant to convey the basic idea that when humans interact, their interaction is typically patterned, organized, systematic; it is not generally random or spontaneous.

Groups, Communities, and Society   Perhaps the most basic of all sociological concepts is the term *group*, defined as a set of two or more persons in reciprocal communication. Thus, the essence of a group is social interaction. One of the most important consequences of human interaction is the formation of stable collectivities called communities and societies. A *community* is defined as an interdependent grouping of relatively like-minded persons living somewhat permanently in a geographically limited area that serves as a focus for a major portion of daily life.

> Wherever the members of any group, small or large, live together in such a way that they share, not this or that particular interest, but the basic conditions of a common life, we call that group a community (MacIver and Page, 1949:8–9).

Although entire nations are sometimes referred to as communities, the term is usually applied only to smaller areas and numbers; the maximum of those involved is occasionally said to be the number who can maintain face-to-face relationships with one another.

Society is another basic concept of sociology, but it must be noted that definitions of this term vary widely. However, most sociologists would agree that the term society refers to the totality of organized human life and is thus often used synonymously with *social order, social organization,* and *social system.* Another common definition of society is smaller groupings of humans who maintain a unique life style and who are self-sufficient. The Crow Indians on the Western plains, for example, constituted a representative type of human society. The USSR is such a society, as are the United States of America, England, and France. All of these constitute societies as the term is used in sociology.

When societies are observed in a systematic way, one of the first things that becomes apparent is that societies differ fundamentally from one another depending on their size and complexity. These phenomena have led to a rough classification of societal types, ranging from the very small to the very large. The smallest societies with the simplest kind of organization are often termed *folk societies.* This concept is borrowed from anthropology and denotes the kind of society that is so small and intimate that all the participants tend to think of one another as "one of the folks." Such a society is, almost by definition, an isolated grouping with a simple technology and is sometimes referred to as "sacred." This term has been suggested because in the folk society it is typical for societal members to regard a very wide range of activities as having religious significance. Therefore, change is a rarity; if something is sacred, it must be eternal.

Once the members of a society interact with members of other societies—in short, when isolation is undermined—it is typical for the society to change technologically. This happens because people tend to borrow tools and techniques from one another. As they do, they enrich the physical aspects of their society and can, therefore, support more people.

If a society develops as most Western societies have, it characteristically becomes very large, complex, and industrialized, thus reaching a stage known as "secular." In the *secular society* practically nothing is sacred. Instead, *utilitarian* or *instrumental* values prevail—values that signify concern with practical results. The modern urban scene represents the essence of the secular society. In the urban environment, large-scale industry predominates and people in general have practically no sense that their fellow societal members are "folks." They are, instead, almost all strangers. Among the strangers, the most important, at least in terms of power and frustration potential, is the *bureaucrat*. This is the omnipresent rule-conscious official so characteristic of the formal social organization.

When classifying societies in terms of size and complexity, some observers prefer to use the terms communal and associational rather than folk and secular. However, the *communal society* and the *associational society* are, respectively, the equivalents of the folk society and the secular society. In Ely Chinoy's words:

> Immediate families and often larger kin groups, small cliques, and perhaps a handful of other subdivisions exhaust the group membership in the communal type of society. . . . Instead of the tight integration characteristic of communal society, the associational society is loosely articulated and the degree of consensus tends to diminish (Chinoy, 1967:48–49).

There are, of course, many degrees of variation possible in the great range from the communal-folk to the mass-secular society. But the trend in human history has almost always been away from community and toward mass society rather than the reverse. Hence folk societies are fast disappearing, and no doubt there will be a day when they exist in memory and literature only. Even societies with small populations, such as the Danish or Swedish, have practically none of the folk aspects left; they too are secularized.

Just and Unjust Societies   Classification of societies in terms of size and complexity is a traditional concern in sociology. This concern, however, seems less than vital to those adopting the humanistic perspective. For humanists, the critical question is not size or complexity per se. It is, rather, what societal types and procedures are associated with degrees of justice or injustice? In this context, justice is defined as fairness or equitable treatment.

Professor Morris Ginsberg (1965), British social anthropologist, has described the just society as one in which 1) arbitrariness (with special reference to power and inequality) is held to a minimum; 2) there is equitable distribution of the means to well-being; and 3) there are adequate measures to permit ready rectification of wrong. With these qualities in mind, many social scientists would probably designate the Scandinavian countries as the most just. Few would choose the United States as the prototype. Indeed, it seems likely that the United States might be placed close to the unjust extreme.

Such a classification would surprise and probably enrage chauvinistic types. However, it is certain that despite the official creed of "justice for all," the United States has been built and maintained primarily through a systematic exploitation of the weak and underprivileged. As British observer Ronald Segal has put it:

> America, once the embodiment, for most of mankind, of liberation and the future, is now become, for most of mankind, the embodiment of captivity and the past. . . . On the pretext of protecting democracy, she clasps to her national interests the most repressive and corrupt of regimes. And when popular disaffection rises in revolt against her clients, she speeds to their support. . . . The cause of a nation masquerades as the cause of mankind, and the morality of privilege wraps itself round in the rhetoric of democracy. If there are shades, how those of George III and Lord North must be fluttering with laughter! (1968:314–315).

Details of the implied exploitation-and-protection-of-special-privileges process will be the concern in the chapters dealing with differentiation and the political–economic order that follow. At the moment, it is sufficient to point out that the much-noted and quite obvious prosperity of middle and upper status America began with literally stealing land and resources from often helpless American Indians (Brown, 1970). With the foregoing as the foundation, it was an easy technical and ideological step toward the development of a form of slavery that has been termed the most depraved in all of human history. The resulting "good life" for those who benefited from the system has been maintained in more recent decades by a regular maldistribution of rewards and punishments (Gans, 1972), by "milking" weaker societies, and, in effect, by raping the environment so as to maximize short-term gains. The latter process, which will be detailed in Chapter 11, has been so extreme that many expert observers are convinced we are close to eliminating the possibility for life itself to continue.

Ideal Types   Societal types—such as the just society, the folk society, the associational society—represent extremes. German sociologist Max Weber suggested that such extremes might well be referred to as *ideal types*. He did not use the word "ideal" to mean something that should be emulated. Rather, he had in mind the point that extreme examples seldom exist in nature; they are, at best, approximated only when conditions are just right (that is, "ideal") to produce the given phenomenon.

Weber advocated the delineation of ideal types as a basic research tool. Such types are chiefly useful as models in terms of which reality can be viewed. Thus, there is no perfectly just society, but it is instructive to describe such a society in ideal typical terms. Actual societies can then be compared to the ideal type and similarities and divergencies noted. The latter can be especially important when it comes to planning and implementing desired social change.

Primary and Secondary Groups   In any society, aside from those with a very limited population, there tend to develop subgroupings which are customarily designated as *primary* and *secondary*. The primary group was first named by sociologist Charles Horton Cooley.

Cooley was very much interested in the fact that certain kinds of groups—family, neighborhood, play—have the greatest impact on personality development. This *primary* influence seemed so important to Cooley that he suggested we should use the term to designate the groups responsible. Other scholars added to this observation by saying it would be logical to use the term *secondary* for denoting groups that are not primary. Both kinds of groups are, therefore, *reference groups*, negative or positive, defined as sets of persons used by individuals as points of reference for evaluating important aspects of life. For example, white society constitutes a negative reference group for Black Panthers, and social scientists a positive reference group for historians.

Sociologists working independently of Cooley made observations similar to his. French sociologist Emile Durkheim concentrated on the nature of the social bond in traditional as compared to modern societies. He termed the traditional bond *mechanical solidarity*—the nonchoice basis of cohesion in the small, homogeneous society that stresses family, "blood," community; he spoke of *organic solidarity* to indicate that the heterogeneous society is analogous to an organism in the sense that its parts are specialized and interdependent. Some sociologists have used the terms *we group* and *they group* to denote primary and secondary groups respectively. *In-group* and *out-group* are sometimes used for the same purpose, but this can be hazardous since an in-group is any set of persons designated when someone says "we," hence can be as large and impersonal as all Americans as distinguished from the relevant out-group consisting of all non-Americans.

In Germany, Ferdinand Tönnies suggested *Gemeinschaft* (German for "community") and *Gesellschaft* (German for "society") to refer to these two kinds of groups. Today, the same terms are often used to designate polar types of interaction as well as types of groups. When applied to interaction, Gemeinschaft denotes intimacy and fullness, with the participants dealing with one another as ends rather than as means. Gesellschaft relationships, on the other hand, are those which are segmented, partial, instrumental, the participants concentrating on means rather than ends. Thus, the prototype of a Gesellschaft relationship is that which prevails in a typical buyer–seller situation. In contrast, the ideal type parent–child relationship is the prototype of Gemeinschaft.

Primary and secondary groups are described in similar terms. Members of an ideal type primary group generally engage in face-to-face relationships, dealing with one another as whole persons deserving of support no matter what the circumstances. This can be exemplified in the response of a Michigan mother who, when informed that her son had killed four strangers, retorted: "I know he did a terrible thing. But he is my son and I intend to hire the best lawyer I can find and do everything I can to help him." Students taking a particular college class usually constitute a secondary group. Typically, they know little about one another or their teacher. Their reason for getting together with the teacher is simply practical. Once the teacher and students have gotten what they want from one another, they cease to meet. Relationships in a secondary group, thus, are relatively formal, temporary, fragmented, and instrumental.

The modern world is such—with constantly increasing population, urbanization, industrialization, and bureaucratization—that people have to function more and more in terms of secondary groups and Gesellschaft relationships. Such a trend, superficially considered, appears to run totally counter to humanistic goals. It is in pursuit of such goals that a number of young people have joined together to form communes. However, communal residents have often found, as have those of many a *Main Street* (Lewis, 1920), that full-fledged self-development is often less of a possibility in an intimate setting than in the large and impersonal city. One reason is that *social control*—formally defined as any process conditioning or limiting the actions of individuals or groups—is typically most rigid and narrow in a smaller, more personalized setting. In the small town where "everyone knows everyone else," the slightest deviation from what is traditional arouses widespread gossip, and the threat and thrust of gossip tends to keep people "in line." But such an informal mode of social control has no impact in the large city where anonymity prevails; under such conditions, the only practical social controls are formal ones, such as police action. It is therefore ironic that in the impersonal "dehumanized" setting of the city one often has the best chance of achieving certain humanistic goals.

THE CULTURAL ORDER

Culture   A society has been defined as a relatively independent group
that maintains a unique way of life. The formal term for such a life style
is *culture*. Thus, there is a Crow culture, an American culture, an
English culture, and so on.

When used in the socio-anthropological sense, culture obviously does
not mean what Matthew Arnold meant when he asserted that culture
consists of acquainting oneself with the "best" that has been known and
expressed in world history. In contrast, to sociologists and anthropologists a humble cooking pot is as much an aspect of culture as is a
Beethoven sonata—to use anthropologist Clyde Kluckhohn's apt example. This is because culture, as used in sociology and anthropology,
denotes the *total* way of life of any given human society, and a total way
of life is naturally all inclusive.

The socio-anthropological use of the term culture differs from the
Arnold use in still another way. Arnold implied, if he did not say
outright, that there is an absolute natural standard that should be used
for judging the relative merits of different cultural products and systems.
On the other hand, most sociologists and anthropologists believe that
there is no respectable evidence for the existence of any ultimate
standards except those humans create and decide to adopt.

Cultural Relativism   In relation to their feeling that there is inadequate evidence about the possible existence of ultimate standards, many
social scientists find it compatible to adhere to the philosophical position
known as *cultural relativism*. This point of view is accepted by a large
number of Western sociologists and anthropologists.

It is important to note what cultural relativisim is not, as well as what
it is. It *is* the idea that there is no known scientific basis for making
ultimate judgments about culture; even such universal values as the
desire for health, which some have suggested as a common standard to
be applied to all (Means, 1970:57–58), vary when it comes to details of
interpretation and implementation. Despite such observations, cultural
relativism is *not* a covert way of saying that "anything is as good as
anything else." To make such an assertion would be to assume the
existence of the very kind of absolute that relativism denies. Rather than
being compelled by logical imperative to accept complacently whatever
exists, the cultural relativist can—without fracturing logic in the
slightest—opt for given standards purely on the basis of desirability. And,
when particular standards are adopted, it then makes sense to speak in
terms of associated "oughts." Such oughts can, as mathematician J.
Bronowski has pointed out (1965:40–42), be tested in terms of "does it
work?" "Does it help us to get where we want to go?"

The relative nature of culture is, from a sociological perspective, one of its most important characteristics. Another is that it is totally learned, and cultures are, therefore, also relative to the learning process. The learned nature of the human way of life stands in sharp contrast to the basic nature of the life of other social organisms. For example, termites, like humans, participate in a communal life that is highly organized; unlike people, termites live the way they do because their genes program them to live that way. Humans, however, must be taught to behave in terms of the demands of their culture—and, as we have seen, societies typically devote a lot of time and effort to see that such teaching is done "properly" and thoroughly.

Subcultures   An important aspect of large-scale, complex societies is the *subculture*—the way of life of a group that is part of a larger society but set apart from it in some sense. For example, there is a black subculture in the United States just as there is a French subculture in Canada. The essence of the typical subculture is that those for whom it is a way of life participate in the larger society, yet maintain a life style somewhat different. It is characteristic, therefore, that the black subculture includes distinctive modes of speaking, dressing, eating, worshipping, singing, and so forth. And it is also characteristic that most of such expressive behaviors are the end products of a long-term discrimination and segregation process. When a given people are forced to live apart from others, and when they are subjected to constant unfair treatment, in the long run they quite naturally develop special methods of coping with their situation. This does not imply that *all* subcultures arise from discrimination and segregation, but many of them do.

Even though a subculture may be a product of repression and almost totally derived from the prevailing culture, it can with time achieve an independent standing that enriches the overall society. This is equally true for aspects of given subcultures; the "jive talk" heard in many black American communities is an example. This special way of speaking has the double function of serving as the medium of communication among in-group members and as a barrier against outsiders. Jive talk has its own high-pitched, excitable sound, and a unique vocabulary including a wide range—to outsiders, a confusing array—of words for items regarded as especially important. Thus, *money* may be termed bread or jack or cake; or it can be described as grape, dust, blood, wine, pounds, or apple. *Women* are designated as chick, fish, fox, stone fox, leg, hammer, side, mink, bear, bat, deal, or snag. *Whites* are honky, Mr. Charley, ofay, gray boy, paddy, whitey, the man, Mickey Mouse, and so forth.

Culture as a Complex of Values   Culture was originally an anthropological concept; hence, in anthropology, one sees the most detailed analyses of the meaning of that concept. There are even anthropologists so involved with the concept that they refer to themselves as "culturologists." It is routine to see, in anthropological literature, finely honed descriptions of various aspects of culture, such as *culture traits* (the functionally most simple elements in a given culture), *culture complexes* (interrelated sets of traits), *culture patterns* (enduring organizations of traits and complexes), and the *culture base* (total array of traits in a given culture). The importance of these aspects of culture is that they heavily influence the nature of life in particular societies. A relatively simple society—simple in terms of number of traits—tends to be static. A society with a richly diverse culture base generates *inventions*, new arrangements of existing sociocultural items; inventions, in turn, are a significant factor in bringing about sociocultural change. The dependence of invention on the culture base is suggested by the phenomenon known as *simultaneous invention*. This refers to the established fact that since any given invention usually appears shortly after all the elements needed for it become available, it is often developed simultaneously by a number of inventors working independently of one another. The availability factor frequently applies in several cultural settings at the same time, so that some inventions—the automobile, for example—are evolved in several countries at once.

Values Despite the importance of the physical aspects of culture, such as technological invention, sociologists generally give more attention to *cultural values*. A *value*, in the sociological sense, denotes any phenomenon that has special positive or negative meaning to the members of a particular group. The importance of hard work in the Puritan value scheme is a typical example; diligent work is regarded as a positive sign of favor from above. Such values constitute the essence of culture; they are the heart of a given way of life. As it has been said, "If I know what a man values, I can accurately predict almost every one of his important actions."

But relating action to values does not mean that values themselves somehow generate particular behavior patterns. This was once thought to be the case. The current view, however, reverses the order. It has been found that what is most crucial about a given culture is that the prevailing behavior patterns are a function of the social structure; such patterns are rationalized, explained, and justified in abstract formulations called "values." Thus, instead of values explaining behavior, it seems that, generally speaking, behavior explains values. It is, nevertheless, instructive to study values because they symbolize both the behaviors predominant in a given culture *and* the rationalizations for such behaviors.

Norms as Values Regarding Behavior   The two most important sets of values in any culture are those relating to behavior and those relating to people. Values regarding behavior are usually referred to as *norms*. Norms are the behavioral expectations prevailing in a particular society. Note that norm is not a synonym for "normal." The latter refers to average behavior (for example, it is normal for people to retire at 11 P.M., let us say, but this "normal time" is a summation of all relevant bedtimes, ranging from early in the evening until early in the morning). In contrast, a norm is not an average or summation—it is simply what one is expected to do in a given situation, whether or not one does it. For example, it is a norm for Americans to marry before they have children.

Kinds of Norms   The four terms *folkway, mores* (pronounced morays), *tecnicway*, and *law* are generally used to designate different kinds of norms. A folkway is a customary way of behaving which, if not observed, results in some inconvenience (frequently a minor one). Table manners are a typical example. In middle America, one is expected to eat mashed potatoes with a fork. But we do not send for the police if a guest uses a finger instead. It is most probable that we say nothing. However, if we are hung up on formality, we say, "Let's not invite that slob to dinner again."

It was pioneer sociologist William Graham Sumner who suggested the term *folkway* for customary behavior (1906 [1960]). He made the suggestion because, when he set out to find why given groups behaved in particular ways—for example, why West Africans always pass the salt with the right hand—he found that the ultimate answer in any group was inevitably, "We do it because that's the way our folks did it." The merits of such traditional behavior are typically unquestioned. As Sumner put it, "In the folkways, whatever is, is right" (1906:28). That is, by definition, people do not think about their folkways and decide whether or not to comply—for example, "Should I eat with my fork or with a stick?" Once a folkway is generally so questioned, it usually loses its social control power and, therefore, sooner or later ceases to be expected behavior.

If the social control power of folkways and other types of norms is undermined when questioned, then it would seem that a system of norms is based on agreement; this is the belief of many observers. Others find that normative systems are the consequence of ascendancy relations among the different elements in a society (some people dominate while others are subordinate). These two conclusions are the fundamental orientation of the two major social science schools of thought delineated in Chapter 3. Advocates of the schools are often termed conflict and consensus (or functional) theorists, as appropriate;

they are élite-dominance theorists or pluralists when addressing themselves to questions involving political–economic power. To reiterate, consensus (functional) theorists assert that order is primarily due to concurrence on norms; conflict theorists say that order is imposed by the dominant. Both theories, Rosenberg says (1972), are one-sided answers to the question, "What holds society together?" He recommends a middle ground stance, since he finds that few if any societies have an all-or-nothing quality. They are not totally oppressed or totally free, not all conformist or all spontaneous, not completely static nor always changing. And, if in the course of time a society does become overbalanced in a particular direction—in the direction of centralized control, say, or of lack of control—then there is a strong tendency for the opposite condition to be generated. As sociologist Joseph Bensman has paraphrased Rosenberg's position in brief form:

> . . . no society is possible without some minimal form of consensus, and no society exists without some external form of social control. All societies are therefore in some way repressive, but all repression breeds the desire for freedom (Rosenberg, 1972:xi).

Despite the mollifying nature of Rosenberg's middle ground position, the present writer is inclined to believe that the conflict view produces a more realistic picture of human society. At the same time, it must be admitted that social order has elements of consensus as well as of conflict, the latter referring to order imposed by those who hold power. This is illustrated by the process known as *internalization*, which means the acceptance by individuals of the norm system of their society as their personal value orientation. To the degree that people in a society manifest such agreement, then, other things being equal, to the same degree that society is cohesive. But how does such consensus arise? It arises out of a process that includes conflict as an important element. The conflict part of the process can be quite subtle; it often consists of no more than an implied threat, on the part of those who have power, to withhold rewards from, or impose punishment on, those whose actions indicate "faulty" internalization. As described by J. F. Scott:

> . . . the learning of norms is never complete, and always involves expectations that sanctions will be applied. Thus even when norms are thoroughly learned, when moral commitment is strong and a sense of obligation is reported as keenly felt, the maintenance of both conscience and conformity depends on the exercise of sanctions (1971:xiii).

In addition to introducing the term folkways, Sumner suggested the Latin word *mores* for norms that are thought to be particularly important (though he did not use the term norm). In every group there are "must behaviors," Sumner noted, things that one must do or must not do. These are the mores, which is the plural form, the singular being *mos*. And the key to whether a given behavior is a mos or an ordinary folkway is the sanction applied. If the negative sanction for a violation is very severe, then by definition the norm is a mos. For example, the Ten Commandments were the mores of the Jews of antiquity: "Thou shalt. . . ," and "Thou shalt *not*. . . ." The general prohibition against murdering a fellow group member is a positive mos in every society. (One must qualify the statement because killing out-group members under certain circumstances is sometimes permitted and even rewarded, as in war.) And the negative sanction for murder is severe indeed.

The term *tecnicway* is sometimes used to denote folkways that arise out of technical innovation. Early in this century, for example, it was a folkway to use a vehicle drawn by horses if one wanted to travel any distance. But horses were quickly supplanted by motor-driven vehicles. Early in the game, motor travel was a tecnicway while it was still a novelty, yet very common. It is typical that, after a time, the tecnicway of motor travel came to be regarded much as one does other customary behavior—as a folkway.

The term *law* designates still another type of norm. In the most general sense, a law is an orderly and dependable sequence of events; thus, in science generally a law is a statement that takes the form, "If such and such conditions prevail, then such and such consequences will follow." Relative to norms, a law is a rule of conduct enforced by government. There are two major types of such rules: *statutory* law and *common* law. A statutory law is one that is codified—formally written down in legal terms—whereas a common law is simply based on custom, although it, too, is enforced by government action.

When the relative social control power of folkways and laws are considered, an interesting paradox becomes apparent. The paradox can be phrased thus: Generally speaking, in any given society a law is effective only to the degree that it is based on a prevailing folkway; but on the other hand, a folkway needs no law to enforce it (although a law may help to systematize enforcement). This principle is often illustrated by the American experiment with prohibition against alcoholic beverages. Although this prohibition was made an amendment to the Constitution in 1919 and thus became part of the basic law of the land, it was commonly ignored. The point is this: If it is in the folkways for a people to drink, or to smoke pot, then drink or smoke they will, no matter how many laws are enacted and almost totally without regard to the danger of doing what they wish to do.

On the other hand, a widely accepted folkway is fully effective without the need for law enforcement. Let us consider one example. There is no law prohibiting people from picking their noses in public, but few aware people do it—or, when they do, they try to be discreet.

Even in "polite society" the police are not called when someone violates this folkway. People simply turn their backs on the person gauche enough to be so "vulgar." This shunning process is typical in that it effectively keeps people in general from violating the folkways about which feelings are relatively keen.

These observations explain why the police must expend so much time and energy enforcing traffic laws. To most, these laws are not clearly related to the folkways; hence they are violated regularly and with free conscience by multitudes of people when they feel they can do so with little danger. In contrast, most people do not refrain from murder simply because punishment is provided. They refrain from it because they have been taught to regard it with horror. "Thou shalt not kill." To violate this rule is an abomination unto the Lord—is regarded as tampering with the ultimate forces of the universe and thus tempting fate. Such forces, with their presumed control over all significant sanctions, will be challenged by few, and then only under conditions of extreme provocation.

Values Regarding People   Participants in all cultures are taught to view their fellow members, and outsiders, in particular ways. The typical teaching is that members of the in-group are good and others are viewed differently, frequently as bad. The concepts we use to signify and sum up important aspects of these teachings and feelings are consciousness of kind, ethnocentrism, prejudice, and stereotype, all described below.

Consciousness of kind refers to the tendency of people to recognize others who have similar values and to gravitate toward them. Early in the twentieth century, this concept was suggested by a New York sociologist, Franklin Giddings, after he saw, out of his Columbia University office window, that sparrows gathered on certain window sills, while pigeons congregated on others and juncos used still others. Values, of course, played no part in the process, but the result was the same as if the birds had particular values.

Most societal members are taught that their own society and culture or subculture is more defensible and natural. The consequence is that people typically use their sociocultural order as a standard for judging others, usually in a damning sense. The term *ethnocentrism* is used to denote this entire process and its results. Ethnocentrism is frequently thought of in totally negative terms, but it is unlikely that any group could cohere if its members did not see the group as somehow deserving of loyalty and effort. On the other hand, from the humanistic perspective, it is clear that forms of ethnocentrism, such as nationalism or patriotism, racism, and sexism, have had particularly ugly consequences. It is special loyalty to a given nation–state that permits its leaders to generate the hatreds that are necessary before citizens will let themselves be coerced into engaging in international war. And surely racism, with its categories of those who are presumed inferior or superior, is one of the root causes of human misery.

When people take an intellectual position irrespective of the nature of possibly relevant information, they are engaging in a judgment process the consequences of which are usually called *prejudice*. This phenomenon is of course a general one—a person can be prejudiced about anything. But at the moment our concern is with prejudice in relation to people. This kind of prejudice, like any other, can be either positive or negative; it is the latter that generally has the most obvious social results. However, any kind of prejudice affects the social process. The reason it does so was summed up in the W. I. Thomas theorem, previously stated: "If men define situations as real, they are real in their consequences." Thus, even if a given group of people produce a constant run of Nobel Prize winners, Phi Beta Kappas, and Olympic champions, they will nevertheless be discriminated against if they are *defined* as inferior.

The basic thing to understand about negative prejudice against people is that it has little if anything to do with the actual behavior of the persons involved. For example, anti-Semitism can be found among North Dakotans who have never once seen or met a Jew. Old-style Mississippians have been heard to criticize blacks both for not producing enough professionals and for being pushy when they produced some. In both cases, the immediate problem is that the North Dakotans and the Mississippians noted above are governed by what is technically called a *stereotype*. This term was suggested by journalist Walter Lippmann, who spoke about "pictures in the mind." Such pictures are group-shared ideas about the alleged essential nature of those who make up a whole category of persons.

The most significant stereotypes are emotion-charged negative evaluations—for examples, Jews are greedy, blacks are lazy, and Orientals are crafty. Stereotypes of this sort ". . . represent institutionalized misinformation, distorted information, and caricatured ideas . . . " (Cuber, 1968:242; italicized in the original). They nevertheless profoundly affect social interaction, as Robert Merton has indicated so cogently:

> So much for out-groups being damned if they don't (apparently) manifest in-group virtues. It is a tasteless bit of ethnocentrism, seasoned with self-interest. But . . . Can one seriously mean that out-groups are also damned if they *do* possess these virtues? One can.
>
> Through a faultlessly bisymmetrical prejudice, ethnic and racial out-groups get it coming and going. The systematic condemnation of the out-grouper continues largely *irrespective of what he does*. More: through a freakish exercise of capricious judicial logic, the victim is punished for the crime.

> Superficial appearances notwithstanding, prejudice and discrimination aimed at the out-group are not a result of what the out-group does, but are rooted deep in the structure of our society and the social psychology of its members (1968:482).

But how can this be? Merton answers that in-group members, when judging out-groupers, use a special form of moral alchemy that transforms virtues into vices. For example, they might grammatically decline the word *firm:*

> I am firm,
> Thou art obstinate,
> He is pigheaded.

Applied to specific individuals, the process may take this form: When Abraham Lincoln worked far into the night, he was industrious; when Abe Cohen does the same thing, he is regarded as motivated by greed.

THE SOCIOCULTURAL ORDER AND FREEDOM

Sociology and Revolution   The social control aspects of culture—its patterned, systematic nature, and especially its norms—led one observer to make a statement to this effect:

> To the persistent question, why do people act as they do, the most exciting and complete, albeit brief, answer offered by sociology and anthropology is *culture.*

People behave as they do primarily because their culture or subculture prompts them to behave that way. Culture thus puts a form of damper on individual freedom. The question arises, then, do the social control features of culture necessarily undermine the humanistic goal of building a society where every individual can most fully realize his or her potential?

The answer to the question is a complex yes and no—complex because certain control aspects of culture do indeed undermine humanism; but this is not unequivocally so. Norms do more than control. They also free societal participants from having to sustain interest in making a multitude of trivial decisions. Thus, ". . . society protects our sanity," as Peter Berger observes, "by pre-empting a large number of choices—not only choices of action but choices of thought" (1971:4). He adds: ". . . social life would be psychologically [as well as physically] intolerable if each of its moments required from us full attention, deliberate decision, and high emotional involvement."

There is another dimension of freedom that is associated with the sociocultural order, but this results from knowledge about the order rather than from participation in it. This is a difficult point to discuss because, as with the more intangible aspects of religion, one must almost "be it" in order to "see it." However, to make the point as clear as possible, it can be described in the following terms: the more one honestly and thoroughly studies a particular phenomenon, in general the less possibility there is for the phenomenon to have an emotional hold on one. As it was put in ancient times, ". . . the truth shall make you free" (John, VIII:32).

When this process takes place among students of society and culture, it is usually manifested as anti-establishment radicalism, sometimes coupled with revolutionary implications. This occurs when the more sensitive and knowledgeable among the students of sociocultural systems learn that it is typically "respectable" value systems and "decent" people that are most responsible for the prevalence of despair, inequality, racism, repression, and war. Knowledge about such matters—if the knowledge is more than superficial—makes those involved painfully aware of the narrowmindedness of most chauvinistic claims about the alleged superiority of this or that system. This awareness, in turn, frees the aware from thoughtless ethnocentric notions about "blood, God, and country."

It is no wonder, thus, that students of society and culture who begin their studies as conservative citizens so often end with a declaration that they can no longer, in good conscience, give prime loyalty to any less inclusive a group than humanity as a whole. These citizens of the larger world are much like the "authentic" individuals described by Maslow:

> . . . such a person, by virtue of what he has become, assumes a new relation to his society, and indeed to society in general. He not only transcends himself in various ways; he also transcends his culture. He resists enculturation. He becomes a little more a member of his species and a little less a member of his local group (1968:11-12).

Thinking of the traditional dominance of the "value-free" stance, Maslow added: "My feeling is that most sociologists and anthropologists will take this hard."

Sociology and Counterrevolution   The liberating aspects of sociological knowledge are often regarded with suspicion by flag-waving chauvinistic people who glory in a superpatriotism. They are prone to mutter darkly about the subversive nature of sociology, and have even advocated screening job candidates to weed out those who have had courses in the discipline (Berger, 1971:1). The writer is reminded of a student in a recent class—a Mormon, who told her bishop she was signed up for an introductory sociology course. "Oh you poor child," said the bishop. "It is certain to make an atheist of you."

The bishop's fear is at least partly groundless. He is not aware, nor are the chauvinists, of the ironic fact that the findings of sociology have counterrevolutionary as well as revolutionary implications.* These counterrevolutionary implications by no means boil down to conservative support for a traditional distribution of power and privilege. The "conservatism" of sociology, if that can be used as a proper descriptive term, is far more profound. It has to do with *order* in general, not just the law and order of an established regime.

If sociological knowledge reveals anything at all, it tells us that the heart of human life is its orderliness and patterned nature. Not perfect order, of course—that is achieved, if at all, only in a totalitarian state. But life without order in general is jungle life, and the law of the jungle is that of tooth and claw. Without order there is no predictability, and without predictability there can be no intelligent coping with challenge. International relations are a perfect example of what life is like without order—"nasty, brutish, and short" (quoted from Thomas Hobbes concerning war). Order is so important to humanity that it is impossible to point to any significant examples where people on the local level have lived without order for any but the briefest chaotic moments. They simply refuse to live that way, given a choice, even if their only alternative is lynch law or vigilantism. Revolutionists have learned this quickly or they have not succeeded; if they do not restore order almost instantly, they are quickly supplanted.

The imperative of order means that any reasonable sociologist ". . . thinks daringly but acts carefully" (Berger, 1971:1). One's thoughts about ordinary established order may be close to revolutionary, given the typically enormous gap between the promises and performances of current establishments; but the sociologist does not, therefore, easily join some handy movement whose leaders pledge they will tear down the establishment and build a utopia out of the pieces of debris. Generally, we do not, because to our skepticism about the establishment we add skepticism about the new establishments promised by self-proclaimed. messiahs who prate endlessly about the need for a continuing revolution and about the alleged benefits of a form of "mass political democracy" that would necessitate everyone's being constantly in meetings about everything. And of course it is chastening to know that when impatient true-believer saviors assume control, it is quite typical of them to become, sooner or later, leaders or members of a new privileged élite

---

* I am indebted to Peter Berger (1971) for his brilliant discussion of the dual nature of sociology.

living off the sweat of the masses just as have their predecessor élites from the beginning of time.

The Task of Humanistic Sociology   Knowing what has been discussed, the humanistically oriented sociologist is understandably often discouraged. But we would give the lie to our professed belief in human potential if we surrendered to cynicism just because of "man's inhumanity to man." That is the challenge we face! No tradition is forever; change is the very essence of life.

Although we produce a full measure of those who are cruel and exploitative, we also create idealists who point to a better way, emboldened by the fact that what seems utopian in one era ". . . has repeatedly become the basic norm of decency for the next" (Lynd, 1968:219). It is one of humanistic sociology's basic tasks to help accelerate this process of making the "impossible" dreams possible. The acceleration process may often require cooperation with existing regimes; it may sometimes, when all more orderly methods have failed, necessitate thoughtful, radical, maybe even revolutionary, action. In any case, the humanistic goal is always the same: achievement of a time

> When . . . all men's good be
> Each man's rule and universal
> Peace be like a shaft of light
> Across the land.
>   Alfred Lord Tennyson

REFERENCES AND FURTHER SOURCES

Berger, Peter L.
1971 "Sociology and Freedom." The American Sociologist 6 (February): 1–5.

Bronowski, J.
1965 Science and Human Values. New York: Harper Torchbooks. Revised edition.

Brown, Dee
1970 Bury My Heart at Wounded Knee: An Indian History of the American West. New York: Bantam.

Chinoy, Eli
1967 Society: An Introduction to Sociology. New York: Random House. Second edition.

Cuber, John F.
1968 Sociology: A Synopsis of Principles. New York: Appleton-Century-Crofts. Sixth edition.

Gans, Herbert J.
1972 "The new egalitarianism." Saturday Review 55 (May 6): 43–46.

Ginsberg, Morris
1965 On Justice in Society. New York: Cornell University Press.

Lewis, Sinclair
1920 Main Street. New York: Harcourt, Brace and World.

Lynd, Helen Merrell
1968 On Shame and the Search for Identity. New York: Harcourt, Brace and Company.

MacIver, R. M. and Charles H. Page
1949 Society: An Introductory Analysis. New York: Rinehart.

Maslow, Abraham H.
1968 Toward a Psychology of Being. Princeton, N.J.: D. Van Nostrand. Second edition.

Means, Richard L.
1970 The Ethical Imperative. Garden City, New York: Anchor.

Merton, Robert K.
1968 Social Theory and Social Structure. New York: Free Press. Enlarged edition.

Rosenberg, Bernard
1972 The Province of Sociology: Freedom and Constraint. New York: Crowell.

Scott, John Finley
   1971   Internalization of Norms: A Sociological Theory of Moral Commitment. Englewood Cliffs, New Jersey: Prentice-Hall.

Segal, Ronald
   1968   The Americans: A Conflict of Creed and Reality. New York: Viking Press.

Sumner, William Graham
   1906   Folkways: A Study of the Sociological Importance of Usages, Manners, Customs, Mores, and Morals. New York: Mentor Books. 1960 reprint of the original.

6

Social Differentiation

INTRODUCTION

***My Fair Lady* Revisited**   When Henry Higgins first saw his "fair lady," Eliza Doolittle, he remarked to Colonel Pickering, "Look at her—a pris'ner of the gutter; condemned by ev'ry syllable she utters."

Eliza responds, "Garn."

Higgins says to the colonel, "Garn. I ask you, sir, what sort of word is that? It's 'Aoow' and 'Garn' that keep her in her place, not her wretched clothes and dirty face."

The interaction between Professor Higgins and Miss Doolittle illustrates some aspects of *social differentiation*. This is the process whereby people and groups acquire characteristics that make them unique and thus set them off from one another. One of these characteristics is speech pattern. Professor Higgins claims he can place where a person comes from within a few miles simply by the way that person speaks. And, if the home is London, the professor says he can place it within a few blocks, sometimes within two streets. He goes on to boast that, as a linguist, within six months he could teach "this guttersnipe" to speak and act in such a way that she would be taken for a duchess at an embassy ball.

When the professor and Colonel Pickering wander off, Eliza and her friends and father manifest other characteristics of the poor and disadvantaged. They sing of their highest ambition as a "room somewhere"—a room where one can have a warm face, warm hands, warm feet. That would be loverly! But such takes a little bit of luck, the elder Doolittle observes. Good fortune occurs only with the fall of the cards,

121

so there is not much point in regular work. With a little bit of luck, he says, you will give in to temptation and you will not be in when your neighbor asks you to help. You'll indulge in a little fillanderin', perhaps, but the bloodhounds will not find out. And, though the gentle sex was made for marrying, with a little bit of luck "you can have it all and not get hooked."

The modest hopes of Eliza and her friends symbolize the truly important consequences of social differentiation. It is not superficialities like speech patterns that matter; it is the differential distribution of advantage. As subsequent discussion will indicate, the final result of social differentiation in almost all large-scale societies is great disparity in life chances between those who are privileged and those who are not. The latter, in most cases, far outnumber the former; in the familiar phraseology, the multitudes grovel while the ruling class lives in luxury. The arbitrariness and injustice of such a disparity in life style is set forth below.

Three Dimensions of Social Differentiation   The Doolittles, it is clear, have few privileges and no power to speak of; they are also totally lacking in prestige. These three things—*power, privilege,* and *prestige*—are the three most critical dimensions of social differentiation.

For present purposes, *power* is defined as the means whereby people control aspects of their environment, including one another; thus power permits individuals or groups to control other individuals or groups against the latter's will. The coercive potential of power distinguishes it from *authority*, which is usually defined as an established and widely accepted right to control others. Thus, a person with power can exercise, in the short run, control without regard to right; a person with authority controls others only to the degree that he is regarded as having the right to do so. *Privilege* is here defined as a special advantage available only to selected persons or groups; and *prestige* is the regard or honor associated with particular social positions.

The relationship between the three dimensions of social differentiation is a complex one, as I have shown in Figure 1. In this figure, an attempt has been made to indicate that the three dimensions of differentiation are interlocked and interacting, but that of the three, power and privilege are by far the most important, prestige being a consequence of the other two. Gerhard Lenski asserts that power alone is the critical dimension. He says, ". . . to explain most of the distribution of privilege in a society, we have but to determine the distribution of power" (1966:45). C. Wright Mills similarly emphasized the power dimension. The basic theme of his *The Power Elite* (1956) was that critical decisions in American society are made by relatively few individuals—two to three hundred at most. It is the members of this élite alone, Mills claimed, who make critically important decisions about such basic matters as American foreign policy, the economy, war, peace, and the ecological order, to name but a few.

Despite the importance of the power dimension of social differentiation, it is clear that privilege too is basic. Those who, for one reason or another, have privileges also have access to power, just as those who have power are able to command privileges. Few would disagree with the contention that those who have either power or privilege also generally have prestige. But this is not always the case, as illustrated, for example, by union leaders who may wield immense power yet have almost no prestige in the eyes of the general public. On the other hand, one can imagine an impoverished person who has high prestige solely because of family background; yet such a person might have few privileges and almost no power.

The arrows in Figure 1 indicate that when a person has power, the power typically gives access to privileges and vice versa; also, a person with power or privilege sometimes has prestige and occasionally vice versa. Then, over time, the possession of power and/or privilege and/or prestige leads to an accumulation of more power and privilege and possibly prestige—with the final result that, for a select few, life is an

Figure 1.   Relationship of Three Dimensions of Social Differentiation

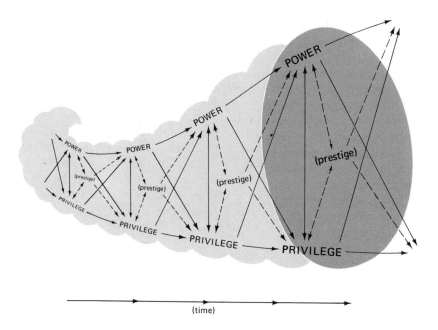

overflowing cornucopia of good fortune. This is a rather formal way of expressing the folk observation that the rich get richer while the poor get babies.

The Life and Death Aspects of Social Differentiation   Social differentiation is not simply an abstract matter of interest only to professional social scientists. To multitudes of people, differentiation can be a vital matter. This was brought home to the writer and a colleague in a most graphic manner. Following the Korean War during the early 1950s, while looking over a list of the war casualties from the Detroit area, we were struck by the apparent overrepresentation of people who had come from poor neighborhoods. We decided to test our casual observation by doing a systematic study (Mayer and Hoult, 1955); a related study that obtained similar results has been completed for the Phoenix, Arizona area in relation to the Vietnam war (Willis, 1973); still another study concludes, "Men from poor families are overrepresented among troops killed in Vietnam . . ." (Zeitlin, 1970:174–175). Although these studies are concerned with particular wars and specific locales, the findings are probably applicable to modern American communities in general.

The basic hypothesis of the original study was that the higher the economic well-being of a Detroit population grouping, or the lower its proportion of nonwhites, the lower its casualty rate. The basic findings of the study are depicted in Tables 1, 2, and 3. The first table shows that when the casualties are categorized in terms of median income, without exception the index of the casualty rate becomes progressively lower as income level rises, the rate of the highest level being about one-third that of the lowest. When the casualties were categorized by value of home, as shown in Table 2, the indices of casualty rate did not go down as evenly as those shown in Table 1. However, the direction of difference in rates is obvious; the rate in areas where home values averaged $15,000 was approximately one-fourth the rate in areas where home values averaged less than $4,000. Table 3 shows the indices of casualty rates among economically comparable whites and nonwhites (the latter, in Detroit, are 95 percent black). As indicated, the total nonwhite rate was almost twice as high as the white rate. In comparable economic areas, as represented by average value of homes, the nonwhite rates were almost 50 percent greater than the white rates.

The hypothesis of the study was obviously confirmed beyond any doubt. Interpretations of such findings vary in accordance with the value positions of the individual observer. Our interpretation was that the findings were a concrete expression of the critical significance of certain aspects of social differentiation. As for explaining the differential casualty rates, they were most probably due to differential education;

Table 1.   Korean War Casualty Rate Indices (by Median
Income of Census Tract, Detroit, Michigan)

Median Income in Dollars	Casualty Rate Index
Under 2,500	14.6
2,500-2,999	10.8
3,000-3,499	9.1
3,500-3,999	8.6
4,000-4,499	7.5
4,500-4,999	6.6
5,000-5,499	5.8
5,500 and over	4.6

Source: Adapted from Mayer and Hoult (1955: Table 3).

the higher the educational or technical competence of a man, the more likely he was stationed in a relatively less exposed combat area. In addition, it is known that relatively more men from disadvantaged groups have volunteered for the armed forces and are thus more "available" to become casualties. But such higher volunteer rates, and relatively low educational attainments of the disadvantaged, are products of social differentiation, so the realities of differentiation are not explained away.

There are many more evidences of the vital realities associated with social differentiation. For example, a recent book by Heribert Adam (1971) describes apartheid, the South African system of racial segregation. As Adam and others point out, in South Africa no so-called nonwhite, regardless of talent, can have authority over any white, no matter how untalented. The supremacy of whites is maintained through brutal repression. In Johannesburg alone an average of 600 nonwhites are arrested and sentenced to prison daily simply for not carrying identity documents. All opposition to the prevailing regime is prosecuted under an act prohibiting "communism." The mining barracks, where blacks earn one-twentieth the wages paid whites, are described as places of "fierce horror." In the urban areas, black workers from the countryside are not permitted to bring their families for the first ten years; it is not surprising that in such areas violent crimes are commonplace. The associated result is that South Africa's annual executions account for close to 50 percent of the total for the entire world.

Another example much closer to home consists of the studies dealing

Table 2. Korean War Casualty Rate Indices (by Average
Value of Home, Detroit, Michigan)

Economic Level as Indicated by Average Dollar Value per Home	Casualty Rate Index
Under 4,000	16.4
4,000-4,999	15.5
5,000-5,999	13.1
6,000-6,999	15.1
7,000-7,999	9.2
8,000-8,999	5.3
9,000-9,999	5.3
10,000-10,999	5.4
11,000-11,999	7.2
12,000-12,999	5.7
13,000-13,999	6.1
14,000-14,999	6.7
15,000-15,999	4.3

Source: Adapted from Mayer and Hoult (1955:Table 4).

Table 3. Korean War Casualty Rate Indices (by Value of Home
and Race, Detroit, Michigan)

	Indices of Casualties	
Dollar Value of Home *	Whites by Value of Home	Nonwhites by Value of Home
Under 8,000	11.5	16.8
8,000-14,999	5.4	7.7
15,000 and over	4.3	—
Total	7.7	13.3

Source: Adapted from Mayer and Hoult (1955:Table 5)

with brain function and nutrition deprivation and their high degree of
relation to each other. Biochemists have found that the human brain
accomplishes 80 percent of its growth during the first three years of life.

*Because of the relatively small number of nonwhite cases, stable indices could be ob-
tained only by consolidating the 13 average dollar values of home categories shown in
Table 2 into the 3 categories shown here in Table 3.

The brain begins to develop in the mother's womb, producing new cells by means of a chemical reaction involving a number of crucial ingredients, especially amino acids. The aminos are supplied by the mother, who derives many of them from the protein in her own diet. After birth, the infant can receive them from the mother's milk, which is rich in protein. If at any point in the sequence of growth the supply of aminos is deficient, brain growth is affected. Quite obviously this has critical implications for the poor of any country, including the United States. It means that some types of malnutrition can lead to the mental degradation of many members of economically deprived groups. Deprivation among black Americans has been widely noted. But the recent census reports (1970) are more discouraging than ever. They show that the much heralded indicators of black economic progress during the 1960s were largely illusory (*New York Times* News Service, December 21, 1971). There were gains for black families where both husband and wife worked, but there was nothing but long-term poverty for a swelling number of families headed only by a mother. It is these families that provide the cases, which considered collectively, led child development specialist Urie Bronfenbrenner to make the following observation:

> Though the Negro infant is not biologically inferior at the moment of conception, he often becomes so shortly thereafter. The inadequate nutrition and prenatal care received by millions of Negro mothers result in complications in pregnancy which take their toll in extraordinarily high rates of prematurity and congenital defects. Many of these abnormalities entail neurological damage, resulting in impaired intellectual function and behavioral disturbances, including hyperactivity, distractability, and low attention span. Of particular relevance is the significant role played by paranatal and prenatal factors in the genesis of childhood reading disorders (1967:913).

Bronfenbrenner's observation has been confirmed by a number of careful studies. Amante and his colleagues, all psychologists or social workers, compared 219 black and white children from two disadvantaged groups living in western Michigan and came to this conclusion:

> It is apparent, then, that the black population of children is characterized not only by higher overall rates of brain damage relative to the white population; it is also characterized by more severe cases of brain damage (1970:126).

The investigators cautioned that conclusions associated with race per se are not warranted. They hypothesized that if racial groups are screened neurologically before I.Q. tests are applied, then ". . . the supposedly obvious or inevitable I.Q. differentials between the groups might collapse to zero and/or statistical insignificance" (p. 129).

Epidemiologists Benjamin Pasamanick and Hilda Knoblock also assert that it is unwarranted to point to *racial* factors on the basis of differential brain damage among racial groups. On the basis of a series of studies conducted by them and others, they postulated: ". . . prematurity and pregnancy complication rates increase exponentially below certain socioeconomic thresholds" (1966:19). Similar findings have been reported from Mexico, Chile, and Guatemala (*Life,* January 24, 1969:52). Up-to-date details are related by Paulo Freire in his *Pedagogy of the Oppressed* (1970). A Brazilian educator, Freire observed that the deprived Latin American masses are "living corpses," "shadows of human beings." They are hopeless men, women, and children victimized by endless strife in which their ravaged bodies are devoured systematically by infant diarrhea, tuberculosis, schistosomiasis, and the multitude of other diseases associated with poverty.

Brain damage from nutritional deficiencies is complicated by other factors. *Environmental Action* (February 19, 1972) reported that air sampling in eight large cities indicated that inner city poor people, in comparison with more affluent suburbanites, are subjected to much more deleterious air pollution. It was noted:

> In Chicago, the one-hour carbon monoxide standard of thirty-five parts per million is exceeded forty-eight times per year. The eight-hour standard of nine parts per million is exceeded seven hundred and thirteen times per year. In Washington, D. C., the one-hour standard is exceeded eighty-seven times per year, and the eight-hour standard ninety-nine times.

In contrast, federal law stipulates that the standards should not be exceeded more than *once* per year.

STATUS AND ROLE

Status   In all societies, even those with the smallest populations, there is social differentiation in the form of *status,* formally defined as the relative rank of a person in a particular group. In the case of Professor Higgins and Eliza Doolittle, the group is English society. In that society, the professor has a relatively high rank, especially in comparison with the Doolittles, who have a low rank.

The basis for the status form of differentiation varies with time and with the society and its structure. In many societies the most important status differentiations are associated with the *division of labor*—the separation of a total work process into interdependent tasks. Thus, in a given society the division may call for fishermen, sailmakers, boatbuilders, fish processors, and so on. It is typical that, depending upon a society's history, the different tasks will be regarded as having differential importance. And those who do the most important tasks will generally have the highest status—that is to say, the greatest power with its associated privileges and possibly prestige. To phrase it another way: Generally speaking it is those who do the work regarded as most significant who are given special privileges, and these in turn are typically associated with the acquisition of power, which, of course, provides more privilege, which leads to more power, and so on (see Figure 1, page 123).

In 1963, a study done by the National Opinion Research Center indicated the prestige rating accorded by Americans to different occupations. Although the study may seem old, it is the most recent available. More important, its findings probably still apply since it included a comparison with 1947 research and found that there was a very high degree of stability in occupational prestige over time (correlation coefficient of .99). In any case, NORC found that Supreme Court justices were given the top rating. Close behind them were physicians and state governors. Tied for fourth place were federal cabinet members, foreign service diplomats, and college professors. Airline pilots and priests were ranked the same even though the former obviously earn considerably more money than the latter, and certainly more than college professors. This illustrates that money alone is not sufficient cause to give one a higher ranking over another in American society. However, in general the occupations rated highest were also those that commanded the highest income. Other factors in high ratings included specialized and lengthy professional education like that required for surgeons.

One of the most significant things about status is that it permits participants in a social system to interact meaningfully even though they know nothing about one another aside from their respective statuses. If one sees a uniformed policeman, for example, one knows immediately that such a person has the legal right and power to direct one in traffic or to stop one for questioning. It is the policeman's status that gives him this special combination of power and privilege. Or again, if one sees a man disciplining a small child, one does not generally interfere if it is reasonable to assume the man is the father of the child. In most Western societies, at least, the status of father confers on the individual the privilege of disciplining his children. This is not true in some societies, such as the Zuñi, where the discipline privilege is reserved for the mother's brother or some other member of the family. But, in any case, the task of engaging in disciplinary action is a function of differential status.

Ascribed and Achieved Statuses   Many observers find it useful to differentiate between two basic forms of status. One of these is usually termed *ascribed status*—one that is conferred without reference to desire or accomplishment. The most important ascribed statuses are usually bestowed at birth; racial status is an example. Others are sex status, age, nationality, and frequently such characteristics as religion. Less common ascribed statuses are those associated with physical anomalies such as dwarfism.

The other basic form of status is the *achieved*. This is the kind that results from meeting certain requirements. For example, marital status is achieved; one marries or stays single according to one's inclinations and life style. Marital status is thus not conferred on one haphazardly, at least in Western societies. In such societies other important acquired statuses are those associated with education, occupation, political party membership, and the like.

In a modern, complex society, a typical person has many statuses, a number of which vary with time and circumstance. In addition to one's unchanging statuses—sex membership, race—there are temporary statuses such as student or mother of small children. And, along with unchanging and temporary statuses, there can be an occupational status such as machinist or housewife. Later in life, one may achieve the status of grandparent. Simultaneously, one can have the status of communicant in a particular church, a lodge member, a participant in a voluntary service agency, an athlete, a customer or a salesperson in a store, to name but a few.

Injustices associated with many ascribed statuses have often been noted. These injustices are particularly significant because ascribed statuses generally come first in point of time and thus constitute the framework within which the socialization process takes place for given individuals. Ascribed statuses, therefore, determine the goals toward which people aim and the means that can be used to achieve those goals. Thus, if one knows a child's ascribed statuses—sex, age, type of family, religion, nationality, and so forth—one knows pretty well what his chances of reaching his aspirations in life will be. The example of sex status has come to public attention in recent years. Beginning at least as far back as Karl Marx in the mid-nineteenth century, it was noted that male domination meant women generally had the status of serfs whose chief duty was to act as cheap and controllable labor. To insure this result, men have seen to it that laws, socialization processes, and educational organizations have been such as to help "keep women in their place."

Another example is the injustices associated with aging; they have become notorious in most Western societies. One's age is ascribed; there is nothing one can do about it. And, if one happens to live in a society that worships youth, then increasing age means increasing disability in far more than a purely physical sense. A recent hospital patient wrote:

. . . my aged hospital neighbors inculcated a new fear of old age. Even worse than the physical debilitation and pain are the scorn and shame connected with old age in America. The national youth cult decreed it a crime to be less than efficient, to have wrinkles and infirmities, to have too many memories and little future prospects of power and productivity. The old are not seen as storehouses of wisdom and knowledge as in other cultures. Just to be slow moving is an annoyance (*Streetpress*, September 7, 1971).

A status as "abnormal human being" is less common than that of being aged; but the results can be no less debilitating or poignant. A relatively short (5 feet 4 inches) sociologist has written about "heightism." Professor Saul Feldman (1971) points out that America has an obsession with height: "There is nothing cute about a short man or a tall woman in our society." He indicates that in a study of recent graduates of the University of Pittsburgh it was found that men who were six feet two or taller received an average starting salary 12.4 percent higher than men who were under six feet.

Role   The other side of the status coin is called *role*. A role is made up of the behaviors associated with a given status. Thus, in Western society, a man who has a status as father is traditionally expected to play a certain role—to provide support for his children, and to guide and protect them until they are at an age where they can be considered as on their own. If one's status is that of teacher in a college classroom, the prescribed role is to take charge of given groupings of students, to direct them in appropriate study, and to grade them in accordance with prevailing standards. On the other hand, if one's status is that of college student, then the prescribed role usually calls for attending class, reading textbooks (at least once over lightly), preparing papers, and taking tests.

Perhaps the most significant aspect of roles is that they are usually parts of tradition-dominated social structures and thus very confining. Boston University faculty member Seymour Sarason (1971) has described schools as a typical example of the social setting wherein roles are carefully defined and thereby shape the behavior of those who play them. Given such a structure, Sarason is not surprised to find that young teachers who are enthusiastic and innovative in the beginning, so often quickly become apathetic participants in educational procedures that boil down to dull and compromising routine. The change in the outlook and related behavior of young teachers is due to several major factors. First, they discover they must make a compromise between the ideal of helping all children and the realities of coping with a classroom filled with those in need of various degrees of help. Second, the desire to be innovative is undermined by the necessity to maintain a schedule, sometimes involving daily lesson plans prepared in detail and in triplicate. Third, they find that if they attempt to get help with their fears and problems, they are very likely to evoke job-undermining negative evaluations. The result is that for many new teachers the first two years on the job become a baptism of fire, consuming idealism and experimentalism. But—

> the important point is that what happens in these years . . . cannot be understood by narrowly focusing on the teacher, but by seeing the teacher as part of a matrix of existing relationships, practices, and ideas (Sarason, 1971:171).

Bureaucracy   In larger societies, it is common to find social phenomena called bureaucracies. The most notable feature of the bureaucracy is that it is a *formal* social organization. To say that an organization is formal means that it includes carefully specified behavioral rules and relationship regulations. Such rules and regulations are most evident in the bureaucracy, which is an organization of officials whose work related statuses and roles are spelled out in fine detail. Among the details there is typically a specific description of the decision-making power of participants in the system so that an unambiguous chain of command can be achieved.

It is characteristic for formal organizations like bureaucracies to be governed by purely rational values—by a businesslike attention to implementing the goals of the organization. Thus, there is usually a very impersonal application of rules without regard to sentiment or individual needs of the moment. There is also a routinization of tasks assigned to participants in the system so that given individuals can be easily replaced. The dispensability of particular persons is enhanced by the file system that can reveal to new personnel all that is significant on a particular topic. The file is the carefully collated and systematized collection of papers recording the rules, previous commitments, correspondence, and future duties of the organization. A visitor from Jupiter might well conclude that the file is akin to an altar, so many are concerned with it, collect around it, hover over it, and make offerings to it.

Although people often speak disparagingly of bureaucratic red tape, it is clear that complex social systems could not function effectively without many of the elements of a bureaucracy. Indeed, a bureaucracy is in essence little more than the division of labor, together with its differentiation of status and role, carried to the logical extreme. Without some such task specialization, few largescale social systems could reach their desired ends. As it has been said, too many cooks spoil the broth. Broth can be made both tasty and with efficiency only if the various cooks—in case there is more than one—divide up their work appropriately, with each attending to his own business so that mutual interference does not impede achieving the wanted goal.

Unfortunately the bureaucracy associated with a complex society frequently achieves a life of its own; the result is that it is often impossible to pin down who is responsible for what. It is a common experience for people to observe that dealing with a well-established bureaucracy is like trying to pin the proverbial jellyfish to a wall. Also, it is rather typical for the long-established bureaucracy to gradually shift attention from the ends of the organization to sheer day-by-day perpetuation. This can lead to massive frustration for those attempting to get something done. A living illustration has been provided by the editor of *Arizona*, a weekly newsmagazine. In the February 20, 1972 issue, the editor described the results of his attempt to have his name removed from a public relations list maintained by a large airline. With tongue partially in cheek—but *only* partially—the airline vice president in charge of public relations wrote:

Dear _____ :

. . . According to our figures, we have been sending to you only 20 releases per year. At a cost of 20 cents each, this amounts to only $4 a year.

To remove your name would require the efforts of a secretary to notify the mailroom, a mail clerk to fill out a notification to the punched-card department, a messenger to take the card to the data processing center, a computer programmer to locate the program card which will instruct the $10 million computer how to remove your name from our files, and a $15,000-a-year computer operator to electronically banish you from our lives. . . .

Total cost of removing your name is $400, or the approximate cost of sending you our press releases for 100 years. Inasmuch as I hope to retire in nine, I would have much preferred that you had held this suggestion for my successor.

However, since you have asked, we will comply. But don't think you have done us any favors.

SOCIAL STRATIFICATION

General Observations   In larger societies, people of the same general social status tend to associate with one another in broad groupings. The whole process of forming such groupings, together with the results of the process, is roughly analogous to geological stratification with its layers of sediment. Similarly, the typical largescale society also has layers—that is, groupings of people who have varying amounts of the three components of social differentiation (power, privilege, prestige). Such groupings may, therefore, be regarded as "higher" or "lower" in the sense that people with larger amounts of the components tend to dominate—that is, have the say over those with relatively smaller amounts of the components.

The term *social strata* is most generally used to describe status groups that are the central structural aspect of given stratification systems. There are various kinds of such strata, termed social classes, castes, or estates. To be designated such, a stratum must include people of both sexes and all ages. It may seem that such social strata are the same as the subcultures previously described in Chapter 5. However, there is this difference: In a social system made up of various strata, any given stratum is a critical part of the system and, thus, the system would not be such if the particular stratum were to disappear. The members of a stratum are fully a part of the general social system. In contrast, the members of a subculture such as French Canadians in Maine participate only marginally in the social system of which they are a part. Therefore, if in a society a subculture vanishes, the society at large may not be fundamentally altered.

The most essential difference between the various types of social strata—class, caste, and estate—is their relative rigidity as far as vertical mobility is concerned. *Vertical mobility* denotes an individual's or group's alteration of status when such an alteration is a relatively permanent movement from one rank to another in a status hierarchy. An example of a movement of this sort would be a change from the status of low-income worker to high-income worker. The relative possibility of such change in various stratification systems is graphically indicated in Figure 2. Mobility realities in the United States will be discussed in the next chapter.

Caste Stratification   As indicated in Figure 2, the society characterized by the caste type of social stratification has the least possibility of vertical mobility. In such a society, one's stratum membership is

Figure 2.   Social Stratification Systems Related to Vertical Mobility Possibilities*

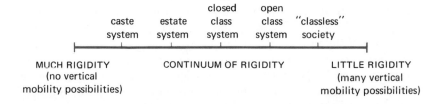

* Positions on the continuum are relative to one another only and are not meant to suggest specific amounts or lack of rigidity.

ascribed at birth and interstratum mobility is all but impossible. As Lenski observed, "When class and caste are used as contrasting terms, castes are thought of as groups out of which and into which mobility is virtually impossible" (1966:77). In addition, the caste system typically restricts the nature of social interaction, if any, between the members of particular strata.

Caste stratification, or important elements thereof, has appeared in many societies, including South Africa, Japan, Guatemala, and the United States. However, the ideal type caste society is, of course, India. It has four broadly inclusive castes each of which encompasses a multitude of subcastes. There are also more than 40 million "untouchables" who are regarded as being so lowly that they have no caste status at all. Although untouchability was legally proscribed in 1949, sacred tradition has preserved many aspects of it.

India's caste system has an all-pervasive effect on individual life-choices. Marriage partner possibilities are prescribed and the occupations in which given caste members can engage are carefully delineated, with special attention given to differentiating between "clean" and "unclean" work. Even clothing and ornamentation have been regulated. All such differences among the members of the various castes and subcastes have been regarded as so important that members of the highest status (Brahmins) traditionally felt polluted if they were touched by even the shadow of an untouchable or a person of low caste.

The Indian caste system is intricately bound and associated with the Hindu religion. At this point, however, one does not know whether the religion underlies the caste system or vice versa. The answer is probably something along the lines of both/and. In any case, the two phenomena are mutually supportive. The religion teaches that although a Hindu can be a believer in gods, or an unbeliever, there is one undeniable requirement that will insure a happier future: the observation of caste rules. The happier future is a possibility because of *reincarnation*—a belief in the transmigration of souls (that is, spirit movement among bodily hosts).

The Hindu version of the widespread belief in reincarnation is that souls never die since they are a part of Brahma, the indestructable ALL. Brahma is conceived as everything that is subjective as well as everything objective. Since people are part of the ALL, souls constantly remanifest themselves in new birth, but not necessarily on the same plane. Therefore, the soul of a man of low status may be reborn as a prince or as a worm, depending upon another belief—the *Law of Karma*. According to this law, one's future is determined by one's thoughts, words, and deeds. In the literal interpretation, the Law of Karma means that everything a person does, thinks, and believes is entered into a balance sheet that determines an ultimate fate from which there is no appeal. Therefore, whatever one's lot, it is felt to be the result of actions that occurred in a former state. This is a particularly significant point because it is the final justification for a caste system that gives great privilege and power to a few, and pain and misery to the great masses. As Noss has described it:

> When the caste system was linked up with the Law of Karma, the inequalities of life had at once a simple and comprehensive explanation. The existence of caste in the social structure immediately acquired a kind of moral justification. If a man was born a Sudra, it was because he had sinned in previous existences and deserved no better lot. A Brahmin, on the other hand, had every right to exalt his position and prerogatives; by good deeds in previous existences he has merited his present high station (1969:108).

Thus, anybody who questioned the caste system was in effect expressing heresy because such questions imply doubts about the law of reincarnation and the sacred Law of Karma. It is not surprising, therefore, that there is a strong strain of escapism associated with Hinduism. The escapism strain is manifested in the three traditional ways to avoid the miseries of everyday life: the Way of Works, the Way of Knowledge, and the Way of Devotion. The Yoga system of mental and bodily discipline was also developed to aid the Hindu in seeking "release and liberation" from the trials of material life.

The rigidity of any caste system is undermined by industrialization. Imagine what it would be like if, in a modern factory, a worker suddenly left an assembly line to take a ritual bath of purification because the foreman, who is of lower caste, has let his shadow fall on that worker. Obviously it would be impossible to conduct a successful business under such conditions. Therefore, there has been strong pressure, where caste has prevailed, to pay only lip service to many of the old restrictions. However, despite this, and despite other recent developments that have moderated many of the ancient caste laws in India, the Indian masses continue to believe in the essentials of the religious ways of their ancestors.

The Estate System of Stratification   Another historically important form of social stratification is known as the *estate system*. It is called this because its major strata were known as "estates of the realm." The ideal type estate system appeared in Europe during the early Middle Ages. At one end of the power–privilege–prestige continuum were two estates consisting of the landowning nobility and the clergy. Close to the other end were the peasants; indentured servants (serfs) had even less of the three major components of social differentiation.

A unique feature of the estate form of stratification is that membership in the various estates, together with the duties, powers, and privileges of the members, was defined by law as well as by custom. Thus, the system was very rigid. Like the caste form of stratification, estate membership was usually ascribed by birth; generally speaking there was nothing a given individual could do about estate membership. If a father was a lowly serf, then his children were also. Or, if one were lucky enough to be the child of a lord, then one would also be part of the nobility. However, unlike a true caste system, in the estate form of stratification individuals could occasionally alter their stratum membership. This could be done by a change in the law, or by engaging in some special service, the reward for which would be membership in a higher, more privileged grouping.

Some historians attribute the growth of the estate form of stratification to the social disorder and limited occupational possibilities resulting from the fall of the Roman Empire. Peasants could do little but till the soil; at the same time there was no semblance of central government; hence personal protection could be insured only by pledging fealty (loyalty in service) to a powerful lord who controlled a given district by force of arms.

As the economy changed and as centralized government began to reappear in the later Middle Ages (about A.D. 1200), the estate social system began to break down. The growth of trade and commerce produced a group of bankers and merchants who could maintain themselves in town and, therefore, did not need to be dependent on a land-owning noble. Then, as the Industrial Revolution gradually developed, beginning roughly about 1750, persons of lowly estate found occupations that were not bound to the land. Finally, manufacturing facilities became more important than land as a source of wealth, so that the agrarian-based social system was significantly undermined.

The Class System of Stratification   The previously indicated commercial and industrial developments were accompanied by compatible religious and attitudinal changes. During the Middle Ages, a dominant value was that pursuit of material goods was an unworthy venture; spiritual salvation alone was glorified. Gradually, however, new views prevailed. By the 1500s, Martin Luther was preaching that each person has a "calling" from God to do a particular job; hence, moral behavior consisted primarily of doing good works in a material sense. At the same time, John Calvin was preaching that the only sign of being saved was material prosperity; hence, his followers placed great emphasis on *work*. The devil occupies the idle! God is glorified when people strive to control all of nature; believers were exhorted to know nature so that it might more readily yield up its secrets and treasures. Such philosophies, collectively known as the *Protestant ethic*, were quite naturally associated with worldly success. Subscribers to the Protestant ethic, churches and individuals alike, prospered and eventually dominated the highly industrialized nations of the Western world (like England, Belgium, and Germany).

The get-ahead ideas which both created, and were created by, commercialism, industrialism, and the Protestant ethic were antithetical to the estate system of stratification. The latter system was based on the principle that individuals are *inherently* unequal and, therefore, should not strive to better their lot in life. The new view, the view that permeated the commercial, industrial, and Protestant religious world, was that humans are what they become. Striving then is both sensible and necessary. It is true that many advocates of the new view adhered to it only superficially. As expressed by Shakespeare:

> That lowliness is young ambition's ladder,
> Whereto the climber-upward turns his face;
> But when he once attains the upmost round,
> He then unto the ladder turns his back,
> Looks in the clouds, scorning the base degrees
> By which he did ascend.
>
> (Julius Caesar, II:1)

Nevertheless, the challenge to the estate system was sufficient to undermine it. In its place there grew a system, termed *class stratification*, that still prevails throughout industrialized society; only in parts of Africa and the Middle East can one find remnants of stratification by estate.

The essence of stratification by class is that membership in any given stratum is a function of possessing characteristics possessed by established members of that stratum. The easiest way to come into such possession is, of course, to have the appropriate parentage. Hence class stratification, like caste and estate, is largely a matter of inheritance. But theoretically at least, in a true class system stratum outsiders can become insiders by acquiring relevant characteristics.

According to the Marxian view, the class system of stratification has two major components: workers on the one hand, and owners on the other. Thus, according to Marx, the class standing of given individuals depends primarily upon their relationship to the means of production. Later observers have insisted that the class system is more complicated than that envisaged by Marx. Class standing is affected by a multitude of variables, including religion, education, race, and the like. However, even those most critical of the Marxian point of view admit that economic factors are the prime ones in a class system.

Sociologist Max Weber was especially critical of Marx. Weber asserted that economic classes—large groupings of people with generally the same material status—have little practical importance because they are not homogeneous and thus do not usually act in unison. In contrast, Weber described collectivities which he termed *status groups*. The members of a typical status group recognize each other as social equals and interact with one another regularly. The existence of a status group is, therefore, dependent upon continuous social contact among the members of the group—status groups then are community phenomena. In contrast, the economic classes envisaged by Marx are vast collectivities whose members frequently have little in common except their relationship to the production and acquisition of material goods. At the same time, Weber fully admitted that the members of the status groups he described were economic equals, but their economic similarity is never, said Weber, their most critical characteristic. Status, to Weber, depended upon prestige, and prestige evaluations are seldom made in purely economic terms. One example of this is the traditional failure of the *nouveau riche* (new rich) to be accepted into high society.

However one views the class system of stratification—whether from a Weberian, a Marxian, or other standpoint—it is clear that this system is less rigid than its estate counterpart. But class systems themselves vary in rigidity. The most rigid among them is termed a *closed class system*. The ideal type example of this is traditional English society. Although there is said to be "room at the top," still the Cockney remains a Cockney lifelong, in contrast to the noble who, sitting in the House of Lords, continues to confer great power, privilege, and prestige on his family and descendants. Such people have little to do with the Eliza Doolittles of the world. Indeed, Eliza exists in fiction only. It would be "shocking, simply shocking" for an Eliza to appear in the reserved boxes at the races or at an embassy ball attended by people with high status. Eliza's language—"Kick the 'orses bloody arse"—would make the good ladies from the privileged classes faint dead away.

It is only in the less rigid *open class system* that there is any realistic possibility for telling a rags-to-riches story. Ideal type open class stratification is illustrated by the American frontier, where it was not what a man's name was or his father's standing that counted. What was important was what a man could do. Could he shoot straight and well? Could he wield an axe effectively? Could he participate in a cattle drive? If he could, then he was accepted in all the circles that mattered. And he was then free to use his energies and talents to build whatever little empire he was inclined to create.

Thus, we had the "Horatio Alger myth," the American dream, that has given so much hope, sometimes unrealistic, to so many generations of Americans. This is the idea that any man can become president, any enterprising young person can become a captain of industry. From rags to riches in a single generation! All that is needed is the Puritan virtues of planning, hard work, and thrift.

The Horatio Alger story is termed a myth because, for the great majority of people, reality is quite different. Statistics clearly indicate that the practical way to become a captain of industry is to have a father who made it possible for you. The way to become a millionaire is to inherit a million. The way to move in the "best" circles is to have parents who do so. The exceptions to these rules are so rare that they are touted in *Reader's Digest* as examples of "the opportunities typical of American society."

Classless Society Finally, there is the so-called *classless society*. This is the aim of the classical Marxist who dreams that when the perfect society is created, when everybody wishes the good will of everyone else, governments will wither away and there will be no more special privileges or unequal distributions of power. In such a classless society, utopia will prevail. The possibility of achieving such a society is, of course, slim. No matter how ideally a society is organized, there are going to be jobs and other matters that are evaluated differentially. Surely the society that values stable cleaning on the same basis as open heart operations will not motivate very many people to submit themselves to the rigors of learning fine surgery. And, if people having different tasks are differently evaluated, then they will tend to develop differential amounts of power, privilege, and prestige. And having such differential amounts, they will tend to associate with others having similar orientations and interests.

Such differential associations and access to rewards are the basic requirements for a stratification system. So, it seems that stratification in one form or another is going to be an aspect of any mass society. This is illustrated by an American sociologist, John Biesanz, who was traveling in Europe during the 1930s. When he reached the Russian border, he asked for a "third class railroad ticket" such as he had used in many other countries. The train clerk answered sternly, "In the Soviet Union we do not have classes, so I cannot sell you a third class ticket. However, we have third category tickets."

A rose by any other name!

At the present time, the most privileged class in the Soviet Union is made up of managers and technical and professional workers. They earn high salaries in comparison to the earnings of ordinary workers, and they eat and dress better. The most powerful among them have luxuries such as country villas and fine automobiles. Other privileged persons are those who are designated "Hero of the Soviet Union" or "Hero of Socialist Labor." In the other major Marxist country, the People's Republic of China, social stratification takes the form of worker "ranks," such as technicians, factory workers, teachers, and state executives, with each rank subdivided into differentially rewarded "grades." However, the reward variations are small when compared with those in capitalist countries; and in the Soviet Union, since 1950 the declining difference in the annual incomes received by various worker categories has been so precipitate it has been described as an "income revolution" (Simirenko, 1972:156–157).

The indicated recent experience of socialist nations suggests that the inevitability of stratification in a large society does not mean that there must be gross differences in the power and privileges associated with the various social strata. Indeed, it can be said that in a modern society, with universal education and the mass media of communication, long-term social stability is possible only to the degree that there are relatively few major differentials in the advantages available to the great majority of societal participants. Therefore, the hopes of the multitudes are given substance by the intelligent among the advantaged. The intelligent are aware of the explosive potential when dreams are too long postponed. "What happens to a dream deferred?" Langston Hughes (1951:71) asked:

> . . . Does it dry up
> like a raisin in the sun?
> Or fester like a sore—
> And then run?
>
> Does it stink like rotten meat?
> Or crust and sugar over—
> like a syrup sweet?
>
> Maybe it just sags like a heavy load.
>
> *Or does it explode?**

* Excerpted from Langston Hughes, "Montage of a Dream Deferred." Copyright 1951 by Langston Hughes. Reprinted from *The Panther and the Lash*, by Langston Hughes, by permission of Alfred A. Knopf, Inc., and Harold Ober Associates Incorporated.

REFERENCES AND FURTHER SOURCES

Adam, Heribert
1971 Modernizing Racial Domination: South Africa's Political Dynamics. Berkeley: University of California Press.

Amante, Dominic, Phillip H. Margules, Donna M. Hartmann, Delores B. Storey, and Lewis John Weeber
1970 "The epideminological distribution of CNS dysfunction." Journal of Social Issues 26 (Autumn): 105–136.

Bendix, Reinhard and Seymour Martin Lipset (eds.)
1966 Class, Status, and Power: Social Stratification in Comparative Perspective. New York: Free Press. Second edition.

Bird, Caroline
1968 Born Female: The High Cost of Keeping Women Down. New York: Pocket Books.

Bronfenbrenner, Urie
1967 "The psychological costs of quality in education." Child Development 38 (December): 909–925.

Centers, Richard
1949 The Psychology of Social Classes. Princeton, New Jersey: Princeton University Press.

Davis, Kingsley and Wilbert E. Moore
1945 "Some principles of stratification." American Sociological Review. 10 (April): 242–249.

Feldman, Saul
1971 "The presentation of shortness in everyday life—height and heightism in American society: toward a sociology of stature." Paper presented at the national meeting of the American Sociological Association, Denver.

Freire, Paulo
1970 Pedagogy of the Oppressed. Translated by Myra Bergman Ramos. New York: Herder and Herder.

Hughes, Langston
1951 Montage of a Dream Deferred. New York: Henry Holt.

Jackson, Elton F. and Harry J. Crockett, Jr.
1964 "Occupational mobility in the United States: a point estimate and trend comparison." American Sociological Review 29 (February): 5–15.

Jones, F. Lancaster
1969   "Social mobility and industrial society: a thesis re-examined." Sociological Quarterly 10 (Summer): 292–305.

Laumann, Edward O., Paul M. Siegel, and Robert W. Hodge (eds.)
1970   The Logic of Social Hierarchies. Chicago: Markham.

Leach, E. R. (ed.)
1960   Aspects of Caste in South India, Ceylon and North-West Pakistan. New York: Cambridge University Press.

Lenski, Gerhard E.
1966   Power and Privilege: A Theory of Social Stratification. New York: McGraw-Hill.

Mayer, Albert J. and Thomas Ford Hoult
1955   "Social stratification and combat survival." Social Forces 34 (December): 155–159.

Mills, C. Wright
1956   The Power Elite. New York: Oxford University Press.

Noss, John B.
1969   Man's Religions. New York: Macmillan. Fourth edition.

Pasamanick, Benjamin and Hilda Knobloch
1966   "Retrospective studies on the epidemiology of reproductive causality: old and new." Merrill-Palmer Quarterly of Behavior and Development 12 (January): 7–26.

Riley, Matilda White and Anne Foner
1968   Aging and Society. Vol. 1: An Inventory of Research Findings. New York: Russell Sage Foundation.

Sarason, Seymour B.
1971   The Culture of the School and the Problem of Change. Boston: Allyn and Bacon.

Simirenko, Alex
1972   "From vertical to horizontal inequality: the case of the Soviet Union." Social Problems 20 (Fall): 150–161.

Weber, Max
1946   Essays in Sociology. Edited and translated by H.H. Gerth and C. Wright Mills. New York: Oxford University Press. See especially pp. 196–244.

Willis, John
1973   "Social status and casualty rates." Unpublished.

Zeitlin, Maurice
1970   "A note on death in Vietnam." Pp. 174–175 in Maurice Zeitlin (compiler), American Society, Inc.: Studies of the Social Structure and Political Economy of the United States. Chicago: Markham.

Social Stratification
in the United States

Social stratification in the United States is a near-classic example of many of the differentiation principles delineated in the previous chapter. This is particularly true with reference to stratification by class. A graphic representation of such a class system is shown in Figure 3.

The figure has three major layers—upper, middle, and lower, with each subdivided into two. The black–white dichotomy is also shown. Although it has been customary to depict U.S. stratification as shown in this figure, the depiction has two major limitations. First, it tells too little about the various strata; second, it inadvertently conveys the impression that there are hard lines between the various horizontal strata. No such hard lines exist in a class system, at least theoretically; hard lines are characteristic of a caste system.

In Figure 4 there is an attempt to depict the stratification system of the United States in a way that more closely approximates reality. The figure shows that about 5 percent of Americans have high status, as indicated by their relatively greater power, privilege, and prestige. Most of the people—about 75 percent—have power, privilege, and prestige that fall in the medium range. And then there are, of course, those of the lowest status—close to 20 percent of the population—that have practically no power, privilege, and associated prestige. In addition, there is a caste-like division in the society depicted by the curved line beginning at the lower left and moving toward the upper right. This line depicts the division between black and white Americans; it also indicates that there are some blacks who, having achieved a fairly high amount of power and privilege, interact readily with whites on a basis of practical social equality. In contrast, relatively speaking, the vast

Figure 3.   Customary Graphical Representation of Social Stratification in the United States

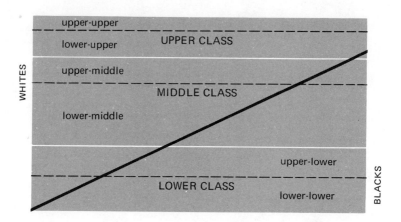

majority of whites, even those of the lowest status, have more power and privilege than blacks. What is not plotted in the diagram are complications such as the power and privileges available to societal elements other than whites and blacks—people of Mexican descent, Orientals, American Indians, and other minority groups.

CASTE IN THE UNITED STATES

It has been noted frequently by many that the black–white dichotomy in American society has been in many respects a caste system. This was true without any question during the days of slavery in the South, in particular. There was a "lower" caste whose members were often and with impunity treated with monumental cruelty, and there was a "higher" caste, many of whose members lived a life of luxury based almost entirely on the labor of exploited slaves. Stories relating what life was really like for numerous American slaves are enough to make even the cynical cringe: newly imported slaves deliberately separated from all their fellow tribesmen so they would be rendered cultureless and, therefore, malleable; children torn from their mothers' arms and sold; families casually broken up in the interests of greater profit. Solomon Northup, in his *Twelve Years a Slave* (1968:57–60, reprint of the 1853 original), told some of the most poignant stories. His description of "Eliza's" forcible separation from her two little children, Emily and Randall, is enough to draw tears from a stone.

Figure 4.   Graphical Representation of Social Stratification in the United
States

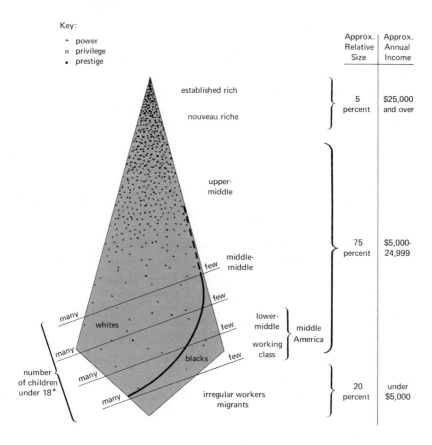

Source: Data from the 1970 Census of Population, General Social and Economic
Characteristics, U.S. Summary (Washington: U.S. Govt. Printing Office, 1972), 178.

The black–white caste system was not substantially changed after
emancipation. Certainly, at least until recently, one belonged to one of
the two great social strata solely by accident of birth. And, with the
exception of the rare few who could "pass" (that is, whose appearance
permitted membership in either group), everybody remained a life
member of his or her stratum.

This caste-like stratification has had many of the same characteristics
of India's caste system. In the vast majority of cases, "caste" determined
occupational goals and possibilities. It affected one's health and who one

---

* The more minor children in a given family, the lower its effective living style, except for
families so affluent that the number of children has no gross effect on income.

could marry; it even found religious sanction. In the traditional deep South it was quite common to hear Bible-pounding preachers assert that since God made blacks and whites different, surely he meant they should live apart from one another. And, it would be added, since blacks obviously had few privileges, then God must have ordained that too.

But the radical black power movement of the 1960s, together with change in the consciousness of white youth, have affected many of the traditional attitudes. At the same time, there has been massive resistance to such change. Bayard Rustin, long-time moderate black civil rights advocate, observes:

> The truth about the situation of the Negro today is that there are powerful forces, composed largely of the corporate elite and Southern conservatives, which will resist any change in the economic or racial structure of this country that might cut into their resources or challenge their status; and such is precisely what any program genuinely geared to improve . . . [the Negro] lot must do (1971:75).

These "powerful" forces are not merely resisting change, says Rustin. During the early 1970s, with Richard Nixon occupying the White House, the racial gains made during the previous decade were assaulted. Rustin added:

> It has been Nixon's tragic and irresponsible choice . . . of building a political majority on the basis of white hostility to blacks.

The "Southern strategy" of the national administration in power during the first half of the 1970s has found varied expression: the rollback on school integration efforts, the watering down of the 1965 Voting Rights Act with the effect of a cut in the black franchise, the Supreme Court nomination of men such as Harrold Carswell and Clement Haynsworth, no-knock and preventive detention legislation for the capital city, and so on. These blatant appeals to white supremacists were allegedly countered by the President's Philadelphia Plan, which provided that on jobs involving more than $500,000 in federal money, a contractor is required to hire a quota of black workers. However, the plan made no provision for training, nor did it provide a means for blacks to attain the journeyman status needed for job security. Further, on the same day that the President described the Philadelphia Plan, he ordered a 75 percent reduction in federal construction. He thereby simultaneously depressed wages and reduced relevant job availability, making a cruel mockery of the Philadelphia Plan. Thus, with the supportive backing of the dominance of law and the ultimate power of government, there has been a concerted, albeit fragmented, attempt to insure continuance of the subordinate caste status of the American black.

CHARACTERISTICS OF MAJOR STRATA IN THE UNITED STATES

The Lower Class   It is common to hear the expressions *lower class,* *middle class,* and *upper class* applied to elements of American society. However, it is erroneous to conclude that the members of such broad strata are homogeneous. The heterogeneity of America's so-called lower class is especially evident and important. Although all members of this stratum are "lower" in the sense of being subject to the power of a multitude of others, there are important differences between relatively more advantaged and the most disadvantaged members of the lower class.

The most disadvantaged group is frequently referred to as the lower-lower class. A less invidious term would be unskilled or irregular workers. The central characteristic of such people, according to a popular middle-class stereotype, is an addiction to instant pleasure. It is true, the very poor find, that if you do not "do it" *now*—eat it, drink it, say it, have it—tomorrow may well be too late. And, since life without some enjoyment is unendurable, it makes good sense to take pleasure when and where available. But the truly important central fact of life for the very poor is that the structure of society is such that they must live in terms of what has been called "the culture of poverty." Living in terms of such a culture boils down to a ceaseless, relentless, all-consuming struggle for survival. For many participants in a culture of poverty, one is on the brink of disaster *every* day, not just on selected days. The social consequence is weak and unstable families and a general belief, based on harsh experience, that expending energy does not pay off, so, "Why strain your milk?" As Alfred Doolittle remarks, if it isn't in the cards, if you don't have a little bit of luck, then it's not going to happen.

In some ways worlds apart from those caught in the culture of poverty, there are lower stratum members who are often referred to as *working class.* The basic characteristic of this group is that it is made up of labor force participants regularly engaged in manual occupations. As sociologists Miller and Riessman (1961) have described the members of this social group, they are tradition-oriented—old-fashioned, often religious, and believe in male dominance and close family life. They like order, discipline, and strong leadership. They desire a good standard of living, but are not attracted to middle-class ideas that stress propriety and high status. And, the typical manual worker " . . . reads ineffectively, is poorly informed in many areas, and is often quite suggestible, although interestingly enough he is frequently suspicious of 'talk' and 'new fangled ideas' " (Miller and Riessman, 1961:90).

Miller and Riessman believe that the outstanding weakness of steady manual workers is lack of education. They strongly desire practical instruction for their children and show concern about school work, but each

> . . . feels estranged and alienated from the teacher and the school, as he similarly feels alienated from many institutions in our society. This alienation is expressed in a ready willingness to believe in the corruptness of leaders and a general negative feeling toward "big shots" (p. 91).

Perhaps most significant of all for workers is that that which they most crave—stability and security—is that which they have least. Working-class families, unlike many of those in the middle class, have no bright future ahead.

> Their economic future cannot get better. It might get worse. Realistically, they can nourish none of the confidence of the middle class that promotions or new careers will make the future more exciting. Little in the experience of the lower-middle class promotes living for the future (Novak, 1972:25).

Each payday has a dreaded quality about it since the pay envelope may include a notice that one's job is automated out of existence, or that the factory will move hundreds of miles away or perhaps go out of business. The attendant insecurity, Miller and Riessman speculate, accounts for some of the ambivalence of the working class toward formal education. They favor it, but their experience is that it does not contribute to security. This is especially true of liberal arts education since it is not specifically career-oriented. A job, on the other hand, is "money in the bank."

Middle America   There is no firm line dividing the working class from the middle class. Rather, it can be said that, in terms of power, privilege, and prestige, the working and middle classes overlap one another, as depicted in Figure 4 on p. 149. It is thus impossible to say precisely where one leaves off and the other begins. Indeed, in certain important senses it is meaningful to conceptualize the working class and the *lower* middle class as a single group (except that many blacks who are "natural" members of it are often not full participants because of racial considerations). This is the group that is frequently referred to as middle America; it is so designated on Figure 4. Karl Marx called an important part of the group the petite bourgeoisie.

The most significant thing about this group at the present time is that it is made up of people who, though they are keenly irritated with the established distribution of power and privilege, do not reject the system as such. They do not reject it because they believe the revolution has been won—the *economic* revolution, which is the only one that really interests most of them—"Economics is the worker's basic reality; politics is a luxury" (Novak, 1972:228). They do not know that their share of the system is inequitably small and tenuously held, and they do not realize that economic security is almost always short term unless accompanied by political arrangements that prevent the powerful from abusing the weak. Thus misinformed, they become potential followers for a strong leader who promises to safeguard the system by wresting power away from "the establishment" and returning it to "the people." This is the basic theme of the populist orator. He cries, "power to the people" and they respond enthusiastically, not knowing that the typical populist leader, once he achieves power, "returns" it to himself and his cronies alone. During the late 1960s and early 1970s, the populist-oriented clustered around such figures as Governor George Wallace of Alabama, a Presidential hopeful. In him they saw one of their own, a man who seemingly scorned intellectuals and the Eastern establishment—the well-off liberals, for example—and who said, in effect, "We're tired of supporting all those welfare cheats" (mostly referring to blacks and hippies). This does not mean that middle Americans are necessarily racist in the full negative sense of the term. The racism of American ethnics—that is, the largely Catholic descendants of immigrants from southern and eastern Europe, plus many of Irish descent, who constitute a very large part of middle America—is a protective group feeling in contrast to, for example, the Nordic sense of superiority. Ethnics see that black Americans have great difficulty and are, therefore, quite deserving of help; but ethnics feel that the burden of such help should not fall disproportionately on "poor slob immigrants" who are themselves frequently just one step above the poverty line (Novak, 1972:11–14).

Even the least demagogic politician is often tempted to engage in populist rhetoric because it appeals to "mass man." There are 30 to 40 million such Americans if one thinks purely in terms of workers. They constitute vast numbers of the nation's blue-collar labor force, plus multitudes of civil service workers, small entrepreneurs, shopkeepers, farmers, clerks, and sales personnel. They and their families add up to more than 80 million people. They earn from $5,000–$15,000 a year, but are usually heavily in debt on credit for cars, appliances, and homes. They feel that all they have going for them is a work ethic made fun of by those living on unemployment checks and welfare and by upper-middle class youth who speak disdainfully of scrabbling for "bread."

Therefore, many of these people are angry; they feel they have had to work very hard and now their reward is to have to support the poor. They feel victimized by inflation. When there is international difficulty, their children are drafted while the children of the affluent go to college and those of the poor are exempted because of educational deficiencies. Their work is often personally unsatisfactory since it is mindlessly repetitious and does not even have the virtue of paying well, at least not consistently. And, adding insult to injury, the worker's paycheck has decreased in buying power during the very time when taxes have been increased, partly so that school and other advantages for the well-off may be better subsidized.

Such harried members of the lower-middle echelons of society have repeatedly demonstrated their political inclinations when, in their view, things get bad enough. In Germany, in 1932, they turned to Adolf Hitler; in Louisiana in 1928 they followed Huey Long. They have turned, at various times in recent decades, to similar demagogues in Italy, Spain, Argentina, Portugal, Brazil, Egypt, France, and Greece. The lesson is clear. Angry, frustrated, insecure workers stand ever ready to listen to a magnetic spellbinder who promises relief. If pushed far enough, it seems possible that America's angry workers could finally erupt in a rage that will make student riots look as benign as a baby shower.

The Privileged Middle Class   Populist appeals do not attract the more privileged members of the middle class, with one exception. The exception consists of many of the once-affluent who are living on a fixed income and thus are subject to the fears and insecurities plaguing lower-middle class society. Hence the populist orator can count on a wide and enthusiastic hearing in the typical retirement community. He will not get such a hearing in affluent suburbia. Secure members of the middle class prefer things just as they are. And why not? They have prospered. Their professional, technical, and managerial occupations, or higher-rank bureaucratic positions, give them relatively stable incomes that adjust with inflationary pressures. Having adequate incomes, they can command the services that spell gracious living.

The security and prosperity of the more privileged members of the middle class are associated with the Protestant ethic. Indeed, members of the "middle-middle" constitute a living embodiment of the ethic; those who are upper-middle are not so compulsive about it. But all believe in most details of the ethic and conduct their lives in accordance with it. The ethic also has historical importance; its values are interlocked with the development of industrialism and capitalism. Given the ethic's past and current significance, it is appropriate to spell out its five prime features:

1. *Individualism*—All people should make their own way; one should wrest all one can from the world of nature and thus come out number one. God helps those who help themselves. It is the immediate family that counts; improvident relatives may learn a

needed lesson if they are left to suffer the consequences of their lack of foresight. "If you help every spendthrift in the family, how are you going to get ahead?"

2. *Hard work*—Outstanding performance is very much admired. Even athletic achievement is applauded; it is how you play the game that counts. But academic excellence and the acquisition of skills with market value are especially admired. One should never let down. Even in sexual activity one should strive to be proficient (see "Sex as Work"; Lewis and Brisset, 1967).

3. *Asceticism*—The best things in life are obtained only with the expenditure of effort and time; hence it is unrealistic to expect instant reward. Rome was not built in a day. So be thrifty; a penny saved is a penny earned. Do not indulge yourself even in your leisure time; your recreational activities should be wholesome ones that help you to improve so you become a stronger and better person.

4. *Rationality*—Success is achieved only to the degree that activities are controlled in a businesslike way. Plan ahead; a stitch in time saves nine. Do not waste your time, budget it. Allocate your resources efficiently. Cultivate influential people. Learn how to make friends and how to influence others; only thus can you utilize your talents efficiently.

5. *Respect for property*—Material goods, including land, are extremely important. Possession of them is a sign of achievement; therefore, people should strive to gather property and to have complete control over it. Without control, one might have to give in to the claims of others. Property is sacred. It should therefore be kept in good repair. And, so that property rights and duties are known to all, precise accounts and records should be kept. One's home is particularly important; it is a living testimonial to respect for property, hence should be maintained with great care and attention to detail.

> . . . a middle-class home is, to a great extent, a carefully ordered museum of artifacts for display, representing a great deal of "congealed labor." Their function for conspicuous consumption depends upon the preservation of their original state and upon ready recognition of their value, and middle-class children are trained to respect such objects and the order in which they have been lovingly arranged (Cohen, 1955:93).

The Upper Class   The people with the most extreme amounts of power, privilege, and prestige are usually termed the upper class. There are two basic varieties—either nouveau riche or old, established families. The former have great wealth but no proud heritage or important family connections; the latter may not have unlimited income, but they have something that is worth more than money to those in the know. This consists of their ties, through kinship and marriage, to the "best families," both currently and historically. People with such ties constitute the highly influential "first families of Virginia," "the 400," and the New England gentry among whom are the Cabots who talk only to the Lowells who, in turn, talk only to God.

Political scientist Edward Banfield (1970:48–50) has described the upper-class personality, with special reference to the "old rich." The central characteristic of the personality is its future-orientation. The individuals with such an orientation think in very long terms, seeing themselves as part of an unending process, as exemplified in the family line. They look back to their ancestors as the solid base on which they and their descendants can build to insure a firm, successful future. This future is also dependent on a stable community and nation, so there is powerful incentive to keep things in order and to make investments promising large and long-term gain.

Upper-class individuals are self-confident and self-sufficient. They place a lot of emphasis on self-control and independence and, therefore, on developing all personal talents to the utmost. But they are not victims of the righteousness and the feeling of being up-tight that affects so many members of the middle-class. They tend to be free of gross bigotry and to be tolerant about unconventional behavior in the arts and politics, and even in sexual expression. They admire rationality and, therefore, reject violence as unseemly. They are paternalistic to the less fortunate—expressed as *noblesse oblige* (the "obligation" of the privileged to be generous to the underprivileged) or as political–economic liberalism. Cynics sometimes remark that the very rich can well afford such liberality, especially since its mass monetary aspects are usually subsidized by the less wealthy who pay the great bulk of taxes.

Members of the upper class generally live a life of such opulence that it is hardly understandable to outsiders. But in Western countries today, "opulence" does not imply the public display satirized by Thorstein Veblen in his *Theory of the Leisure Class* (1899); such display is associated with the nouveau riche who are not fully informed about upper-class values. The essence of the old rich living pattern is quiet elegance. In given cases it includes several completely equipped large homes maintained by professional staffs; multiroom cottages tucked away in guarded settings; casual use of priceless heirlooms, including displays of works of art by old masters; family and corporate connections giving ready entrée to the most exclusive clubs; deluxe travel, frequently by private or corporate conveyance, whenever and wherever desired; and so on.

VERTICAL MOBILITY IN THE UNITED STATES

The concept of vertical mobility was previously defined as an individual's or group's generally permanent change of relative rank in a status hierarchy such as a set of occupations that are differentially regarded and rewarded. The hod carrier who becomes a wealthy contractor has engaged in upward vertical mobility; the contractor who becomes a hod carrier has experienced downward mobility. Such mobility, up or down, is differentiated from *horizontal mobility*—job alteration that does not involve a change in status (for example, a teacher who moves from one school to another).

The hod carrier–contractor example illustrates *intragenerational mobility.* Another version of the same kind of mobility is the family that goes "from rags to riches in a single generation." A different form of vertical mobility is that termed *intergenerational.* This type includes low-status workers whose descendants achieve high status. For example, a garment worker may refer to his offspring as "my son, the doctor."

In a change-oriented society the important question relative to vertical mobility is: What is the opportunity to engage in it? Part of the American dream has been that there should be such opportunity. The general consensus has been that ability alone, not family background, should govern opportunity. However, if such an abilitocracy were to prevail, one wonders if it would be favorably regarded. To people in general, an aristocracy of ability might not seem preferable to one of birth since either system condemns the vast majority to a less privileged existence.

Regardless of what is concluded about the relative merits of various forms of aristocracy, the question remains: What are the possibilities for upward vertical mobility in American society today? Despite the significance of the question, there is no clearcut response that would satisfy all observers. One can find an incredible range of answers, varying from the conclusion that opportunity is dead in America, to the idea "America *means* opportunity" (as Ralph Waldo Emerson put it 100 years ago). One sociologist, J. O. Hertzler (1952), has argued that representative data clearly indicate a tendency toward building a closed class system in the United States. Another sociologist, Gideon Sjoberg (1951), feels that the data point to growth of more openness in the class system.

In spite of the conflicting data and opinions, the total information available suggests this general conclusion: working-class and middle-class *white* Americans have had and still have a modest opportunity to engage in both intra- and intergenerational upward vertical mobility. The term "white" is emphasized because it is clear that upward vertical mobility possibilities for black Americans are limited. Indeed, their mobility, what there is of it, is more downward than upward. A United States Department of Health, Education, and Welfare study concluded:

> The Negro man originating at the lower levels is likely to stay there, the white man to move up. The Negro originating at the higher levels is likely to move down; the white man seldom does. *The contrast is stark* (*Toward a Social Report*, 1969:24; italics added).

The HEW study, based on a carefully drawn national sample, showed that most black American men, *regardless of their fathers' occupations*, work at unskilled or semiskilled jobs. Even the children of men who have been in professional, managerial, or proprietary positions are typically operatives such as service workers or laborers. In contrast, the majority of white men with higher white-collar backgrounds remain at their father's level in the job market; and up to half of those whose fathers were in clerical or sales work, or had a farm or blue-collar background, move into higher-status professional or managerial occupations. Blacks with similar origins do not; and, what is perhaps most important, the reason is associated with racism. According to the HEW report,

> . . . Negro men with the same schooling and the same family background as a comparable group of white men will have jobs of appreciably lower status. It is surely attributable in part to racial discrimination in hiring, promotion, and other job-related opportunities (*Toward a Social Report*, 1969:25).

The data discussed in the HEW study were gathered by the U.S. Bureau of the Census in a 1962 (the most recent available) survey of "Occupational Changes in a Generation." The data have been extensively analyzed by Professors Peter Blau and O. D. Duncan (1967). They found that the occupational achievements of the great majority of sons are not explained by their fathers' occupations. When Blau and Duncan summed up the factors affecting occupational achievement, they found that fully 60.7 percent are not accounted for by family background or education. They do not spell out what the "other factors" are, but in any case the implication is that there is some opportunity for vertical mobility.

Blau and Duncan account for such mobility on the basis of three structural conditions prevailing in industrial societies. The first of these is technological improvement that eliminates the least challenging jobs and creates new and better ones. The second is the stress on achievement that seems to motivate relatively high-status people to have fewer children, thus leaving room at the top. Finally, industrial societies depend on rational values, among which is utilization of the talents of individuals and groups without regard to their general social standing or family background.

Blau and Duncan test the idea that there is a "culture of poverty" that inexorably holds people in its grip and thus eliminates any possibility for the poor to better their lot. Using a sophisticated analysis technique, Blau and Duncan show that a father's education and occupation have less effect on a son's mobility than does the son's educational achievement and first job experience. It should be noted that this finding applies to whites only. It, therefore, has little practical meaning for those most in need of mobility—the poor, that is, who in America are to a large extent nonwhite.

In contrast to the Blau and Duncan finding that almost 40 percent of occupational achievement is associated with education and family type, a recent report by Christopher Jencks and his associates (1972:226) asserts that family background and educational attainment account for only 12 to 15 percent of income difference. Such a gross opinion clash between experts suggests once again that social "science" still has many of the preference aspects of art. "I don't know what is good; I just know what I like." And what Jencks and his associates "like" is an interpretation that a 28 percent income difference is not very important. According to the data cited in the Jencks volume (1972:222–223), college-educated individuals earn about 28 percent more than their lesser educated peers; but Jencks' values lead him to conclude that such an income differential is not sufficient to support a generalization that education is vitally associated with income. Further, the Jencks study fails to control for age and place of residence even though income varies greatly according to age, and *real* income is heavily influenced by cost of living variations in different geographical areas (for example, according to the U.S. Bureau of Labor, in 1970 an intermediate living standard for a four-person urban family could be maintained in Austin, Texas with an annual income of $9,200; in Honolulu, the cost was $13,000). Also, the statistical formulations of the Jencks study include types of income, such as social security, that have little to do with individual productivity. In sum, the Jencks study has a number of questionable methodological features—enough so we need to question the conclusion that inequality in schooling and family background are not meaningfully related to income.*

Despite their concentration on the various aspects of inequality, Jencks and his associates (1972:Chs. 6 and 7) corroborate the Blau and Duncan conclusion that vertical mobility possibilities are available to

---

* Although the Jencks study has some methodological shortcomings, the work taken as a whole is a heartening example of science used in the service of humanistic values. The prime interest of Jencks and his associates is equality, especially income equality (Jencks, 1972:260–261), and they are, therefore, concerned with the ineffectiveness of most alleged cures for income inequities.

large numbers of American whites, especially males. Occasionally—too seldom to make a statistical difference, but often enough to keep the myth alive—the son of a small-time grocer and the son of a Greek immigrant restaurant owner can become President of the United States and Vice President, respectively. American society is, however, very far from achieving true equality of opportunity since irregular workers and their children, along with blacks and browns in general, have no realistic chance for improving—and sometimes for even maintaining—their occupational status. There is, therefore, a discouragingly large gap between reality and the equalitarian ideal, at least in the short run. The long-run trend is more encouraging, as the following discussion will indicate.

A MAJOR TREND IN STRATIFICATION

It is hazardous to speak about drifts in social stratification because there are so many variables that it is easy to make rather gross errors. Nevertheless, it seems justified to point to one major long-term trend: the gradually, and lately precipitately, increasing challenge to the idea of hierarchy, particularly arbitrary hierarchy, in human affairs. Some have referred to this trend as the move toward democracy; others have spoken of progressivism, or liberalization, or equalitarianism. All such movements or efforts may be regarded as examples of the general phenomenon that is here termed challenge to hierarchy. It is appropriate for this challenge to be considered in a chapter that has concentrated on the United States. It is in this country, historically speaking at least, that some of the most significant challenges have occurred.

From the beginning of recorded history, humans almost everywhere have assumed that a hierarchical organization of society is natural. People in general have accepted the notion, without any sense of fundamental injustice, that it is perfectly all right for a few people to have extreme amounts of power and privilege while the great majority has almost none. The idea seems to have been that those who have power, and the privileges associated with power, must deserve it or else they would not have it.

The hierarchical principle was not significantly challenged for many centuries of man's life, aside from a few isolated incidents such as the early slave revolts in Rome. But, in A.D. 1215 the signing of the Magna Carta, which put some restrictions on the arbitrary powers of the ruling head of England, was a truly significant challenge to the hierarchical principle. Since that time, the principle has been challenged increasingly, and with increasing significance, especially in Western Europe and North America. In some respects, the American Revolution was an example of such a challenge. Although this revolution was essentially a struggle for political rather than for general equality, it included a number of more basic elements. Central among these was the Declaration of Independence, which claimed that it is "self-evident" that "all men are created equal." This assertion proved to be somewhat hollow, considering later political events, but it played a significant part in a process that imbedded the *ideal* of social equality in American society. The ideal

> . . . does not, of course, severely limit income or power differences. . . . But as Tocqueville and others have noted, Americans act as if they believed that such differences are accidental, not essential. . . (Lipset, 1962:32).

The French Revolution, in its early stages (1789–1791), was a radical challenge to the hierarchical principle. It tried to eliminate the ruling class itself, along with its special privileges. Liberty, equality, fraternity, the masses cried, hoping and believing they were creating a fundamentally new social order. Failing, they tried again in 1848; and again in the Paris communes of 1871; and again during the worker–student uprisings in 1968.

There are a multitude of other examples of challenge to the hierarchical principle. Two notable ones were the struggle against slavery and the abolition of serfdom. Still another was the growth of unions which tried to equalize the power available to employees and employers. A more recent example has been termed *The Decline of the Wasp*. In a book of that title, sociologist Peter Schrag (1972) chronicles the decreasing power of the white Anglo-Saxon Protestant in American society. And he describes the rise of the ethnic as a partial fulfillment of the American dream (also see Novak, 1972).

Other examples of the decline of hierarchy are the rise of Protestantism and the movements to obtain suffrage, first for men in general, then for women, and more recently for the young. The antitrust laws, attempting to restrict the size of businesses that could control the lives of millions, are another example. More recent instances are women's liberation, the student revolt against arbitrary rules, widespread anti-papist developments in Roman Catholicism, and the humane aspects of the color movements—black, red, and brown.

The various eighteenth century challenges to hierarchy are viewed by historian R. R. Palmer as a unitary revolutionary movement

> . . . for which the word "democratic" is appropriate and enlightening; a movement which, however different in different countries, was everywhere aimed against closed elites, self-selecting power groups, hereditary castes, and forms of special advantage or discrimination . . . (1964:572).

The central theme of the democratic movement, Palmer says, was ". . . the assertion of 'equality' as a prime social desideratum" (1964:572). And he suggests that since 1800 the same general idea has been the guiding light of the major political–economic struggles in Africa, Asia, and Latin America. The situation is essentially the same today, as Yale sociologist Wendell Bell has observed. Using the West Indies as a laboratory, he concluded:

> . . . much of the political, economic, and social change going on throughout the world in the last half of the twentieth century can be understood as a continuation of the democratic revolution—especially as an extension of the drive toward equality—to which Europe and America of the latter part of the eighteenth century gave birth as a realizable human aspiration (Horowitz, 1969:239).

The great variety of serious challenges to the hierarchical principle does not imply that there are no contrary examples; there are many. The American Revolution produced a Constitution the central purpose of which was to protect the propertied classes. The French Revolution failed completely, resulting in a rule from the top that was more totalitarian and exploitative than the traditional aristocracy ever dreamed was possible. Businessmen have found a multitude of ways to subvert antitrust laws. In some large unions, entrenched bureaucratic officials dominate ordinary workers almost as thoroughly as did the robber barons. And the populist petite bourgeoisie, though they cry out against the special privileges of bankers and Eastern intellectuals, are often not opposed to hierarchy in principle; many simply want to change their relative position in the prevailing hierarchy. Upper status people generally are opposed to any practical implementation of equalitarian ideas; people with power have never been known to give it up gracefully. It has always had to be wrenched away, either through legal tactics or through revolution.

Despite these contrary examples, the writer still asserts his belief that the general, long-term trend—and considering the whole history of humankind—is away from hierarchy and toward equalitarianism. It is true that there are some horrible examples of opposing trends, including especially racism, imperialism, Nazism, and Stalinism. And it is no doubt true that dominance by a power élite in the United States has recently increased at an alarming rate. As famed historian Henry Steele Commager has observed, "It would be an exaggeration to say that the United States is a garrison state, but none to say that it is in danger of becoming one" (*Look*, July 14, 1970:19).

Nevertheless!

When one considers the tyranny of some over others in the past—a tyranny that included absolute monarchy, divine right, colonialism, feudalism, slavery, serfdom, totally rigid caste stratification, official "untouchability," an unchallengeable clergy, aristocracy, robber barons, the nobility to which all commoners had to accede—when all this is considered, then, surely it is realistic to claim that there has been progress toward establishing the equalitarian ideal. To the degree that this is so, then recent trends suggesting a frightening increase in political repression, and disturbingly widespread acceptance of such repression, are properly viewed as short term. But even the long-term trends do not justify a claim that there is an inevitable movement toward realizing the equalitarian ideal. The slow gains toward such realization have been achieved only to the extent that it has been worked for, fought for, sacrificed for. As it has been well said, "The price of liberty is eternal vigilance."

A HUMANISTIC COMMENT ON SOCIAL STRATIFICATION

In the foregoing discussion of social differentiation, humanistically oriented value judgments have been expressed at several points. Such judgments have been prompted by the vast gulf that exists between the humanistic ideal of maximizing individual opportunity for self-development, on the one hand, and traditional stratification systems on the other. These systems are almost invariably arbitrary, hence unjust; their arbitrariness lies in the fact that they are not based on reason but rather on customary distributions of power and privilege. Therefore, in the relatively rigid systems, even the talented and ambitious lower-status person has few chances for full self-development.

Opposition to such harsh realities has prompted humanists to hail the long-term trend that has challenged various aspects of hierarchy. They have sympathized deeply with the labor movement and with the cry for black liberation and women's rights. They no doubt participated as revolutionaries in the French struggle of 1789. They have cheered the various governmental measures putting restrictions on the incomes and associated power of the rich and superrich. As sociologist S. M. Lipset has expressed it:

> My own politics derive from the belief that while differences in the distribution of status, income, and power (stratification) are inherent in the nature of any complex social system, such inequality is punitive and unfair. . . . And since I feel that inequality, though inevitable, is *immoral*, I support all measures which would bring the utopian "equality of status and of opportunity" closer to realization (1962:31–32).

The measures referred to by Lipset are supported by the prudent among the highly advantaged. They know, as Karl Marx noted long ago, that one can organize a society in terms of almost any principle; but a society cannot survive if sharply contradictory principles prevail. And this is what has come to pass in the modern world. Major elements of the hierarchical principle are continued in force by the short-sighted few who have an overabundance of power; at the same time, modern education and mass media have made the deprived aware of their deprivation and, more important, aware that previous challenges of maldistributions of advantage have sometimes succeeded. Therefore, "The contemporary world today is a little like the modern city," columnist James Reston observed:

> . . . part black, embittered and revolutionary slum, and part white and prosperous. The main difference is that in urban America the poor are a minority, and in the world at large, now being rushed together by modern transportation and communication, they are the vast majority (*Arizona Republic*, November 10, 1971).

Thus, the time is close at hand for an immense struggle for power between the haves and the have nots. Such struggles have occurred many times in world history. But now, for the first time, the battle promises to be a global one, a world war of class between the rich northern nations and the poor but heavily populated majority in the Far East and in the "underworld of the sunny slums below the Equator" (James Reston's phrase). And in this struggle the consistent humanist, though perhaps bemoaning the associated violence, has no alternative but to side with the downtrodden. Their moves to throw off the chains of exploitation constitute the shape and cry of the future, and they will be joined by all who have a sense of justice or a grasp of the direction of historical forces. "This storm is our storm," Judge Dorothy Kenyon wrote, "the storm of human beings crying for fair play everywhere, and we cannot stand aside. We must move with the wind" (*Civil Liberties*, April 1972:3). In the poignant phrases of Martin Luther King, Jr., penned just before his assassination:

> We shall overcome because the arch of the moral universe is long, but it bends toward justice. We shall overcome because William Cullen Bryant is right, "Truth crushed to earth will rise again." We shall overcome because James Russell Lowell is right, "Truth forever on the scaffold, wrong forever on the throne, yet that scaffold sways a future." And so with this faith, we will be able to hew out of the mountain of despair a stone of hope. We will be able to transform the jangling discords of our nation into a beautiful

symphony of brotherhood. This will be a great day. This will not be the day of the white man, it will not be the day of the black man, it will be the day of man as man (1968:12).*

---

* Excerpted from Martin Luther King, Jr., "The Role of the Behavioral Scientist in the Civil Rights Movement." Copyright © 1967 by Martin Luther King, Jr. Reprinted by permission of Joan Daves.

REFERENCES AND FURTHER SOURCES

Baltzell, E. Digby
1971   Philadelphia Gentlemen: The Making of a National Upper Class. Chicago: Quadrangle.

Banfield, Edward C.
1970   The Unheavenly City: The Nature and Future of Our Urban Crisis. Boston: Little, Brown.

Blau, Peter M. and Otis Dudley Duncan, with the collaboration of Andrea Tyree
1967   The American Occupational Structure. New York: Wiley.

Cleaver, Eldridge
1968   Soul on Ice. New York: Dell.

Cohen, Albert K.
1955   Delinquent Boys: The Culture of the Gang. Free Press of Glencoe.

Domhoff, G. William
1970   The Higher Circles: The Governing Class in America. New York: Random House.

Gordon, Leonard (ed.)
1971   A City in Racial Crisis. Dubuque, Iowa: W. C. Brown.

Hertzler, J. O.
1952   "Some tendencies toward a closed class system in the United States." Social Forces 30 (May): 313–323.

Horowitz, Irving Louis (ed.)
1969   Sociological Self-Images: A Collective Portrait. Berkeley, California: Sage Publications.

Jencks, Christopher, Marshall Smith, Henry Acland, Mary Jo Bane, David Cohen, Herbert Gintis, Barbara Heyns, and Stephan Michelson
1972   Inequality: A Reassessment of the Effect of Family and Schooling in America. New York: Basic Books.

King, Larry L.
1971   Confessions of a White Racist. New York: Viking Press.

King, Martin Luther, Jr.
1968   "The role of the behavioral scientist in the civil rights movement." Journal of Social Issues 24 (January): 1–12.

Komarovsky, Mirra
1964   Blue-collar Marriage. New York: Random House.

Kronus, Sidney
1971   The Black Middle Class. Columbus, Ohio: Charles E. Merrill.

Lewis, Lionel S. and Dennis Brissett
1967   "Sex as work." Social Problems 15 (Summer): 8–18.

Lipset, Seymour Martin
1962   "My view from our left." Columbia University Forum 5 (Fall): 31–37.

Miller, S. M. and Frank Riessman
1961   "The working-class subculture: a new view." Social Problems 9 (Summer): 86–97.

Northup, Solomon
1968   Twelve Years a Slave. Edited by Sue Eakin and Joseph Logsdon. Baton Rouge: Louisiana State University Press. Originally published in 1853.

Novak, Michael
1972   The Rise of the Unmeltable Ethnics: Politics and Culture in the Seventies. New York: Macmillan.

Palmer, R. R.
1964   The Age of the Democratic Revolution: A Political History of Europe and America, 1760–1800; the Struggle. Princeton, New Jersey: Princeton University Press.

Rustin, Bayard
1971   "The blacks and the unions." Harper's Magazine 242 (May): 73–81.

Schrag, Peter
1972   The Decline of the Wasp. New York: Simon and Schuster.

Sjoberg, Gideon
1951   "Are social classes in America becoming more rigid?" American Sociological Review 16 (December): 775–783.

Straus, Murray A.
1962   "Deferred gratification, social class, and the achievement syndrome." American Sociological Review 27 (June): 326–335.

Toward a Social Report
1969   Washington, D.C.: U.S. Government Printing Office.

Veblen, Thorstein
1899   The Theory of the Leisure Class. New York: Vanguard Press. 1927 reprint of the original.

Institutionalization: Process and Consequence

People everywhere develop standardized ways of responding to basic needs. Such regularized response modes, especially relatively long-term ones, are usually called *institutions*. A marriage ceremony is one example. It is a complex, stylized procedure demanded of men and women who wish to live intimately together with full social approval. In no known human society do men and women in general *casually* live together as sex partners; they cohabit only under certain conditions which include a specification of the rules governing such a living pattern.

Because they are often associated with fundamental needs such as satisfying the sex drive, and because they usually force people to act in prescribed ways, institutions are one of the most important aspects of culture. Yet they are difficult to deal with in a conceptual sense. One of the difficulties is that the term institution is commonly used to denote anything rather well established. Usage is so broad that it applies to phenomena as disparate as large organizations (Sears, Roebuck) and single individuals ("Oh yes, Mr. Chips is an institution here.").

Sumner's Approach   A number of professionals have been similarly casual in their use of the term institution. William Graham Sumner is an early and typical example. In his fundamental work, *Folkways* (1906), he implied that anything established—whether a group, a building, or a procedure—is properly regarded as an institution. However, he distinguished between what he referred to as the *crescive* and the *enacted* institution.

To Sumner, a *crescive* institution is a well-established organization or process that has no specific, traceable beginning.

> They are crescive when they take shape in the mores, growing by the instinctive efforts by which the mores are produced. Then the efforts, through long use, become definite and specific (Sumner, 1906:62).

Religion is a commonly mentioned example. No one knows when or how religious beliefs and practices began; all we know is that they have, in general, grown by accretion—that is, very gradually, often imperceptibly.

There are also *enacted* institutions—that is, those that are consciously developed by people having a specific purpose in mind. An example is provided by almost any given family, say "the William J. Brown family." Usually such a family has a precise, traceable beginning. In contrast, "the family in general" is almost purely *crescive*. Similarly, banking is a crescive institution, but The Third National Bank of Dayton is enacted. Baseball is crescive; the San Francisco Giants are enacted.

MacIver's Approach   Sociologist-philosopher Robert MacIver was not satisfied with Sumner's and others' analyses of institutions. He felt the concept was loosely used and ill-defined by professionals themselves, not to speak of the complexities introduced when laymen spoke of jails, cocktail parties, hospitals, or even gas stations as institutions.

MacIver's basic contribution was to suggest the utility of differentiating between two phenomena that are always involved in the meeting of basic human needs: associations and processes. An *association* is an organized group; a *process* is a series of steps or changes leading toward a particular end. MacIver suggested that certain processes alone should be called institutions.

> . . . we shall always mean by institutions the established forms or conditions of procedures characteristic of group activity. When men create associations, they must also create rules and procedures for the despatch of the common business and for the regulation of the members to one another within the ambit of the organization. Such forms are distinctively institutions (MacIver, 1931:16).

Professor MacIver attempted to clarify two possibly confusing points: One involved the similarity and relationship between the institution and the folkway. Although both entail customary behavior, institutions have an organizational aspect not inherent in the folkway. As for confusing institutions and associations, MacIver asserted that if a phenomenon in question can be joined, then it is an association. "Do we think of it in terms of membership, as something which people belong to, then it is in our reference an association." Also, "We cannot *belong to* an institution" (MacIver, 1931:17).

A New Approach   Although Sumner's and MacIver's views on institutions are now many decades old, they have a timeless quality about them so that they continue to provide at least groundwork for further analysis. Surely there is a difference between a particular bank and banking, between a particular church and religion, between a given university and higher education in general. This difference was symbolized by Sumner with the terms enacted and crescive. But, as MacIver suggested, it is also clarifying to differentiate between procedures on the one hand and, on the other, the groups utilizing those particular procedures.

Despite MacIver's advice, many sociologists and others have continued to speak of particular organized groups as being institutionalized. This seems sensible, given what is meant by *institutionalization*. As generally used, the term denotes the degree to which any human phenomenon is organized, systematized, and stabilized. These three characteristics (relative to associations or to particular procedures) are defined as follows:

1. Organization—specification of the statuses, roles, and relationships of those involved.
2. Systematization—specification of rules governing relevant things that should, may, and/or may not be done.
3. Stabilization—fixity; steadiness; tendency to remain the same irrespective of the presence of particular participants at any given time.

With the foregoing considerations in mind, it is herewith suggested that the best features of Sumner's and MacIver's views can be combined for a new and more inclusive conception of institutions. In this synthesized view, it is proposed that Sumner's crescive and enacted categories be retained, along with MacIver's differentiation between processes and groupings. However, I depart from MacIver in suggesting that associations as well as processes can be institutionalized (as the term has been defined above).

The suggested view of institutionalization, and of processes and associations, is graphically represented in Figure 5. It will be noted that this figure has two basic categories: (I) Processes and (II) Associations. Each of these major categories is subcategorized into Crescive and Enacted. The three critical aspects of institutionalization—organization, systematization, stabilization—are shown as continua in connection with each subcategory. The minus and plus signs at the ends of the continua are meant to suggest that any process or association is institutionalized *to the degree* that it is organized, systematized, and stabilized.

With the aid of the schema depicted in Figure 5, and provided that sufficient information is available, one can roughly indicate the "institutionalization profile" of any given process or association. Let us take, as an example, the Roman Catholic Church. The first thing to ask is the question suggested by MacIver, "Can you join it?" Since the answer is obviously yes, we go to the second part of the diagram, labeled "Associations." Now the second question: "Is the phenomenon relatively more crescive or enacted?" Here we have an immediate problem. There

Figure 5.   Elements of Institutionalization

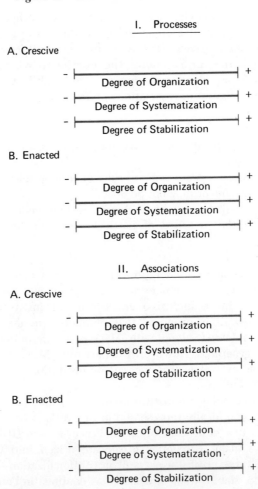

I.   Processes

A. Crescive

Degree of Organization

Degree of Systematization

Degree of Stabilization

B. Enacted

Degree of Organization

Degree of Systematization

Degree of Stabilization

II.   Associations

A. Crescive

Degree of Organization

Degree of Systematization

Degree of Stabilization

B. Enacted

Degree of Organization

Degree of Systematization

Degree of Stabilization

are faithful Catholic adherents who will say that the church was specifically founded by Jesus of Nazareth and is, therefore, enacted. Historians of ancient history, on the other hand, would generally claim the church had no specific beginning but, rather, gradually evolved from the interplay of spiritual ideas and political conditions during the last days of the Roman Empire. This historical view is accepted for present purposes; hence, we classify the Roman Catholic Church as crescive, thus placing us in part A of the Association half of the diagram.

The next three questions concern the degree to which various conditions prevail. Such questions of degree cannot be answered accurately with any precision unless careful measuring techniques are used. Therefore, the answers suggested in the present context should be understood as guess-estimates based on general information rather than on empirical calculation.

The first degree question is: "To what degree does the church specify the statuses, roles, and relationships of significant participants?" Since the church is quite specific about the relative status of parishioners, priests, bishops, cardinals, and so on, and about the appropriate role for each, it seems reasonable to conclude that the church is very much organized. Therefore, if we were actually attempting to establish the church's institutionalization profile, we would probably insert an indicator mark toward the far right (plus) end of the appropriate continuum labeled "Degree of Organization."

The next question is about systematization: "To what degree are there rules governing relevant behavior?" The church has a multitude of rules about what should be done or not done; hence, it seems sensible to assert that the church is highly systematized. This could be indicated by making a small mark toward the far right (plus) end of the appropriate continuum labeled "Degree of Systematization."

Finally, "Is the church stable?" It seems certain that this question would be answered with a resounding *yes* by almost all observers. Although the church undergoes change and has at times been shaken quite literally to its foundation, still it has a stability that remains beyond the life of particular participants. This fact could be indicated on the diagram by inserting a mark toward the right end of the appropriate continuum labeled "Degree of Stabilization"; however, in comparison with the other two indicator marks, I would place this one a bit more toward the center since the stability of the church seems less evident (to me) than does its degree of organization and systematization.

And so, relative to the proposed schema, the Roman Catholic Church is patently an association; and, equally patently, it is decidedly institu-tionalized since it manifests a high degree of the three prime characteristics of institutionalization. Its institutionalization profile, according to the foregoing discussion, would be something like this:

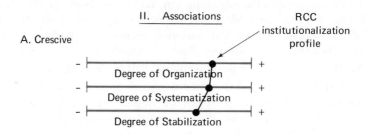

Let us take sandlot baseball as another example. Generally, you have a group of youngsters who gather informally on a field somewhere and, after choosing up sides, begin to play ball. Relative to the proposed schema, where does sandlot baseball "fit"? First, is it a process or is it an association? You cannot "join" sandlot baseball. Therefore, this particular phenomenon is a process. You can only join a given baseball team. So, sandlot baseball fits in the first part of the diagram depicted in Figure 5. Secondly, is sandlot baseball crescive or enacted? It seems doubtful that anyone could point to a specific, conscious beginning for this form of recreation. Hence, if it must be classified one way or another, it is probably more crescive than enacted. Finally, to what degree is it systematized, organized, and stabilized? For the typical sandlot baseball team, the rules are pretty loose. They vary with the group and with circumstance, and, therefore, there is not much systematization. Also, sandlot baseball is, almost by definition, loosely organized. There is no careful specification of the statuses or roles of players. Finally, sandlot baseball probably has a good deal of stability in the sense that, as a process, it continues pretty much the same despite change in personnel and time. Therefore, we have a crescive process that is somewhat stable, but not at all systematized or organized. It seems reasonable then to term this phenomenon relatively noninstitutionalized. This would be especially the case if one were to compare it with major league baseball. The latter is highly systematized, organized, and stabilized; it is, therefore, very much institutionalized.

For clarity's sake, perhaps one more example might be in order. Let us consider class registration at a typical university. Here we have what must be one of the most annoying procedures known to students—and right there we see where registration fits into the suggested schema; it is a process. Now, is it crescive or enacted? It is hard to imagine that anything as irrational as the registration most of us have experienced was specifically created, but generally that has been the case. However, the whole idea of "registration" is probably lost in the mists of antiquity, and therefore it is a puzzle to know how to classify university registration so far as being crescive or enacted. But is it institutionalized? In older universities such as Oxford it is probably institutionalized, at least to a large degree. One imagines that registration at such a school is highly systematized, organized, and stabilized. Not so at a new university such as Arizona State. Here there is some significant change made almost every semester. We hardly learn how to fill out a given set of forms before they are revised. The rules of what should be done change almost day to day. The relationship of those having various statuses and roles is similarly altered. Registration at such an association—that is what a university is, an *association*—is thus not institutionalized to any significant degree.

Bureaucracy and Institutionalization   A bureaucracy, described in Chapter 6 as an example of a formal social organization, is the epitome of a highly institutionalized association. Indeed, "bureaucratized" and "institutionalized association" are synonymous terms. Both denote a specialized collectivity that is highly organized, systematized, and stabilized.

Systematization in the bureaucracy is suggested by the importance of the established rules governing the personnel. To the professional bureaucrat, rules are inviolable guides; in effect, they are holy writ. Thus, to the bureaucratic-minded, the statement "It's a rule" is unchallengeable. There are, therefore, no special cases calling for personal, idiosyncratic decisions. For the bureaucrat, a legal tenet is far more valuable than a person. Hence a paraphrase of Tennyson's sentiment applies: "Ours not to reason why, Ours but to do and die." Or, "We don't make the rules, lady. We just follow them." Or, "I just work here."

In addition to being highly systematized, the bureaucracy is the ultimate in organization. A hierarchical "table of organization" designating who reports to whom is carefully worked out; in this sense, an army is an example of a special-purpose bureaucracy. Armed service symbols of status have their civilian counterparts, as indicated in a recent Nader report on the federal civil service system. According to the United Press description (June 18, 1972), the report points out that lower-grade employees are given small metal desks whereas higher-grade workers receive large wooden ones. Also, those having a rank as low as GS-6 (designation of job classification) are allotted only 60 square feet of work space in comparison with the 225 given to GS-15 supervisory employees.

The typical worker in a bureaucracy occupies an "office," which is a constellation of prescribed duties and responsibilities called a "job description." Since the office is more important than a particular occupant, personnel are easily replaceable. Therefore, a bureaucracy has great staying power. If any questions arise regarding the duties of a given office, reference can be made to the "file" (discussed earlier) where the records of previous decisions, actions, and established rules are carefully maintained.

Institutional Variability   A number of observers have spoken about the "functional prerequisites" of societies. These are the problem areas that must be attended to successfully in any society if it is going to survive as a recognizable entity. A basic list of functional prerequisites includes the following:

1. *Membership replacement*—a method for allocating responsibility for the bearing and rearing of children.
2. *Socialization*—a procedure for insuring that basic values are internalized by the vast majority of societal participants.
3. *Economics*—a method for regulating the production and distribution of goods and services.
4. *Health care*—a method for minimizing the deleterious effects of physical and mental disability.
5. *Harmonizing with nature*—a method for making constructive use of—and for replacing—the gifts of nature, and for making adequate response to natural disaster.
6. *Government*—a method for controlling seriously disruptive forces, internal or external (that is, keeping the peace).

The arrangements for handling such functional prerequisites are institutionalized in all societies, but the institutional arrangements vary tremendously from time to time and from society to society. Health care is one typical example. Although such care is almost always institutionalized, interpretations of ill health and the methods of handling it are almost unbelievably varied. This is illustrated by the general reaction to sickness in modern Western nations, for example, as compared with the reaction among the Manus of New Guinea (Fortune, 1935).

In Manus society, illness is regarded as punishment for breaches of moral standards. The most important offense is loose sexual conduct, meaning any sexual behavior other than the prescribed marital relationship. Therefore, when a Manus falls ill, the first suspicion is that there has been sexual transgression. However, it is not necessarily the ill person who was the transgressor since illness may attack anyone in the families of those who misbehave. Therefore, everyone is interested in the behavior of many others since personal innocence does not guarantee safety.

The prescribed response to illness among the Manus is for an oracle to be consulted by family members. Through magical manipulations, the oracle decides who the guilty persons are. They must confess or the sick individual may die. In the event that the accused refuse to confess, they are regarded as murderers if the invalid does not recover. After confession, the guilty must make compensatory payments to the controlling ghosts of relevant households. Once these payments are made, the sinful behavior is forgotten; any subsequent related illness is treated as due to some other cause.

Generally in the western world, the prescribed reaction to illness is, of course, quite different from that found among the Manus. First, the ill are regarded primarily as victims in contrast to the Manus assumption that the ill may be victimizers. Second, to obtain treatment, the typical Westerner consults a highly trained specialist whose basic orientation is naturalistic rather than supernaturalistic. Finally, the treatment process consists of a direct attack on the illness itself.

The institutionalized aspects of health care in the West are impressively detailed. The specialist consulted—except by those who believe in naturopathic or spiritualist methods—is a person who has been trained in a rigidly controlled setting designed to produce practitioners who will hew to a narrow range of ideas and activities. To help insure the desired results, the practitioners must pass a licensing procedure and must practice in accordance with the rules of various associations. If they prescribe medicine, much of it must be obtained from other licensed people who dispense it under controlled conditions. If the ill person is sick enough, he is sent to a hospital which is obviously a highly institutionalized setting. The typical hospital is run by a staff that is arranged in a strict hierarchical order, with medical doctors and high-ranking administrators at the pinnacle, followed by registered nurses, practical nurses, orderlies, and students, and with maintenance personnel at the very bottom. Each rank has its insignia of office: stethoscopes for M.D.s; business suits for top administrators; caps for trained nurses; colored garb for practical nurses, orderlies, and students; and clean-up paraphernalia for maintenance workers, Any treatment undertaken in the hospital is strictly controlled as to how, when, and where it shall be administered. Rules are specified relative to who can move about the hospital, where they can go, who can visit whom, and when. All of the above and more is prescribed in a typical hospital.

It should not be concluded that the naturalistic emphasis of Western medical treatment means it is free of magical practices such as those found among the Manus. According to sociologist Julius Roth's description, the typical tuberculosis hospital is a setting where concern for administrative ease results in procedures that are largely ritualistic; these procedures in turn lead to ". . . irrational practices that can properly be called 'magic' " (Roth, 1957:310). Among the many examples of ritual found in the hospital, one of the most interesting is that which is officially listed as procedural rules for controlling the transmission of TB. Observing these rules is ceremonial because they are not observed on any rational basis but solely depending upon extraneous social conditions. For example, Roth found a very definite relationship between the rank of a hospital employee and the degree to which protective clothing, particularly the face mask, is worn. This relationship is depicted in Table 4. Those who do wear the mask often pull it down so that the nose is uncovered, thus making breathing easier. According to Roth, ". . . the mask then takes on the status of a charm necklace" (p. 312).

There are also examples of institutional magic. In the state hospital observed by Roth, the patients must wear masks when they go for a haircut, an X-ray, or to see the services director or social worker. They do not have to wear masks, and never do so, when they go to occupational therapy, visit with their families, go to socials, movies, and the library, or play bingo. Thus, the patients are required to wear a mask when they are "on business" but not when bent on "pleasure," even though they use the same parts of the building for business and pleasure and come into contact with many of the same people. Roth comments, "The rules suggest that the tubercle bacillus works only during business hours" (p. 314). This seems to be the conclusion of ward employees. They commonly wear protective clothing when attending to their duties, but discard such clothing when socializing with the patients, even though social as compared with work contacts involve more prolonged and intimate contact with the sick. In sum, the Manus are not alone in resorting to magical practices and other heavily ritualized behavior.

Table 4. Wearing of Protective Clothing by State Hospital Personnel

	Times Entered Room	Percentages Wearing		
		Cap	Gown	Mask
Doctors	47	5	0	5
Registered nurses	100	24	18	14
Practical nurses	121	86	45	46
Aides	142	94	80	72
Students	97	100	100	100

Source: Adapted from Roth (1957:312).

The Institutionalization Process   The process whereby associations and procedures become institutionalized is graphically illustrated by the experience of many religious groups. The Quaker religion, founded by George Fox in seventeenth century England, is representative.

Fox was scandalized by what appeared to him to be the corruption of the official Church of England. He, therefore, called for a return to the principles of primitive Christianity. His preaching inspired a number of followers who referred to themselves as the Society of Friends. They accepted Fox's belief that "there is that of God in every man"; hence all men are essentially equal. With this idea in mind, the Friends concluded that they should not adhere to a common practice of their day which called for those of low status paying deference to those "above" them in the social order. Such deference was symbolized by the peasant tipping his hat to members of the nobility, by the elaborate clothing of wealthy people in contrast to the rough working garb of commoners, and by differential ways of addressing people, informal pronouns being used by gentry when speaking to children, servants, and laborers.

Dramatizing their opposition to such customs, the Friends began to wear what they called "plain clothes" even when they could afford more elegant apparel. They spoke in "plain talk," using the same forms of address for all people including high government officials. They refused to doff their hats, even keeping them on in court and while attending religious services. They asserted that Jesus's command for men to love one another meant that they should not hurt others; hence, the Friends refused to give military service when called.

During one of the many times when George Fox was in court charged with a violation of law or custom, the presiding judge took him to task for his pacifism. Legend has it the judge told Fox that if, as a supposed religious leader, he had a proper sense of proportion, he would tremble at having the audacity to defy his "betters." Fox's response was to point his finger at the judge and speak to this effect: "It is you who should tremble—nay *quake*—in the sight of the Lord." The judge came back with, "I'll let you do the quaking. Thirty days for all you quakers." And from that moment, the term was adopted by the Friends as a symbolically useful nickname.

It is obvious that Quakerism began as a radical dissenting sect. Today, however, the best known Quaker, a birthright member, is *Richard Nixon!*

Here is a name that prompts many to think bitterly about napalm, Cambodia, Kent and Jackson State, Hanoi, and Haiphong Harbor; there are also frightening thoughts about such things as wire tapping, no-knock entry legislation, preventive detention, Watergate coverup, official attacks on a free press, and demagogic manipulation of anti-communist hysteria. It is, therefore, appropriate to ask: What happened? What happened to the loving message that George Fox's converts accepted so completely and followed so carefully?

An accurate answer would be complex, but surely it would include the institutionalization process as an important element. As with the Methodists, Latter-Day Saints, Jehovah's Witnesses, Christian Scientists, and so forth, the informal relationships and procedures of the original Quakers were soon regarded as inefficient and inadequate. Organized and systematic activity is more effective because it designates responsibility, facilitates coordination, and spreads the risks involved in advocating something new. But such organization immediately changes an unworldly endeavor to a worldly one. What could be more materialistic than choosing leaders, making assessments, and assigning duties? Moreover, if ideals are kept too high and rigid, the good word will be accepted by only a few true believers.

Thus, gradually, often imperceptibly, the out-group becomes an in-group (even if, as with the Friends, it remains relatively small). As German social scientist Robert Michels pointed out relative to democratic social movements, "Organization is, in fact, the source from which the conservative currents flow over the plain of democracy, occasioning there disastrous floods and rendering the plain unrecognizable" (1962:62). The growth of conservatism among Quakers was greatly speeded by their deeply felt ideals of honesty and love for all. With such ideals, Quaker businessmen soon achieved a well-earned reputation for integrity, leading in turn to almost certain success. With success came involvement "in the world." And, being involved with things as they are, dissent no longer seems reasonable. Why change that which brings satisfaction? Finally, the symbols of dissent were abandoned. Even "the old folks" gave up plain talk and clothing. The Meeting House which had originally been maintained with an unpaid ministry typically became a "Quaker Church," an establishment designation that had once been avoided.

The final result, with a few noticeable exceptions such as that embodied in the American Friends Service Committee, is seen in Whittier, California, a city where the author, as well as Richard Nixon, once resided:

> On the other side of the city there is a group which struggles to preserve some of the shattered remnants of Quakerism. But the demands of city living have been too much. To attract members, the old meetinghouse where Friends once joined together at unprogrammed gatherings to ponder things of the spirit has become a full-fledged church. In place of the cooperative leadership of the past, there is now an efficient and salaried minister who conducts services much like those found in most Protestant churches. Only a few gentle old ladies and saintly old men still use "thee" and "thou," talk about the historic "peace testimony" . . . of the Society of Friends, and

come to the old-style "silent meeting" at 9:00 A.M. Their children and grandchildren attend the more conventional 11:00 o'clock programmed service. When they reach adolescence almost all of the grandchildren, . . . acculturated American youngsters, become concerned with such things as drag strips . . . and approve entering the armed forces when called (Hoult, 1958:155–156).

With institutionalization, thus, the procedures, goals, character, and personnel of organizations become radically altered.

Satirizing Institutions   Three satirical analyses of institutionalization have received widespread attention in recent years. Although written humorously, the views of C. Northcote Parkinson, Laurence Peter and Raymond Hull, and Robert Townsend had the serious purpose of making the general public aware of the follies and foibles of human organization. First, Professor Parkinson wrote *Parkinson's Law* (1957). The essence of the "law" is that work expands to fill available time; hence, there is no realistic relationship between an amount of work to be done and the size of staff needed to do it. Underlying the law are two factors: 1) officials want to multiply subordinates, not rivals; and 2) officials make work for one another. In just a few sentences, thus, Parkinson "explained" institutional growth.

To understand the workings of the law, Parkinson gave a simple but representative example:

. . . we must picture a civil servant, called A, who finds himself overworked. . . . For this real or imagined overwork there are, broadly speaking, three possible remedies. He may resign; he may ask to halve the work with a colleague called B; he may demand the assistance of two subordinates, to be called C and D . . . . So A would rather have C and D, junior men, below him. They will add to his consequence and, by dividing the work into two categories, as between C and D, he will have the merit of being the only man who comprehends them both. It is essential to realize at this point that C and D are, as it were, inseparable. To appoint C alone would have been impossible. Why? Because C, if by himself, would divide the work with A and so assume almost the equal status that has been refused in the first instance to B; a status the more emphasized if C is A's only possible successor. Subordinates must thus number two or more, each being thus kept in order by fear of the other's promotion. When C complains in turn of being overworked (as he certainly will) A will, with the concurrence of C, advise the appointment of two assistants to help C. But he can then avert internal friction only by advising the appointment of two more assistants to help D, whose position is much the same. With this recruitment of E, F, G, and H the promotion of A is now practically certain.

Seven officials are now doing what one did before. This is where Factor 2 comes into operation. For these seven make so much work for each other that all are fully occupied and A is actually working harder than ever (1957:4–5).

Parkinson also recorded his views on status-conscious bureaucratic officials and their fancy offices and headquarters buildings. He wrote:

> Every student of human institutions is familiar with the standard test by which the importance of the individual may be assessed. The number of doors to be passed, the number of his personal assistants, the number of his telephone receivers—these three figures, taken with the depth of his carpet in centimeters, have given us a simple formula that is reliable for most parts of the world (1957:59).

Parkinson concluded, "It is less widely known that the same sort of measurement is applicable, *but in reverse*, to the institution itself." For example, a well-ordered building is a sign of a dead institution. In the really live endeavor, there is no time for planning the perfect setting. "The time for that comes later, when all the important work has been done. Perfection, we know, is finality; and finality is death" (Parkinson, 1957:61). Examples cited include the Palace of Westminster where the House of Commons meets, the British Empire government buildings at New Delhi, and the Pentagon. Westminster was completed at the end of Parliament's dominance of the English government. New Delhi was brought to perfection just as England's control over India was relinquished. And the Pentagon, which was built to house the massive military headquarters needed to fight World War II, was finished just as the war ended.

Second, the "Peter Principle," formulated by Laurence J. Peter and popularized by Raymond Hull, concentrates on the individual participant in a bureaucratic organization. The first written description of the principle was in a ten-page article in *Esquire* (Hull, 1967); the interest aroused was so widespread and so intense that the brief piece was expanded into a book (Peter and Hull, 1969). The heart of both article and book was this statement: *In a hierarchy each employee tends to rise to his level of incompetence.* The ultimate result is that in a typical hierarchical organization, almost every job is handled by an unqualified person. Professor Peter explains:

> Suppose you own a drug-manufacturing firm, Perfect Pill Incorporated. Your foreman pill-roller dies of a perforated ulcer; you seek a replacement among the rank-and-file pill-rollers. Miss Cylinder, Mrs. Ellipse and Mr. Cube are variously incompetent and so don't qualify. You pick the best pill-roller, Mr. Sphere, and promote him to foreman.
>
> Suppose Sphere proves highly competent in this new job: later, when deputy-works-manager Legree moves up one step, Sphere will take his place.
>
> But if Sphere is incompetent as foreman, he won't be promoted again. He has reached what I call his level of incompetence and there he will stay till he retires.
>
> An employee may, like Mr. Cube, reach his level of incompetence at the lowest rank: he is never promoted. It may take one promotion to place him

at his level of incompetence; it may take a dozen. But, sooner or later, he does attain it (Hull, 1967:76).

Finally, Robert Townsend, in his *Up the Organization* (1970), describes how the more stultifying effects of institutionalization can sometimes be avoided. Townsend spoke from personal experience since he was the executive who made Avis Rent-a-Car the successful No. 2 business in that field; he has also held top management positions with American Express, Dun & Bradstreet, and CRM Communications. In dealing with the entrenched bureaucracy of these organizations, Townsend found he was stymied if he let too many others get wind of a new problem-solving idea before it was implemented. "It's a poor bureaucrat," Townsend notes, "who can't stall a good idea until even its sponsor is relieved to see it dead and officially buried" (1970:55).

In a chapter titled "Institution, On Not Becoming An," Townsend asserted his belief that a viable organization needs someone to perform a function such that he would be titled vice president in charge of antibureaucratization.

> He must have a loud voice, no fear, and a passionate hatred for institutions and their practices. In addition to his regular duties, it's his job to wander around the company looking for new forms, new staff departments, and new reports. Whenever he finds one that smells like institutionalization, he screams "Horseshit!" at the top of his lungs. And keeps shouting until the new whatever-it-is is killed (1970:84–85).

Institutionalization and Humanistic Values   Although it may be possible, as Townsend asserts, to minimize certain aspects of organization and systematization, it is no doubt unavoidable for a vast number of human associations and endeavors to become institutionalized, at least to some degree. Indeed, any given society, together with its culture, is in effect a complex institutionalized system. But beyond that, even in a paradise there would be those who would say, "We must safeguard what we have achieved and to do this we must organize ourselves efficiently." Thus, Heaven could also be routinized, bureaucratized, institutionalized.

Despite the cynical views of Parkinson, Peter and Hull, Townsend, and others, there is merit in some aspects of institutionalization. For one thing, an institutionalized situation is something a person can count on. The same yesterday, today, and tomorrow! This can be exasperating, but at least one is spared unwelcome surprises. And, as indicated in Chapter 6, the specialization developed in a bureaucratic organization often facilitates reaching desired ends. At the same time, the humanistic goal of individual development is quite antithetical to typical institutionalized arrangements. The truth of this observation will be more apparent to the student who simply considers what usually happens when one attempts to deal with the rules and personnel controlling the typical school. The student who puts high principle above expediency will fail at almost every point. The expedient student, the one who simply goes along with the system whether or not it is just or sensible, will be rewarded by the controlling bureaucracy. In Townsend's almost classic phraseology:

> And God Created the Organization and gave it dominion over man.
> Genesis 1, 30A, Subparagraph VIII (1970:vii)

In an institutionalized setting, it is conformity that counts, not growth or truth or sincerity. According to the Nader report referred to earlier, in the federal civil service the prescribed code of conduct is so status-quo-oriented that anyone who raises questions is regarded as a trouble-maker. As a result, "A veterinarian who attempts to slow plant production to insure a wholesome product is transferred; an inspector who forwards too many reports of violation is investigated; a food inspector whose name appears in a news story critical of inspection programs . . . is threatened with transfer; a ship inspector who reports faulty welding in a combat ship is sent hundreds of miles to examine ferry boats" (UPI, June 18, 1972).

It is disheartening reports of this sort that led some New Left advocates of the 1960s to suggest "participatory democracy" as a solution to the problems created by institutionalization. The concept of participatory democracy first appeared in Paris in the early 1790s when concerned citizens attempted to find an alternate to the traditional rule from the top. The solution was for the entire citizenry to get together daily in section meetings so that they could collectively solve problems of substance. The belief was that out of thorough debate would come consensus. However, it was soon clear that few people have the time or the inclination to be permanently politicized. Therefore, the revolution quickly fell into the hands of the few who were willing to give full time to it, and these few were impatient purists. The sad result was the Reign of Terror during which the guillotine was used almost indiscriminately (Palmer, 1941:27).

It seems that *representative* democracy, with all its faults, is less hazardous, especially if it can be combined with a rational measure of the participatory principle. In any case, it is quite obvious that servicing the health, food, clothing, and shelter needs of the multitudes of all societies today cannot be accomplished, even minimally, except through efficient organization and with systematic procedures. So here again we see one of the many paradoxes of human society: That which is necessary for life can simultaneously be a killer.

REFERENCES AND FURTHER SOURCES

Fortune, Reo F.
1935   Manus Religion. Vol. 3: Memoirs of the American Philosophical Society. Philadelphia: American Philosophical Society.

Homans, George Caspar
1961   Social Behavior: Its Elementary Forms. New York: Harcourt, Brace and World. See especially pp. 360–377, "A Federal Agency: Consultation Among Colleagues."

Hoult, Thomas Ford
1958   The Sociology of Religion. New York: Holt, Rinehart and Winston. Dryden Press Series. See especially Chapters 2 and 4.

Hull, Raymond
1967   "The Peter principle." Esquire 67 (January): 67–77.

MacIver, R. M.
1931   Society: Its Structure and Changes. New York: Long and Smith.

Michels, Robert
1962   Political Parties: A Sociological Study of the Oligarchical Tendencies of Modern Democracy. Translated by Eden and Ceder Paul. New York: Collier. Originally published in 1915.

Palmer, R. R.
1941   Twelve Who Ruled: The Committee of Public Safety During the Terror. Princeton: Princeton University Press.

Parkinson, C. Northcote
1957   Parkinson's Law: And Other Studies in Administration. Boston: Houghton Mifflin.

Peter, Laurence J. and Raymond Hull
1969   The Peter Principle. New York: Morrow.

Roth, Julius A.
1957   "Ritual and magic in the control of contagion." American Sociological Review 22 (June): 310–314.

Sumner, William Graham
1906   Folkways: A Study of the Sociological Importance of Usages, Manners, Customs, Mores, and Morals. New York: Mentor Books. 1960 reprint of the original.

Townsend, Robert
1970   Up the Organization. New York: Knopf.

Three Major Institutions: Religion, Marriage and the Family, Education

When sociologists speak of "the five major institutions," they usually refer to the family and related matters, education, and religion, as well as government and the economy. The interrelationships existing among these highly institutionalized aspects of life illustrate the general sociological principle that any one facet of a sociocultural system, however basic and important, is more a product of the system than a shaper of it. This principle is symbolized in Figure 6 below.

Figure 6. Interrelationships Among Five Major Institutions

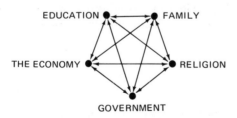

Note in Figure 6 that each institution is represented by a small circle. The interrelationships between the institutions are represented with double-headed arrows. Religion can serve here as an example; it affects education, the economy, government, and family life, as indicated by the arrows running out from religion and pointing to the other institutions. At the same time, religion is affected by the other institutions, as symbolized by the arrows coming from them and pointing to religion.

When attention is centered on religion in particular, the effect is as follows:

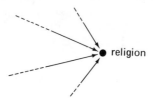

Thus, when seen in the abstract, religion appears to be a product of the influences affecting it, especially those originating in the other institutionalized aspects of the sociocultural system. The same observation can be applied to the other major institutions. The result, quite naturally, is that in any given sociocultural system largescale institutions, even those that are antagonistic to others, have a strong tendency to be mutually supportive. This tendency has been termed *the principle of sociocultural compatibility* (Hoult, 1958:17–19). The principle implies that since most of the constituent parts of one society are products of the same general social forces and cultural norms, they tend to be consistent relative to one another and thus uphold complementary beliefs and practices.

Some of the practical implications of the compatibility principle are that it is unrealistic to assert "religion ought to be the conscience of the nation," or "education is the proper vehicle for social reform," or "the family should become a better refuge from the impersonality of the modern world." It would be pleasant if such assertions could be part of the real world. But the reality, however harsh, is that institutions are largely mirrors: They reflect the social order in general, so that if that order is corrupted, then the institutionalized aspects will also have a strong tendency to be corrupt.

RELIGION

Religion is one conspicuous aspect of the universal culture pattern. It is found in all known human societies at all times. It can be defined as the doctrines and practices associated with belief in, and attempts to relate favorably to, ultimate spiritual forces or transcendental values. When such doctrines, practices, and beliefs become institutionalized, they constitute what we know as organized religion: the Roman Catholic church, the Methodist church, the Church of Jesus Christ of Latter-Day Saints, Society of Friends, and so on.

Organized religion is a particularly clear example of the principle of sociocultural compatibility. For example, this becomes evident when one contrasts what given religious believers are taught with what might well be construed by an alien "man from Mars." In every case, religious advocates are told that there is one particularly effective way—*their* way, the in-group way—to achieve and maintain good relationships with ultimate forces. The Martian would be likely to comment: "It is interesting that the 'uniqueness' of each major religion appears in a form that is almost always strictly in accordance with the cultural norms and social structure prevailing where the religion functions." In short, religion is a particularized expression of underlying sociocultural forces; where it is not, it generally has little success. This applies to any social movement; adherents of a new movement who want it to become a mass phenomenon will be disappointed except to the degree that they convincingly portray their movement as an expression of commonly accepted values. Thus, Christianity did not become the established religion of the Roman Empire until there was a melding of Christian and secular norms; Methodism was nothing but an obscure cult until its adherents began to live in terms of establishment values; the Assembly of God churches were hardly more than a butt of jokes until their members ceased to be "holy rollers"; the Mormon or Latter-Day Saints (LDS) organization remained an odd frontier sect until its officials agreed to refrain from practicing the polygyny and incest that were so generally distasteful to Americans (for incest among early Mormons, see Weinberg, 1955:36).

The LDS church is a particularly interesting example because its growth rate among middle-class Americans has been close to spectacular. It is likely that the growth stems in large part from the special "fit" of Mormon doctrine with middle-class ideas. The Mormon belief that hard work and self-development spell virtue is highly compatible with the Protestant ethic associated with the middle class; and the Mormon exclusion of blacks from the priesthood gives an air of sanctification to the racism so common in America. The declining respectability of racism directed against blacks will no doubt be paralleled by a change in LDS doctrine; the current president of the church has already hinted he expects such a change, saying it will occur at the moment he, or a successor, feels there is an appropriate ". . . divine message from God . . ." (UPI, November 16, 1972).

Another example of the relationship of religion to prevailing sociocultural conditions is provided by the sharp contrast in the way North American and southern European Roman Catholic groups judge fascism. When fascism became a political force in Italy in the 1920s (and in the 1930s and 1940s in Spain, Portugal, Austria, Greece, and southern France), it was not generally opposed by southern European Catholics because it was compatible with the basic social values in terms of which the citizenry had been socialized. In addition, when fascism became dominant in a given area, those who wanted to avoid loss of life or property were forced to give at least nominal allegiance to the controlling political regime. Hence, it is not surprising that the Roman Catholic church signed official agreements with fascist governments in a number of countries. But American Catholic officials, generally socialized in terms of the same democratic ethos that influences non-Catholic Americans, usually objected to cooperation with fascist governments once their totalitarian nature became evident.

Further dimensions of the relationship of religion to other aspects of culture are suggested by the close association between the socioeconomic status of people and their religious beliefs. In almost all cases, a people's religious orientation reflects, legitimizes, or compensates for its material condition. Examples include the historic messianic movements among Jews, the American Indian Ghost Dance, and so-called Negro religion. The Ghost Dance, which asserted that Indian ways would once more become dominant, appeared among the plains Indians just as the buffalo began to disappear; Indian societies not dependent on the buffalo, such as the Pueblo, were indifferent to the new cult. The "Negro religion" that traditionally appealed to lower class black Americans was the essence of "pie in the sky," complete with prophets, bishops, and "daddies" who promised all to those who had nothing at all. The appeal of such religion can be expected to decline in direct proportion to acceptance of the idea of black power, which gives hope for satisfaction in the here and now. The content are less inclined to sing about "Beulah Land," "I Can Hear My Savior Calling," or "When the Roll Is Called Up Yonder."

The religion of the middle class is just what the man from Mars would have expected: To a large degree this religious form gives primary stress to decorum, appearance, and quiet ritual. The religion sanctifies work, delayed reward, dedication—all those factors associated with success, or necessary for avoiding failure. It was among the middle classes of America that the "peace of mind" form of religion became so popular following World War II. Peace-of-mind reassured its adherents that striving for material gain is favored by the Almighty. "Follow these ten [or twelve, or six, and so on] simple rules and you will find room at the top," said their leaders.

Upper-class religion is middle-class with patina. It is practiced in cavernous cathedrals or in other ornate marble halls. It has the depth of age and the self-confidence of wealth and high status. Its smooth, soothing ways celebrate the belief that "God's in his heaven and all's right with the world." Such satisfaction with the existing order legitimizes, even sanctifies, the controlling position of those who dominate "others less fortunate." A gloss is thus placed on things as they are (Pope, 1942:Chs. 8–10). We should therefore not be surprised, one observer remarked, that during the Great Depression of the 1930s, the spire of New York City's Trinity Church, which stands on Broadway at the head of Wall Street, inclined a full eighteen inches toward the brokerage houses where the wealthy or their agents gather to engage in the mysterious rites and incantations of stock trading (Luccock, 1936: 181–182).

It should not be concluded that religion is purely an accepting product of outside influences. Religious values such as love, peace, and devotion, commonly given lip service only, have inspired some believers to support fundamental social reform. Examples range from yesterday's social gospel movement among Protestants to today's radicalism within the Catholic clergy such as the Berrigan brothers; other examples include the early Christians, Essene Jews, the first Quakers, the Mormons, Wahhabi Moslems, and so on. Such individuals and smaller groups not only fail to profit from the established order; they see its values as a fundamental barrier to the spiritual concerns wherein alone, believers assert, one can attain salvation. Like Quaker founder George Fox, they seek

> Not of the letter, but of the spirit; for the letter killeth, but the spirit giveth life.

The desire to be more deeply spiritual, so often thwarted by the largely ritualistic nature of established religion, perennially generates new religious movements whose adherents want to "go back to the original Jesus," or otherwise re-create some aspect of the past. Thus arises a much remarked church-to-sect-to-church-to-sect transition process—that is, a new sect formed by dissidents will, if broadly appealing, evolve into an established church or even into an international ecclesia that may prompt new generations of the disenchanted to begin new sects that continue the never-ending cycle. In remarking on the renewal movements, a cynic observed that those wanting to get rid of all the layers of tradition are faced with a task much like that involved in peeling an onion. When you remove the last layer, you have nothing left but the smell.

Max Weber, the German sociologist, is among those who documented the thesis that religion can have a vital influence on society. Weber centered his attention on the economic order, asserting that religious values are an important variable in explaining the appearance or nonappearance of capitalism. This thesis has been questioned by some scholars (for example, Tawney, 1926; Yinger, 1946:115), who make a counterclaim that capitalism produced Protestantism rather than the reverse. As summarized by MacIver:

> . . . it might easily be claimed that the rise of the Protestant ethic itself, with its stern individualism, its "worldly asceticism," and its doctrine of Steward-ship, was the expression in the religious sphere of a pervasive change of social attitudes corresponding to and causally interdependent with a changing socio-economic order (1942:177).

Nevertheless, Weber's claim has not been adequately refuted and it continues to spark some interest.

In his classic work, *The Protestant Ethic and the Spirit of Capital-ism*, Weber wrote, ". . . the essential elements of . . . the spirit of capitalism are the same as . . . the content of Puritan worldly asceti-cism" (1930:180). He felt that two Calvinist doctrines were particularly significant for the development of capitalism. One was the belief that every man has a "calling," a life-task set by God. Catholicism has no such concept, said Weber; the English "calling" and the equivalent German *Beruf* are uniquely associated with ascetic Protestant groups such as, in particular, Calvinists, Pietists, Methodists, Quakers, and some evangelistic sects. One of the modern descendants of these groups is the Church of Jesus Christ of Latter-Day Saints discussed earlier. Nonascetic Protestants, such as Lutherans, interpreted the idea of the "calling" as a commandment to accept the status quo as an expression of God's inscrutable design. In contrast, the Calvinists explained the calling as a command to make the most of one's opportunities. This was a truly new concept; it proposed that worldly activity has positive religious mean-ing. The trusting Calvinist was thus driven to engage in the ceaseless quest that so commonly results in material success. Weber cited Richard Baxter's *Christian Directory* (of Puritan Ethics):

> If God shows you a way in which you may lawfully get more than in another way (without wrong to your soul or to any other), if you refuse this, and choose the less gainful way, you cross one of the ends of your calling, and you refuse to be God's steward, and to accept His gifts . . . (Weber, 1930:162).

The Calvinist belief in predestination, said Weber, was also significant in the development of capitalism. The doctrine of predestination was that the few elect who would achieve eternal salvation were preselected by God. There is no way to attain grace, said John Calvin, if one were not destined for it. But, he added, it is a sign of God's favor if one is successful in everyday concerns. So, unsure about their salvation, Calvinists were prompted to tremendous activity as they tried to convince themselves they were among the saved. As Weber put it:

> The religious valuation of restless, continuous, systematic work in a worldly calling, as the highest means to asceticism, and at the same time the surest and most evident proof of rebirth and genuine faith, must have been the most powerful conceivable lever for the expansion of that attitude toward life which we have here called the spirit of capitalism (1930:172).

The religious devotion of the early Calvinists was representative of spiritual assumptions of that time (A.D. 1000–1500).

> To the Europe of the Middle Ages, it was heaven that vibrated with reality and Jesus who stood in the trembling cloud above us, watching every movement, monitoring the final details workmen lavished on their gargoyles, stone beasts that, once set in place, would be seen by God alone (McReynolds, 1970:23).

But the Calvinists did not know, nor did anyone else, that with the "age of enlightenment" (during the sixteenth through the eighteenth centuries)—with the development of science, widespread secular education, industrialization, urbanization—the power of formal religion to move men would be steadily undermined. As McReynolds has phrased it:

> Sometime between the beginning of the eighteenth century and the end of the nineteenth, God died, though theology could not arrange a formal burial until the 1960's. God died as rationalism arose, celebrated as a goddess by the French Revolution, beloved by our own American revolutionary leaders Jefferson and Paine. Science was seductive. The world could be known; all mysteries finally would be answered. For the first time in history, man looked forward, rather than back, and looked to this planet, and not to heaven (1970:23).

The quotation from McReynolds is an example of what sociologist–priest Andrew Greeley somewhat cynically termed "conventional wisdom." In a highly persuasive account, Greeley asserts there is no good evidence that the most vital aspects of religion have been declining. Indeed, he says, basic religious needs and functions have not changed notably since the Ice Age (Greeley, 1972:1). But Greeley is practically alone in his stand. As he notes himself, his book is a "volume of dissent" (Greeley, 1972:1). The basis of the dissent, however, may be largely a matter of definition. Greeley does not argue that all people need a religion, the sacred, or a church. Instead, he claims only that ". . . there is in the human condition a built-in strain toward evolving an ultimate meaning system and making it sacred" (Greeley, 1972:241). In contrast, those who speak of a decline in traditional religion primarily refer to such things as belief that there is an all-powerful force (called God) who keeps a tally on each person's activities, who can be appealed to for responses that are not just psychic, and who can and does interfere with the physical laws of nature. In reference to such conceptions, it seems quite realistic to observe that the general decline in traditional religious belief is global insofar as the world has been westernized—that is, has adopted the instrumentalism of the scientific point of view. "Science is the infidel to all gods in behalf of none" (Roszak, 1969:211).

But even where westernization has been most intense, there are still many religious believers and participants in religious organizations. In 1970, for example, close to 48 million Americans were termed "full, communicant, or confirmed members" of religious bodies (*Yearbook of American Churches*, 1971:186). However, a multitude of studies completed in the last few decades have shown that conventional religious beliefs now have little behavioral meaning for many, even the most devout. Thus, a study of American college students found that while the students "normally express a *need for religion*," their religious beliefs do "not carry over to guide and govern important decisions in the secular world. Students expect these to be socially determined" (Jacob, 1957:2). God's ". . . place is in church and perhaps in the home, not in business or club or community."

The fact that the above cited study was completed almost two decades ago is symbolic; its findings have been so well established on a general basis that few want to bother researching the question any further, preferring instead to rely on such indices as the religious data gathered by the Gallup poll, data reported by the U.S. Department of Commerce, and trends in new construction of religious buildings. All of these, the *Yearbook of American Churches* observes, ". . . provide indicators pointing in the downward direction" (1971:220). As long ago as the 1920s, social scientists were writing about *The Twilight of Christianity* (Barnes, 1931). More than three decades ago, after considering the results of numerous studies, sociologist L. L. Bernard asserted, with regard to supernaturalistic religion,

> Even today it is nominally the reigning type, but we suspect that in its present form most men have ceased to take it very seriously and realistically and that it has become for them an interesting mythology with which they have strong and sympathetic emotional and artistic traditional associations, rather than intellectual convictions regarding its truth. It is, in other words, so strongly embedded in our literature, art, social conventions, legal forms, and everyday life, that we are not allowed to forget it, although we no longer regard it as anything more than a vast system of social survivals (1938:8).

The decline of supernaturalism is not a static movement. Rather, it comes and goes, as indicated by the wavy nature of the trend line shown in Figure 7. But, as also suggested by the figure that follows, the general, overall movement is away from sacred beliefs and toward secular ones.

"It is now a commonplace," observe Livingston and Thompson, "that one of the central distinguishing characteristics of our age is that we live in a *secular* culture. Most earlier cultures, by contrast, were *sacred* cultures" (1966:80–81). In a secular culture, behavior is judged with reference to nonreligious norms alone; sacred ideas are regarded as less important, if not irrelevant.

But even in the most secularized society, from time to time waves of uncertainty and fear—and sometimes just the dictates of fashion—produce religious movements that in the short run appear to be evidence of a return to religion. One of these waves accompanied the eyeball-to-eyeball diplomacy that characterized the post-World War II era. The result was a great upsurge in religious-body membership and attendance at religious services. Celebrants of the movement hardly got into print before what they extolled declined and disappeared to the extent that religious spokesmen of the early 1960s lamented that organized religion could hardly survive if the trends of the day continued.

And then the mystic inclinations of the youth movement of the late 1960s appeared on the scene. Partly because of their disillusion with the prevailing order, partly because of their disappointment that the hoped-

Figure 7.   Impressionistic Depiction of the Trend in Traditional Religious Belief

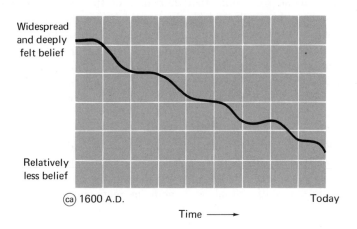

Note: This diagram is purely impressionistic because there is no way to measure accurately the complex historic events and trends underlying the "direction" of religious belief.

for revolution was no longer imminent, and perhaps partly as compensation for their marginal status, many youths turned to an array of occult exotica (Rowley, 1971): Zen, Sufism, Scientology, shamanism, Theosophy, satanism, "Learyism," Subud, Nichiren Shoshu, and various forms of Yoga including Hare Krishna, Meher Baba, Buddhism, and Spiritual Regeneration (through Transcendental Meditation). "In all these zealotries," educator Peter Marin observes, "the driving need is for certainty and purity, for a transcendence of the self." This statement was preceded by a more generally inclusive one:

> The new "millennialism" of the young is a desperate response to . . . public chaos and private isolation. What moves the young is only in part the desire for the simple life, religious ecstasy, and justification. There is a more desolate and organic need, the need to reduce the nightmare complexity of things to a manageable form (1972:58).

The latest example, at the time of this writing, is the Jesus movement. It has wide appeal because it is compatible with many established aspects of Western society and it speaks to the concerns of youth of today. Jesus freaks shout "Right on with Jesus," and some even assert that evangelist Billy Graham, favorite of right-wing politicians, is "a pretty far-out guy." *Newsweek* (March 22, 1971:97) quotes a reformed heroin addict making his appeal: "You want a trip, man? I'll give you a free trip. It's really a groovey high. It's called Jesus Christ and it will really blow your mind."

It is reasonable to assume that defenders of the political–economic status quo have been pleased by the youthful turn toward mysticism. Other-worldly interests subvert this-world reform possibilities. As Marx put it, religion is the opiate of the masses; and Lenin observed, ". . . mysticism becomes the shell of counter-revolutionary sentiments" (1965:10). Give "darkies" time off for religion if for nothing else, said the southern gentry; give industrial workers "a bucket of blood" with every sermon and they'll stay ignorant and servile (Pope, 1942:84–91, Chs. 8–10; Washington, 1964:95–103). Similarly, lower caste and "untouchable" Hindus, despite their often incomparably degraded living conditions, have traditionally avoided participation in secular reform movements; they have been diverted by nirvana-seeking meditation, energy-sapping diets, ecstatic ritual, and medicine-man manipulations (Noss, 1969:Chs. 3 and 7, esp. pp. 203–204; also see Ch. 4).

But, despite some wishes to the contrary, the long-term trends are likely to prevail. Therefore, the Jesus movement, along with the satanists, Subudists, and the like, will probably go the way of previous religious revivals, a cause for lament on the part of many. True, the Rock of Ages has legitimized exploitation and provided numerous fanatics with a rationalization for bestial behavior. But it has also given people in general a comforting place to stand; it was high, firm, and secure, and it gave ready access to the guideposts of the ages. But for many, the Rock has eroded into sand, and as everyone knows, it is difficult and tiring to walk along where the footing is soft and there is no exalted path. Such a path is especially needed now that humanity faces an environmental debacle that will be avoided only to the degree that people and nations turn away from their selfish, exploitative ways. The crisis is so acute that one of the consequences may be a relatively permanent reversal of the long-term trend away from spirituality. As will be indicated in Chapter 11, environmental needs are so universal, so transcendental, that the movement to save the environment partakes of some of the ennobling features of religion, such as love, devotion, and universalism. This prompts Theodore Roszak to observe, "The religious renewal we see happening about us . . . seems to me neither trivial nor irresponsible, neither uncivil nor indecent" (1972:xxii); the renewal is the needed element for making a life-saving—that is, an environmentally oriented—politics (1972:xxiii).

MARRIAGE AND THE FAMILY

The phrase "marriage and the family" is used here to designate the institutionalized arrangements whose function in every human society is to provide for and regulate the various aspects of relatively long-term intimate relationships between given males and females. Those "various aspects" include satisfaction of affectional and sexual needs and the care of children who may be conceived or adopted. It is the family's role in the procreation and care of children, and, thus, the major if not sole source for replacing societal membership, which has led a number of observers to regard the family as the most basic of social institutions.

The function of the family is accomplished by means of a variety of forms depending upon time and cultural setting. The extent of the variety is suggested by the fact that a recent sociological dictionary defines 109 concepts descriptive of various facets of family life and related matters such as dating (Hoult, 1969a:see pp. 366–367 for listing). For present purposes, it is sufficient to note a few of the important types of marriage and family structure.

Types of Marriage   *Monogamy* is the most common form of marriage; the monogamous marital unit consists of one man and one woman. In some parts of the world, polygamous marriage is preferred. *Polygamy* denotes plural marriage in general—that is, forms of marriage in which the marital units can consist of more than two partners at a time. The most common form of polygamy is *polygyny* in which one man may have two or more wives at the same time; *polyandry* is when one woman can have two or more husbands simultaneously, a practice that is quite rare.

Types of Families   Family forms also differ. There are *nuclear families* consisting of a married couple and their dependent, unmarried children, if any; and there are the larger *extended families*. Two major types of extended families are: 1) a kinship group consisting of a married couple, their children, and a number of other relatives, all sharing a common domicile, or 2) a set of marital groupings living in close association and being bound to one another by the fact that either the men in the groupings are related through the male line (called *patrilineal extended*) or the women in the groupings are related through the female line (*matrilineal extended*). The *clan* (sometimes termed *sib*) may be regarded as still another type of extended family; it consists of a group of people who, counting descent from a common ancestor, actual or mythical, think of themselves as a kin group whose members have family-type rights and responsibilities relative to one another. In all of these family forms, including the clan, there is a customary taboo against *incest*, which is defined as sexual relations between close kin. Therefore, families and clans almost always practice *exogamy*, which specifies that mates must be chosen from outside the kin group however construed. Choice of mate within a given group—for example, racial, religious, national—is termed *endogamy*.

The *arranged* vs. *romantic* marriage is still another indicator that family life and related matters are as varied as culture itself. In most traditional societies as in Eastern Europe, parents feel they should choose marriage partners for their children. Only thus, it is believed, can rational matches be insured. Traditionalists point out that young people hardly know their own minds and hearts, let alone those of others. Hence it is just good sense for parents to pick suitable mates for their children. The parents will not be misguided by sentiment or emotion; they will pay all due attention to family values, status, and needs. Marriages of this type, elders claim, are stable, satisfying, and productive.

Nevertheless, romance has become the dominant basis for marriage in Western societies, particularly in the United States. As depicted in Hollywood movies and soap operas, romantic love is essentially a juvenile emotion, a mindless, sweeping commitment adding credence to the folk saying, "Love is blind." As a basis for marriage, therefore, it can be disastrous. Being "in love" is beautiful when it is experienced, but it is a state of being such that many knowledgeable marriage counselors, hearing a sweet young thing declare, "I love him; I want to marry him," would respond, "If you love him, *don't* marry him. You can't possibly know what he is really like if you are so in love with him."

The basic difficulty with romantic love as a foundation for marriage is that, generally speaking, it prevents its victims from analyzing properly the degree to which they and their prospective mates have the characteristics a multitude of studies have shown are among the most important for marital adjustment. These are: similar values, compatible temperaments, determination to surmount problems, and parents who were happily married (Bell, 1971:294–304). A fully rational person, thus, would not ask his or her prospective partner, "Do you love me?" but would ask questions like these: "Were your parents happy?" "How similar are our values?" "Are our temperaments 'compatible'?" "Are we firmly committed to mutually solving the problems we'll face?" A couple for whom the answers to such questions are firmly "yes"— whether or not the marriage partners feel a heart-throbbing attraction to one another—could build a successful marriage and family. Marriages built on such a base tend to generate, among those involved, a mature interpersonal commitment that is inspiringly satisfying. Such deep affectionate attachments can no more be likened to romantic love than can a teeny-bopper—however delightful—realistically be called a thoughtful adult.

It should not be concluded that romantic love is *necessarily* an impediment to happy marriage. If marital partners who are compatible also happen to feel strong romantic attachment for one another, they are blessed with a serendipity. On the other hand, romantic love is not a requirement for a happy marriage; the mistaken belief that it is undercuts many a promising union. Therefore, an astute marriage counselor, hearing this—"He and I get along beautifully; we like all the same things, and even our parents are lifetime good friends; but I can't marry him because I don't 'love' him"—might well respond: "You have been misled by the typical Hollywood romantic ideal, real only on the screen or in books. Mature love, the only kind worthy of adulthood, is not a pulse-racing emotion. It consists of the very things you mention: compatibility, fun, happy parents. So marry him! I guarantee you have characteristics such that you fall in a group made up of people who typically have happy marriages and seldom unhappy ones."

Although family life—as well as processes of courtship and dating—is amazingly stable when considered in toto and over the long run, it is still in a constant state of change. Some of the change is largely evolutionary; some of it is purely a matter of fashion trends; more of it is a consequence of population change or alteration in other aspects of given sociocultural systems. Like religion and other institutions, the family reflects "time and tide." Recent changes in dating among middle class youth are probably evolutionary; however, if there is a relatively swift return to prior patterns, then the changes are best regarded as a matter of fashion. In either case, the formal date so customary a decade or so ago now seems almost archaic. Seldom do today's middle class adolescent boys phone a girl and "ask for a date." More frequently, groups of boys and girls get together and then, as convenient and desirable, pair off for a period of time usually without committing themselves to long-term involvement.

Much more commitment is involved in the paramarriages that are relatively common today. A few decades ago, unmarried young men and women living intimately together was cause for scandal. How many today are really scandalized by such arrangements? That is not to say that the paramarriage has full general approval. It is still a violation of traditional norms; it is also a technical violation of legal statutes in many states. But it appears that a developing new value is giving rise to new norms. The value is taking this form: For those so inclined, living intimately with a person of the opposite sex, with or without marriage, is a good thing to do insofar as the arrangement is not exploitative and is an expression of mutual affection. For an apparently increasing number of people, the developing value is taking this broader form: For those so inclined, living intimately with a person of *either* sex . . . (and so forth). Hence, "accepted" paramarriages, whether narrowly or broadly conceived, should not be compared with promiscuity or a "one-night-stand." They involve mutual emotional commitment and care and they extend over time to a significant degree. The type of relationships implied by such paramarriages has led numerous religious bodies to issue documents indicating that some of even the most conservative elements of society are beginning to accept newly developing values and related norms regarding sexuality. Dr. Mary Calderone, an M.D., cites these representative statements from an Episcopal Church paper—

> Our Lord always stressed the importance of the quality of relations between people. Should not the church likewise be concerned with the inner worth of all relations, whether heterosexual or homosexual?

—and these from a United Presbyterian national study:

> Is abstinence or sublimation the only advice the church will have to give to single persons? Or will it be able to explore new forms of male–female relationships and, while accepting the primacy of marriage and the family as a pattern for heterosexual relationship, be able to condone a plurality of patterns which will make a better place for the unmarried? (1972:62).

Family life changes prompted by change in other institutionalized aspects of life have led some observers to ask serious questions about the future of marriage and the family. Sociologist Barrington Moore, Jr. has written:

I would suggest . . . that conditions have arisen which, in many cases, prevent the family from performing the social and psychological functions ascribed to it by modern sociologists. The same conditions may also make it possible for the advanced industrial societies of the world to do away with the family and substitute other social arrangements that impose fewer unnecessary and painful restrictions on humanity (1958:161–162).

In contrast, answering the question "Does marriage *have* a future?" Sociologist Jessie Bernard writes: "The answer . . . is an unequivocal yes. The future of marriage is, I believe, as assured as any human social form can be" (1972:269).

The apparent gulf between the Moore and Bernard viewpoints is partly a matter of the definition of terms since Bernard defines marriage very broadly. She says there are about twenty-five different liaisons that can be called a marriage, ranging from a temporarily permanent arrangement for child-rearing purposes to a childless association maintained purely for convenience. She favors letting people tailor their relationships in accordance with their individual preferences and circumstance. Perhaps Moore would conclude, "Defining marriage this broadly encompasses what I meant when I spoke of 'other social arrangements.' " In any case, it seems unlikely to the writer that an institution established for so long in history, having so important a biological base, and so interwoven with and supported by many other aspects of life, is in imminent danger. The characteristics mentioned suggest that marriage and the family, including even lifelong commitment and sexual exclusivity, will have a long future. There will of course be further changes; the family has lost its function as a farming productive unit, and its functions as a consumption unit and major factor in the socialization process are being undermined. But it retains some elements of these functions, and it is unparalleled in its potential for satisfying long-term affectional needs.

EDUCATION

Education, like religion, is in general a function of what is implied by the sociocultural compatibility principle. That is, educational endeavors in any given sociocultural system are widely supported so long as they are consistent with other major aspects of the system. Thus universal public education has been fully backed whereas liberal education evokes a grudging acquiescence at best.

The function of every society's public education (elementary and secondary school training) is to complete the socialization process begun by the family. Socialization has already been defined as the procedures whereby the young in a society are taught to internalize the norms—that is, to accept the prevailing norms as their own personal guidelines for belief and action. This process is given further substance, dimension, and support by elementary and high school education which is so conducted that pupils in general have little alternative to concluding that their country, history, ancestors, family-life arrangements, religion, wars, measuring systems, economic systems, and the like, are the "natural," "best," and "most efficient" ways of living. Elementary and high school education, thus, is a barely disguised propaganda scheme that aims to maximize consensus and minimize deviance.

> We call it "education," the "life of the mind," the "pursuit of the truth." But it is a matter of machine-tooling the young to the needs of our various baroque bureaucracies: corporate, governmental, military, trade union, educational (Roszak, 1969:16).

The great majority of formal education is above all not designed to "make people think," as any innovating high school teacher or seriously questioning pupil soon learns, especially if he makes reference to economic injustice, racism, war profits, monopoly, and so on. Ironic as it may sound to those aware, it is not at all unusual for school principals and board members to have their ears bent by irate parents protesting that they pay taxes for schools to engage in career training or to teach "the basics," not to confuse young people by letting them dabble in "matters that should be left to the government," such as engaging in social criticism. Board members are likely to take such protests seriously since controlling boards of educational institutions are typically drawn from the most privileged realms of society.

Control from "the top" is characteristic of higher education as well as of elementary and secondary schools. Educational researcher Rodney Hartnett (1969:58) indicates that fully 94 percent of the trustees of public colleges serve on corporate boards; 43 percent of the trustees at selective private universities have incomes of more than $100,000 per year (Hartnett, 1969:57).

> Trustee politics flow from these economic facts. Overwhelmingly white, Protestant, and in their fifties and sixties, less than a sixth at public universities and less than a fourth at private ones reported their politics as "liberal." Two-thirds of these men at selective public institutions and nearly half at their private counterparts believed that all campus speakers should be officially screened, and over half at the former and a third at the latter favored the requirement of loyalty oaths from faculty members (Miles, 1971:45–46).

The structure of public universities and the nature of state politics, Miles concludes, make the typical board of regents "a wind-swept plain" for reactionary forces. "The trustees are a vector of force for the hard line, particularly at public universities, whose boards are often klatsches for the virulently new rich" (Miles, 1971:48).

The conservative-to-reactionary sensibilities of typical board members are occasionally rubbed raw by maverick university faculty members who accept the ideals and goals of liberal education literally and seriously. Such faculty are inspired by Thomas Jefferson, who wrote, ". . . even under the best [governmental] forms, those entrusted with power have, in time, and by slow operations, perverted it into tyranny" (Jefferson in Lee, 1961:83). The most effective way to avoid tyranny, Jefferson said, if one were not inclined to follow his advice to have an occasional revolution, is to ". . . illuminate, as far as practicable, the minds of the people at large, and more especially to give them knowledge of those facts, which history exhibiteth, that . . . they may be enabled to know ambition under all its shapes, and prompt to exert their natural powers to defeat its purposes."

Thus, Jefferson was one of the first to express the idea that democracy depends on the kind of education that liberates the mind from dogma. This is usually called liberal education. It teaches the value of ceaseless questioning and searching, and the dangers of acceding to arbitrary authority no matter how legitimate. It is in essence the scientific spirit generalized. Such education is of course jeopardized, if not impossible, without the twin safeguards of academic freedom and tenure. Academic freedom and job tenure do not exist for the convenience of muckraking professors; they are intended to insure that society shall continue to have the benefit of searching, critical analyses. These analyses are sadly lacking in schools—and in states—where teachers can be censured or removed on ideological grounds.

However, even in colleges of liberal arts academic freedom is not a crucial issue for most faculty members. They are not much inclined to do battle for liberal education. Truly mind-expanding and freeing education is confined to *selected* classes in philosophy, literature, the arts, and the social sciences. Otherwise, faculty members seem quite content to work on their research contracts, engage in endless and generally useless committee work, participate in faculty meetings which have not changed since Thorstein Veblen, more than half a century ago, described them as "deliberative bodies charged with the power to talk" (1954:282), and collect their pay checks as a well-earned reward for managing to conduct classes without ever seriously challenging the status quo. If any wayward students, teachers, or administrators suggest that a meritocracy which largely confines higher education to the élite is hardly "education for democracy," faculty members in general close ranks in the name of "quality" and "standards." Thus faculties, considered in toto, are quite compatible with dominant forces in general and with the nature of boards of regents and the corporate university. In Miles's words,

> . . . there is nice fit between the goals of a professionalized faculty and the corporate state's objectives for nationalized higher education. The *specialized* talents of the professionals and the funding sources' *instrumental* view of education are complementary. While faculty specialization undermines undergraduate teaching and liberal education in the service of basic research and graduate education, the education managers are intent upon fulfilling manpower needs that are only marginally related to liberal education. Technical and vocational objectives rule the general system of higher education. . . (1971:183).

The generally conservative nature of almost all significant aspects of higher education is in part a consequence of education's relationship to "the new industrial state." Higher education is big business not only on one level, but also in the federal budget it is the largest money expenditure after defense, space, agriculture, and technology; and it has a crucial stimulating effect on the entire economy. In studies conducted for the Brookings Institution and for the Committee for Economic Development, Edward Denison found that almost half the American economic growth rate in the 1950s and early 1960s could be attributed to advances in knowledge applied to production processes (Denison, 1962:Ch. 21) and to educational improvement of the labor force (Denison, 1967:101–108). Harvard economist John Kenneth Galbraith observes that science and education today ". . . stand in relation to the industrial system much as did the banking and financial community to the earlier stages of industrial development" (1971:283). Capital was decisive then; now, the supply of qualified talent is the most vital element. With this point in mind, it is representative that "Stanford [University] is a linchpin of the military–aerospace industry of the West Coast" (Miles, 1971:160).

The industrialization of higher education, in conjunction with youth culture, population changes, and the inspiration of the black revolt, led to the campus upheavals that characterized the 1960s. The riots have come and gone, but education at all levels remains in a state of ferment. One of the problems is suggested by the phrase "unionization or professionalization." For decades, teachers in general have quietly accepted exploitation in return for the psychic income of being termed "professionals." Lately, however, some have pointed out that the main professional prerogatives teachers have are responsibilities; they have few of the privileges such as high income, little control over their own time, and little secure status. Some of them have therefore concluded, "Since we are employees, let us act accordingly. Above all, for our own protection, let us organize and secure collective bargaining rights. If we don't, our employers will continue to reap the benefits of 'divide and rule.' " Such observations have increased teacher militancy except among those who, still believing they can make it on their own, continue to claim it is unprofessional to organize. This sentiment is still very strong among college professors. They are, therefore, much given to engaging in activities they have been told are "professionally respectable"—such as participating in powerless faculty senates where, as Veblen observed, imponderables are weighed and incommensurables are correlated. "It is a nice problem in self-deception, chiefly notable for an endless proliferation" (Veblen, 1954:282).

Erosion of the once-common belief that education is the ultimate solution to practically every social problem has affected schools on all levels. Declining belief in this unrealistic hope has led to taxpayer revolts, failure of bond issues, and cutbacks on legislative appropriations. The most serious results have been experienced in the schools of older cities whose industries and affluent citizenry have fled to the suburbs and beyond. The result in such cities has been the creation of predominantly black and depressingly poor central city areas whose schools reflect all the worst elements of their environment: racism, poverty, alienation, anger, drugs, riots. Proposed solutions, such as free schools, street academies, and "performance contracts" with private businesses, have been notably unsuccessful (re contracts, see Sessions, 1972). Tuition grants ("vouchers") for individuals to spend as desired have shown more promise. However, if their use becomes general, there seems little doubt that business interest in increasing profits will ultimately result in giving private agencies a massive, publicly financed new way to exploit the poor and innocent.

Busing is another proposed solution. But even where the aim is to provide for quality education rather than to achieve racial desegregation, it has aroused deep resistance and widespread debate. In their opposition to busing, right-wing politicians are particularly fond of citing the Coleman report (James S. Coleman, et al., 1966) and some reanalyses of the Coleman data (Mosteller and Moynihan, 1972), all of which allegedly indicate that the nature of schools is irrelevant to their effects on students. "Better elementary schools" supposedly do no more for students than "inferior schools." However, some observers feel there are serious limitations in the data gathered for the Coleman report:

> The methodological, conceptual, and practical problems that the Coleman researchers encountered in arriving at their "no-school effect" conclusion have been documented many times. The wrong kinds of tests were administered and in the wrong ways. School "effectiveness" was too narrowly defined. The sample was biased and the data unreliable (Guthrie, 1972).

Further, one reanalysis of the Coleman data concluded that racial segregation in the classroom accounts for a significant proportion of the poor achievement of blacks as compared with whites (U.S. Commission on Civil Rights, 1967:II, 89–91). Finally, Coleman himself says that by no means are all aspects of school environment irrelevant to pupil progress. Referring to his original study, Coleman recently asserted, "The research results indicate that a child's performance, especially a working-class child's performance, is greatly benefited by his going to school with children who come from educationally stronger backgrounds" (*Saturday Review*, May 27, 1972:59). Such observations have, however, not impressed some ethnic groups and black separatists.

Given the incredible complexities of the current school crisis, it is not surprising that there is no perfect solution. Perhaps the nearest approach to a reasonable answer that does not ignore tradition altogether would be the creation of community-controlled open-enrollment schools equitably financed at the state level, together with busing available for those who choose to attend schools outside their own neighborhood. The model is based on the system created by the late Senator Robert Kennedy for Virginia's Prince Edward County when, during the early 1960s, county officials closed the public schools rather than integrate them.

> Such a model could work in every state. Here's how:
> Each community would elect its own local school board. A city the size of Boston, for example, might be divided into ten local school boards. Each local board would nominate some of its own members as candidates for a regional board of directors. . . . The state supreme court would choose members of the regional boards from candidates nominated by the local boards. The regional boards would set broad policy objectives for their areas and would hire a chief executive to carry them out.
> This model would take control away from the state legislatures and from unrepresentative, unresponsive, and often irresponsible school boards and would give a good deal of control to neighborhood and community groups. It also would make one executive responsible for the administration of the system. If he or she met the annual objectives of the board of directors, he or she would be retained. . . .
> Down the line, a committee of teachers, students, and parents should select the school principal and set objectives for that job. The principal, too, should be measured against them annually: His or her job would depend on successful performance (Sullivan, 1972).

Humanistic values would be best served if one of the measures of "successful performance" were innovative techniques so creative, so compelling and interesting, that compulsory attendance laws would be irrelevant.

There are those who claim that school crisis "solutions" entailing any semblance of traditional classroom attendance and performance are not real answers. They, therefore, want to do away with schools as now structured. One prominent critic, Ivan Illich, an educator and ex-priest, feels that compulsory attendance at tax-supported schools is a major element in maintaining a system that gives many advantages to the few and few advantages to the many. Hence he proposes *Deschooling Society*:

> The first article of a bill of rights for a modern, humanist society would correspond to the First Amendment of the U.S. Constitution: "The State shall make no law with respect to the establishment of education." There shall be no ritual obligatory for all (Illich, 1971:11).

Another well-known critic, educator John Holt, has recently joined Illich in calling for a deschooled society. "It would be a society in which there were many paths to learning and advancement, instead of one school path as we have now—a path far too narrow for everyone, and one too easily and too often blocked off from the poor" (Holt, 1972:190).

By deschooled society, neither Illich nor Holt mean we should do away with schools as such, especially for those who like the school experience. What must be discarded—what is fatal for so many—is forced attendance, regardless of interest, for drill in a standard curriculum. Drill under such circumstances is not rightly termed education; rather, it is expensive, often harmful, confinement in which the education that occurs usually does so in spite of the system rather than because of it. There are of course some things, certain special skills, that are best taught in the traditional manner, especially for those highly motivated. But many things, including reading, are most effectively learned informally in conjunction with particular interests: mechanics relative to car repair, for example, or algebra in connection with computer programming. For those who believe that if not forced into school, the underprivileged would never learn to read, the answer is that vast numbers of the poor are functionally illiterate even after long years in ordinary schools. They are illiterate and prepared for menial work alone because they are compelled to attempt learning within a hostile environment. Experience indicates that they *would* learn to read (in as short a time as forty hours if reading drill is related to a pressing interest [Illich, 1971:18]) and would learn many other things thoroughly if provided with congenial settings where they could freely follow up and express their true inclinations and concerns. To be effective, such settings must be open community resource centers staffed with creative, sympathetic teacher–helpers inspired by the humanistic philosophy and having a high tolerance for ambiguity and informality.

The projected resource centers would be sharply different from traditional schools where terrible things sometimes occur—Kozol's report (1967:9) that black children in the Boston schools are whipped when they don't show "respect" for a teacher who calls them nigger;

Herndon's discussion (1971:107–108) of the western U.S. schools where Spanish-speaking children are classed as "retardates" because they don't do well on I.Q. tests administered in English; Illich's description (1971:5–6) of the way that tax funds intended for compensatory education for the poor are actually used to ". . . cater disproportionately to the satisfaction of the relatively richer children who were 'disadvantaged' by having to attend school in the company of the poor"; Herndon's (1971:Chs. 12 and 13) dismaying revelation that "reading problems" are invented and caused by schools; and there is my own description of the ugly parallels between prisons and the average American high school (Hoult, 1969b). The "prisonization" of schools makes them a poor medium indeed for instructing students in the values and techniques that citizens in a democracy must know if it is to survive. Schools cannot successfully teach such things in a repressive classroom or community atmosphere, but where are the school officials campaigning for the public support needed for "training in democracy"? Where are the courses dealing with civil rights and liberties, constitutional guarantees, and the well-known principle that the welfare of each individual is in the long run dependent upon the welfare of all? Instead of sponsoring such vitally needed programs, typical school officials (but of course not all) concern themselves with discipline, order, and "getting the forms filled out on time."

Although it is clear that schools, especially compulsory ones, are hard to defend, critics lacking adequate sociocultural knowledge are sometimes led into a self-defeating extremism. Thus, it is unreasonable to expect a society's major institutions to be free of the taints affecting that society. As University of Chicago ex-president Robert Hutchins has phrased it, "There is never anything wrong with the educational system of a country. What is wrong is the country" (1937:1). Hence the old idea, "If you want something in a nation, you must first have it in its schools," should be reversed: "If you want something in a nation's schools, it must first be established in the nation." Further, if one proposes replacing a major institution with a new arrangement, a questionable possibility in the short run, it is naive to expect that the new arrangement would not soon be institutionalized and come to reflect the sociocultural system in general. If it did not, it would not receive widespread support.

Finally, the idealistic or the discouraged who would impulsively do away with practically all schooling might well ask themselves this: If the established school system is totally bad, how does it produce some happy children who benefit from the experience? Why does it not stultify the occasional Illich and Holt who are so often creative and exalting? How did it fail to put its repressive stamp on the best of those wonderfully idealistic youngsters who struggled during the 1960s to establish a humanistic counterculture?*

Such examples described above suggest that the present school system still has some redeeming features. If those features are dealt with and maximized, rather than discarded, it is entirely possible that schools can play a part in providing the type of education described by Aristotle:

—an ornament in prosperity and a refuge in adversity.

---

* I specifically exclude the pseudoradicals who played at revolution "for the hell of it." It was such escapists that Lenin described in his *"Left-Wing" Communism: An Infantile Disorder* (1965); he termed them "revolutionary phrase-mongers" (p. 11) who indulge in a ". . . petty-bourgeois revolutionism, which smacks of, or borrows something from, anarchism" (p. 16); they are dilettante extremists who, "on principle," childishly refuse to compromise (p. 23); "there are compromises and compromises" (p. 24).

REFERENCES AND FURTHER SOURCES

Barnes, Harry Elmer
1931   The Twilight of Christianity. New York: Long and Smith.

Bell, Robert R.
1971   Marriage and Family Interaction. Homewood, Ill.: Dorsey Press. Third edition.

Bernard, Jessie
1972   The Future of Marriage. New York: World.

Bernard, L. L.
1938   "Sociological interpretation of religion." Journal of Religion 18 (January): 1–18.

Calderone, Mary
1972   "It's society that is changing sexuality." The Center Magazine 5 (July–August): 58–68.

Coleman, James S., Ernest Q. Campbell, Carol J. Hobson, James McPartland, Alexander M. Mood, Frederick D. Weinfeld, and Robert L. York
1966   Equality of Educational Opportunity. Washington, D.C.: Government Printing Office.

Denison, Edward F.
1962   The Sources of Economic Growth in the United States and the Alternatives Before Us. New York: Committee for Economic Development.

1967   Why Growth Rates Differ: Postwar Experience in Nine Western Countries. Washington, D.C.: Brookings Institution.

Farber, Bernard
1973   Family and Kinship in Modern Society. Glenview, Ill.: Scott, Foresman.

Galbraith, John Kenneth
1971   The New Industrial State. Boston: Houghton Mifflin. Second edition, revised.

Greeley, Andrew M.
1972   Unsecular Man: The Persistence of Religion. New York: Schocken.

Guthrie, James W.
1972   "What the Coleman reanalysis didn't tell us." Saturday Review 55 (July 22): 45.

Hartnett, Rodney
1969   College and University Trustees: Their Backgrounds, Roles, and Educational Attitudes. Princeton, N.J.: Educational Testing Service.

Herndon, James
1971   How to Survive in Your Native Land. New York: Simon and Schuster.

Holt, John
1969   "School Is Bad for Children." Saturday Evening Post (February 8): 12, 14–15.

1972   Freedom and Beyond. New York: Dutton.

Hoult, Thomas Ford
1958   The Sociology of Religion. New York: Holt, Rinehart and Winston, Dryden Press Series.

1969a   Dictionary of Modern Sociology. Totowa, New Jersey: Littlefield, Adams & Co.

1969b   "Don't worry—only the worst become administrators." Changing Education 4 (Spring): 23–26.

Hutchins, Robert M.
1937   "Ideals in education." American Journal of Sociology 43 (July): 1–15.

Illich, Ivan
1971   Deschooling Society. New York: Harper & Row.

Jacob, Philip E.
1957   Changing Values in College: An Exploratory Study of the Impact of College Teaching. New York: Harper and Brothers.

Kozol, Jonathan
1967   Death at an Early Age: The Destruction of the Hearts and Minds of Negro Children in the Boston Public Schools. Boston: Houghton Mifflin.

Lee, Gordon C. (ed.)
1961   Crusade Against Ignorance: Thomas Jefferson on Education. New York: Bureau of Publications, Teachers College, Columbia University.

Lenin, V. I.
1965   "Left-Wing" Communism: An Infantile Disorder. Peking: Foreign Languages Press.

Livingston, John C. and Robert G. Thompson
1966   The Consent of the Governed. New York: Macmillan.

Luccock, Halford E.
1936   Christian Faith and Economic Change. New York: Abingdon Press.

MacIver, Robert M.
1942   Social Causation. Boston: Ginn.

Marin, Peter
1972   "Children of Yearning." Saturday Review 55 (May 6): 58, 60–63.

McReynolds, David
1970   We Have Been Invaded by the 21st Century. New York: Praeger.

Miles, Michael W.
1971   The Radical Probe: The Logic of Student Rebellion. New York: Atheneum.

Moore, Barrington, Jr.
1958   Political Power and Social Theory: Six Studies. Cambridge, Mass.: Harvard University Press.

Mosteller, Frederick and Daniel P. Moynihan (eds.)
1972   On Equality of Education Opportunity: Papers Deriving from the Harvard Faculty Seminar on the Coleman Report. New York: Vintage.

Noss, John B.
1969   Man's Religions. New York: Macmillan. Fourth edition.

Pope, Liston
1942   Millhands and Preachers: A Study of Gastonia. New Haven, Conn.: Yale University Press.

Roszak, Theodore
1969   The Making of a Counter Culture: Reflections on the Technocratic Society and Its Youthful Opposition. Garden City, N.Y.: Anchor.

1972   Where the Wasteland Ends: Politics and Transcendence in Post-industrial Society. Garden City, N.Y.: Doubleday.

Rowley, Peter
1971   New Gods in America: An Informal Investigation into the New Religions of American Youth Today. New York: McKay.

Sessions, Jack
1972   "Performance contracting revisited." American Teacher (January): 15ff.

Sullivan, Neil V.
1972   "How did we lose the wheel? or: It's time for a new system." Saturday Review 55 (16 September): 67.

Tawney, Richard
1926   Religion and the Rise of Capitalism. New York: Harcourt, Brace.

U.S. Commission on Civil Rights
1967   Racial Isolation in the Public Schools. Vol. 2. Washington, D.C.: Government Printing Office.

Veblen, Thorstein
1954   The Higher Learning in America: A Memorandum on the Conduct of Universities by Business Men. Stanford, Calif.: Academic Reprints. Originally published in 1918.

Washington, Joseph R., Jr.
  1964   Black Religion: The Negro and Christianity in the United States. Boston: Beacon Press.

Weber, Max
  1930   The Protestant Ethic and the Spirit of Capitalism. Translated by Talcott Parsons. London: Allen and Unwin.

Weinberg, S. Kirson
  1955   Incest Behavior. New York: Citadel Press.

Yinger, J. Milton
  1946   Religion in the Struggle for Power. Durham, N.C.: Duke University Press.

10

Political-Economic Institutions

INTRODUCTION

A relatively short time ago, United States Secretary of Defense Charles E. Wilson, who had previously been president of General Motors, reportedly declared: "I thought what was good for our country was good for General Motors, and vice versa" (*Newsweek*, January 1, 1973).

The "vice versa" part of the declaration was at the time regarded as a political goof. But in his bluntness the Secretary was quite accurate. His assertion symbolized the most important single aspect of political and economic reality in modern industrialized society. This reality can be described in a single, albeit complex, statement:

> *In today's industrial state, practically all significant political power and economic activity are interlocked and interdependent in a complex which is dominated by a relatively small elite group made up of people whose prime aim is to maintain their preeminence so their own interests can best be served.*

The practical result is that people in general have little control over their own destiny, although numbers of them may, at any given time, live in a physically affluent manner. Major dimensions of their lives and fortunes, despite contrary ideological slogans and oratory, are at the mercy of a ruling group whose members provide numerous indications that they have little interest in the common good.

Such assertions demand documentation. They are documented in the substantive sections that follow. First, however, we must attend to four theoretical matters: basic definitions; theories of political–economic power; the interrelationship of power, legitimacy, and disorder; and the spectrum of political–economic ideologies.

Definitions of the two terms, politics and government, are basic to all that is discussed in this chapter. With special reference to official public affairs in a given area: *politics* is the entire process of obtaining the power to set policy, as distinguished from administering it; *government* is the established system of administering policy, as distinguished from obtaining the power to set it. Despite the subtle difference between these two terms, it is clear that there is a lot of politics in government, and vice versa; hence, the two terms are often used interchangeably, as in the present context.

Two Theories of Political–Economic Power   As indicated in Chapter 5, in the discussion of norms, advocates of the (a) conflict and the (b) consensus (or functionalist) schools of thought, when they address themselves to the question of political–economic power, are usually termed, (a) élite–dominance and (b) pluralist theorists, respectively. The pluralistic view, as espoused in representative works by V.O. Key (1958), Karl Lowenstein (1959), Robert Dahl (1961), and D'Antonio and Form (1965), is that political–economic influence is distributed among a very large number of special interest groups (that are sometimes competing élites [Rose, 1967:2–4]). These groups over the long run, the theory asserts, maintain a rough balance because the acquisition of a dispro-portionate amount of power by one or more groups generates counter-balancing moves on the part of the other participants in the political–economic order. Thus, it is said, the modern political–economic system has a certain inherent stability; because it undermines dominance by particular interest groups or collectivities of such groups, it tends to give widespread satisfaction and thus insures equally widespread commit-ment to its continuance without significant alteration.

Other theorists dispute the claims of pluralists, asserting that politi-cal–economic power is concentrated in the hands of an élite that stands at the peak of a hierarchy. Élite-dominance theorists include Karl Marx, Floyd Hunter (1953; 1959), Robert Michels (1962), C. Wright Mills (1956), and G. William Domhoff (1967; 1970). These scholars, despite their disparity in terms of time and basic ideological orientation, have generally concluded that further development of control by élites is made more likely by the mass aspects of industrialized society. A *mass society* is one with a large population characterized by anonymity, mobility, secondary group relationships, specialization of role and status, and general indifference to traditional values. Such a population is volatile, manipulatable, ever ready to engage in irrational behavior. Under such conditions, existing élites are especially vulnerable; hence, they are highly motivated to centralize and maximize their control;

potential élites similarly seek corridors to power. As Kornhauser has put it,

> In the absence of social autonomy at all levels of society, large numbers of people are pushed and pulled toward activist modes of intervention in vital centers of society; and mass-oriented leaders have the opportunity to mobilize this activism for the capture of power. As a result, freedom is precarious in mass society (1959:41).

The élite-dominance theory, with some reservation, is espoused in the present book. The major reservation is that consensus is here regarded as an element in governmental stability, as indicated below. Further, in contrast with some élite-dominance theorists, I know of no respectable evidence for the claim that élites tend to be self-conscious, homogeneous groups whose members conspire together to maintain their power. This seems particularly unlikely in complex Western societies. Therefore, I would agree with the late sociologist Arnold Rose, a pluralist: ". . . I am willing to admit a large element of a 'powerful men' explanation of power, but not much of a 'conspiracy' or 'secrecy' explanation" (1967:4). Even the "powerful men" idea must be used with care lest it degenerate into the thoroughly discredited "great man" theory of history. The sociological view is that humans are more creatures of their time than architects of it—even the most dominant are not unlimited in their exercise of power.

Power, Legitimacy, and Disorder   In Chapter 6 power was defined as the means whereby people control aspects of their environment, including one another. The most all-pervasive type of power is that embodied in political government, since a government is the agency that holds ultimate control over public affairs in a given area. Such control can be maintained, at least in the short run, by raw power. But the need for employment of such power is minimized if, in addition to controlling the instruments of mass coercion, a government is widely regarded as legitimate. Governmental *legitimacy* is defined as the condition prevailing when there is general belief that a given political authority is appropriate in that it conforms to accepted standards. As Lipset has phrased it, "Legitimacy involves the capacity of the system to engender and maintain the belief that the existing political institutions are the most appropriate ones for the society" (1963:64). With legitimacy, thus, a government has *authority,* defined in Chapter 6 as a form of power that is not dependent upon force; rather, it rests on a public consensus that the individual or agency that has it (authority) deserves to have it—a consensus that is undermined by scandal such as that embodied in the Watergate affair.

The government that has legitimacy as well as coercive power is also likely to be highly stable, especially in contrast with the government depending on raw power alone. Thus there is an inherent limitation on the self-serving inclinations of the oligarchies that, as Michels (1962:342–356) noted, appear in even the most "democratic" organizations. Michels was very nearly a total pessimist, concluding that the "iron law of oligarchy" means humans at large will almost always be ruled by power-hungry autocrats. But, as Robert MacIver has noted, "Power alone has no legitimacy, no mandate, no office. Even the most ruthless tyrant gets nowhere unless he can clothe himself with authority" (1965:63). Friedenberg adds: "Legitimacy is the chief lubricant of the social mechanism; it prevents friction by inducing collaboration among its several parts even in situations in which conflict of interest is apparent" (1969:11). He mentions as an extreme example the cooperation between condemned persons and their executioners. In the totally frightening situation, the condemned take what little comfort they can from identifying with the social system that has selected them to be destroyed. Standing with others, thus, they are not alone in their final moment.

It is important to note that government legitimacy does not necessarily imply effectiveness. It is true that a government's stability depends in part on its effectiveness, but only in part. The purely evaluative matter of legitimacy can be considered just as vital. As Lipset notes, the German army, civil service, and members of the nobility rejected the Weimar Republic because they felt it was illegitimate, not because they regarded it as ineffective. Their conclusion that the government was illegitimate was prompted by their perception that the values of the government were different from their own. *It is value similarity that lies at the heart of legitimacy.* Even the most repressive government will, under certain conditions, have a degree of stability if its citizens feel their basic values are compatible with those of the government.

When a given political–economic system loses its legitimacy, the potential for disorder, if not chaos, escalates. Disorder arises not only from those who challenge the legitimacy of given authorities. Perhaps more significantly, when authorities feel an erosion of their power, they typically use coercive violence to put down those described as underminers of "law and order." Such coercion is said to be necessary solely because of the provocation of those who "lack respect for authority."

Although all government, given its ultimate power, is potentially dangerous, by far the most dangerous is the one in the process of losing its legitimacy. The appropriate analogy is the bully whose fear prompts a defensive aggressiveness. In contrast, the fully self-confident person does not need to push others around; so it is at times with government officials.

It is quite obvious that in recent years the American political–economic system has lost a considerable measure of legitimacy previously taken for granted. Signs of lessening legitimacy include the rioting that occurred during the 1960s, prison disturbances, army officers deliberately killed by their own troops, and the current widespread contempt for officials extending even into junior high schools, all indicators of civil unrest. Another sign, perhaps the most significant of all, is the broad use of surveillance and illegal actions on the part of government agencies and high officials; "Watergate" and "the Pentagon papers" are current examples of intrusion of privacy. Such government activity suggests that noncoercive social bonds are no longer as effective as they were in holding the society together.

The Spectrum of Political–Economic Systems   In Figure 8, the range of major political–economic systems is represented in the form of a circle. This circular depiction is used deliberately so that the ultimate philosophical relationship of "left" and "right" extremists is clearly indicated.

> Extremist movements have much in common. They appeal to the disgruntled and the psychologically homeless, to the personal failures, the socially isolated, the economically insecure, the uneducated, unsophisticated, and authoritarian persons at every level of the society (Lipset, 1963:178).

The terms *left* and *right* were first applied to political–economic phenomena during the French revolutionary days of the 1790s when the supporters of the prevailing regime tended to sit on the right side of the chamber of deputies while those wanting a change in the established order grouped together on the left. Generally, since that time, defenders of established tradition have been termed rightists and challengers have been termed leftists.

Perhaps the most fundamental difference between leftists and rightists is their respective attitudes toward private property, with particular reference to the means of production, including specialist knowledge and abilities (the technostructure, as described by John Kenneth Galbraith [1971:Chapter 6]). Those on the political–economic right are generally committed to the idea that property, including production means, should be in private hands. In contrast, to the degree that people move to the left of the spectrum, they criticize private control of property, especially the means of production.

Several major political–economic orientations are labeled on the spectrum depicted in Figure 8. At the top of the spectrum the label is liberal. The *genuine* liberal is the person who is free—that is, liberated from many dogmas of the past. Thus, that person is somewhat change-oriented while at the same time attached to some aspects of tradition, especially the idea of individual liberty including the right, within reason, to hold and use private property. The liberal, then, is neither left nor right, but a little bit of both. The liberal's commitment to individual liberty, expressed politically, takes the form of general support for a democratic society, including civil liberties and equal educational and occupational opportunities. These beliefs are so virtuous, given traditional American ideals, that many people mouth them without having any real commitment to them. The result has been public confusion leading to the charge that the liberal is the person on *dead* center, unable to move. This is a realistic charge only when applied to establishmentarians who, for politically expedient reasons alone, have—with ludicrous inaccuracy—labeled themselves as "liberal" or "progressive."

Figure 8.   The Spectrum of Political–Economic Ideologies

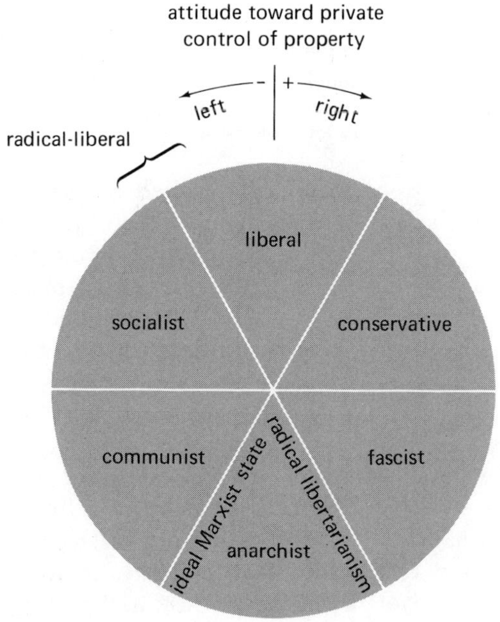

In Figure 8, the conservative position is shown to be at the right of the liberal. The conservative's prime commitment is to the traditionally established distribution of power and privilege, with special reference to private property. Belief in the principle of private control of property is so vital to the conservative that, even while deploring political excess and crudity, he will sometimes support a military government if it promises to put down serious challenges to the established order. Such right-wing military governments are usually termed *fascist.*

However, *mass* support for fascism is found in another group—one that has the mentality Marx termed *petit bourgeois.* The present-day American version of this group is that of "middle America" described in Chapter 7 (also see Lemon, 1970). The American petite bourgeoisie is more inclusive than that pictured by Marx. To Marx, the group was made up solely of small merchants, family farmers, craftsmen, clerks, and the like; it did not include industrial workers and laborers. Today, however, because of union power and government regulations, many regular blue collar workers have had secure though limited incomes long enough so that they have developed a petite bourgeoisie outlook. The essence of this view is acceptance of "the system" because it is believed to give substance to the dream that, with diligence, one can "make it." But the petite bourgeoisie, by definition, have not made it enough to be secure, despite hoping and struggling, so they are uneasy as far as status is concerned.

Their uneasiness occurs in two major areas: anxiety that the powerful (in government or among the business élite) will block opportunities for improvement; and anger against the poor and the deprived who want a share in what achievers have managed to accumulate or hope to amass. When such emotions become strong enough, the petite bourgeoisie typically turn to a strong, central government—one prototype being Hitler's Germany—which promises to crush the "reds" and curb the special advantages of the élite who are alleged to be scornful of "the people." As Lipset has phrased it, ". . . fascism is basically a middle-class movement representing a protest against both capitalism *and* socialism . . ." (1963:131). Lipset quotes historian David Saposs:

Fascism . . . [is] the extreme expression of middle-classism or populism. . . . Their ideal was an independent small-property-owning class consisting of merchants, mechanics, and farmers (1935:395–397).

It would be unrealistic to conclude that since the American petite bourgeoisie *is* American, it is largely free of the fascist taint as described above. Actually, many of the values adhered to by large numbers of middle Americans are proto-fascist at least. The values include favoring the most authoritarian version of law and order, hence support for no-knock legislation, permitting police to break into homes without warning; pretrial detention, and strong police action unhampered by civilian review boards; indifference to constitutional safeguards for civil liberties; nationalistic fervor, lending credence to support for aggressive military action, especially when directed against "the red menace";

education that concentrates on "essentials" rather than on "liberation," "integration," and "welfarism"; welfare measures, if any, based on the philosophy that all individuals are ultimately responsible for themselves. Listing such values brings to mind Huey Long's observation that when fascism comes to the United States, it will come disguised as flag-waving Americanism. The foregoing observations are not made with any feeling of condescension; people, all people—ethnics, blacks, WASPS, and so forth—can, after all, only believe what their life experiences teach them. But the fact that values are understandable, and their holders, therefore, deserving of compassion, does not deny the actuality that given values— fascist for example—are inhumane and must be opposed by all who profess a humanistic faith.

Proto-fascist values such as those already indicated, often termed "populism," have been espoused most vigorously by George Wallace, present Governor of Alabama, especially early in his career, attracting multitudes of Americans to his banner. When an attempted assassination took Wallace out of the national political picture in 1972, many middle Americans, seeking *law and order* candidates, turned to the Republican Party and the Nixon/Agnew team—a bitter choice as later events proved given so many of the team members' ethical and legal standards. Finally, ex-vice president Spiro Agnew, who made his reputation as "Mr. Clean-Against-Permissiveness," had to cop a plea in October 1973 lest he be imprisoned for felonious behavior.

This development is both ironic and dangerous. It is ironic because it gives substance to Marx's observation that the petite bourgeoisie, misled by its dreams of glory, perennially acts against its own true interests; surely the "party of big business" (GOP) is not about to put the interests of "common people" first. The danger of the development is this: With the petit bourgeois vote added in great numbers to the traditional Republican vote, the result is a majority sufficient to create a mandate for a quickened march further to the political far right, perhaps disguised as a presidential pledge to end "the whole era of permissive-ness" and instruct a "pampered" and "indulged" citizenry in "self-discipline" (*Washington Star-News* interview, November 10, 1972). The size of middle America suggests the dimensions of the potential danger—estimates range from a low of fifty-five million to a high of eighty million compared to a gross national population of 210 million. This mass, even given the lowest estimate, plus the value orientation of the group as a whole, prompted social scientist Harvey Wheeler to remark, "The most alarming prospect facing us is not revolutionary chaos but a new wave of counterrevolutionary fascism" (1971:303).

Creation of a right-wing state is a frightful prospect. In addition, such a state would coalesce opposition on the far left, practically guarantee-ing a brutal confrontation between the forces of the extreme left and right. In such a conflagration, citizens in general would, of course, be mere pawns for those who hold or covet total power. Rightists who take comfort from the idea that left extremists have a limited following, since the number of poor Americans has been declining and there are "only" about twenty-five million of them now, had better think again. The poor not only have many nonpoor allies nationally; they are also part of a two-thirds world majority. And, as indicated at the end of Chapter 7, this majority is no longer willing to be exploited. It is on the move; ". . . the time is close at hand for an immense struggle for power between the haves and the have-nots. But now, for the first time, the battle promises to be a global one. . . ."

After considering such critical events, it seems mundane to return to the spectrum depicted in Figure 8. But there are several additional points to be made about it. First, it should be noted that although fascists are obviously far right in their politics, so-called radical libertarians are even farther, as indicated in Figure 8. They are so deeply committed to the principle of individualism, including the unregulated use of private property, that they are opposed to the existence of practically any kind of government (Tuccille, 1971). The antithesis of such views are espoused by socialists (see Figure 8) as the first major political orientation to the left of the liberal. Typically, the socialist is committed to the idea that at least major industry should be socially controlled—that is, controlled by government or socially owned.

The radical–liberal position, as suggested by its location in the figure, attempts to meld the equality emphasis of socialism with the individual freedom emphasis of classic liberalism (see Kaufman, 1968). Combining these two emphases is greatly appealing to the humanist (as the term has been defined in this work). The radical–liberal is generally convinced that the good life can be achieved in society only to the degree that it is both equalitarian *and* libertarian.

Of course, the communist position is farther to the left than the socialist. In areas where communists have taken power, they have opposed most forms of private property except for basic personal effects. To achieve the transition from the traditional commitment to private property, communists from the time of Karl Marx have asserted that a very strong central government is needed to prevent counterrevolution. But the hope is that when the consciousness of the citizenry is totally changed so that all are dedicated to the welfare of their fellows, the need for government will whither away. Thus, the most extreme leftists, like the most extreme rightists, are committed to the anarchist idea, although their commitment to it rests on sharply varied philosophical grounds. That left and right *extremists* are often very similar, despite their seeming philosophical differences, is suggested by the readiness with which some fascists will convert to communism and vice versa. They illustrate the true believer type whose apparent major need is to be caught up in a vigorous social movement that will give one a sense of something larger than self.

Another "anarchist," in effect, is the technician whose ideology amounts to "the end of ideology." He is the specialist, perhaps physicist, chemist, or social scientist, willing to work for any regime because his first loyalty is simply to physical efficiency. Thus, he does not believe in any particular form of government; he simply believes in effectiveness. Such a person stands always ready to sell his talents to the highest bidder. One classic example is the Nazi rocket expert who, without any apparent qualms, joined his former enemies, the Americans, to become *their* rocket expert.

It should be noted that often leftists who succeed in seizing power take on rightist values. The Stalin regime in the Soviet Union is a perfect example. While exploiting leftist slogans, the Stalin government became right-wing extremist in the sense that it was totally committed to the distribution of power and privilege it had established. The Stalinists were not unique; their transformation from radical revolutionaries to establishment reactionaries was quite typical. A similar transformation occurred with the French revolutionary government, American, Indonesian, Indian, Brazilian, Cuban, Spanish, and so forth.

POLITICAL–ECONOMIC ÉLITES

We return now to the assertion that, despite oratory to the contrary, important political–economic institutions in industrialized societies are heavily dominated by self-serving élites. This assertion will be documented in the sections that follow. Attention is centered on the American scene, with special reference to the enormous gap between promise and performance in the political–economic realm. The American situation is heavily stressed for two reasons. First, élite-dominance is nowhere more pervasive than in the United States. This is particularly ironic, because nowhere else (unless it is in the Soviet Union) does one hear such a plethora of slogans asserting just the opposite: free enterprise, government by consent, liberty and justice for all, equality under the law, and so forth.

A second reason for paying almost exclusive attention to the United States is that it is the prototype, the epitome, of the advanced industrial society. Therefore, almost all critical observations directed at the nature and functioning of its political–economic institutions also apply, in general, to almost all other westernized nation–states (Marcuse, 1958:85–92).

It seems advisable to anticipate two possible reactions to the following material. There will no doubt be some who will say the analysis is politicized and, therefore, insufficiently objective. Objectivity has already been discussed in Chapter 4, where it was pointed out that the goals of objectivity are well served if any given analysis is based on adequately handled representative data. We trust that the following analysis *does* involve properly handled representative data; if it does not, then it does not deserve consideration.

A charge that the following analysis is politicized—that is, has a political tone or meaning—is accurate; but the charge is irrelevant. Even the most neutral examination of political–economic phenomena is politicized if considered in terms of its effects—and what matters more than effects? An abstractly empirical analysis of the political–economic order—the kind of analysis common to professional journals, textbooks, and college classes—is a *political act*, in effect, because, to those who benefit most from the status quo, nothing is more useful than analyses that do not cast judgment on things as they are. In short, as India's Ghandi once put it, politics is a serpent from whose coils there is no escape.

A second possible reaction to the following sections is that stressing the purely negative aspects of American society unfairly depicts it as analogous to a Biafran afternoon. Such criticism is understandable. If one is thinking in a relative-historical sense, a good case can be made for the argument that Americans in general have achieved the good life materially. This is certainly true in comparison with the struggling masses of Bangladesh, the Congo, and Vietnam, for example. However, people do not live their lives "relatively-historically." To tell a defeated American black, "Your granddaddy would have been lynched," cuts little ice. As writer James Baldwin has put it (Mead and Baldwin, 1971:169), the black American today is in a trap such that he is often inclined to say, ". . . I can't afford the historical point of view." And to those who say that forgetting history endangers the future, the response is, in effect, "I am in such a bind I don't even care."

Therefore, it seems justifiable—the humanistic thing to do—to concentrate on the political–economic nature of American society, with particular reference made to its shortcomings. The critique is offered with a full consciousness of social critic Peter Viereck's advice that political criticisms, like marital ones, go sour if they are not founded on love. It is out of deep regard for our society that we make detailed note of its weaknesses; only with such a complete diagnosis can the extent of the malady be accurately assessed.

KEEPING THE PEACE

The American Empire   The classic and basic function of government has always been to keep the peace, among societal participants and between them and outsiders. This function, Americans have been asked to believe, has been fulfilled particularly well by various government agencies. The image promoted has been that the United States is a peace-loving nation, resorting to war only to save the world for democracy, or to counter imperialism, or to prevent the further spread of communists bent on fomenting the world revolution.

This is the image; the reality is quite different. As historian W. A. Williams has put it (1966:90), the nation *began* with total war against Indians; the motivation was greed and a self-righteous arrogance that has not altered fundamentally. The ultimate result has been the creation of what amounts to an American empire. Many Americans no doubt resist the word empire, but that is understandable; "Nations rarely recognize that they are imperialist until they themselves enter into their post-imperial age. Americans are thus only beginning to perceive that their relationship with their Latin neighbors to the south has been an essentially imperial one . . . " (Brzezinski, 1971).

To build the American empire, Lens writes,

> The United States has pilfered large territories from helpless or near-helpless peoples; it has forced its will on scores of nations, against their wishes and against their interests; it has violated hundreds of treaties and understandings; it has committed war crimes as shocking as most; it has wielded a military stick and a dollar carrot to forge an imperialist empire such as man has never known before . . . (1971:1-2).

Lens tells a sad story of aggressive wars against Indians, Mexicans, and Spaniards, forcing sovereignty over a vast territory, all in the name of opposition to imperialism.

The brutal aggressiveness of American officialdom was revealed in a most spectacular form in the World War II decision to drop atomic bombs on Hiroshima and Nagasaki; the former city had no war industries whatsoever. The official explanation for dropping the bombs was that they would encourage the Japanese to surrender and, thus, American lives would be saved—a form of public reassurance that brings to mind writer George Orwell's observation that political language is designed to make lies sound truthful and murder respectable. Actually, it was quite clear at the time that the Japanese were on the verge of surrendering before the bombs were delivered. In the words of Herbert Feis (who, as assistant to three secretaries of war, has achieved near-official status as a diplomatic historian), in his *The Atomic Bomb and the End of World War II*:

There cannot be a well-grounded dissent from the conclusion reached as early as 1945 by members of the U.S. Strategic Bombing Survey . . . "that certainly prior to 31 December 1945, and in all probability prior to 1 November 1945, Japan would have surrendered even if the atomic bombs had not been dropped, even if Russia had not entered the war, and even if no invasion had been planned or contemplated" (1966:191).

Feis concludes that the decision to drop the bombs was purely a function of power politics. The American and British leaders wanted to so shock Japan, by sacrificing close to 200,000 civilian lives, that Russia too would be impressed and thus hopefully more compliant after the war.

National Security   Hopes for the governmental function of keeping the peace with outsiders were given a boost during 1972 when President Nixon went to Moscow and Peking and made arrangements for signing arms limitation treaties. It is unrealistic, however, to expect too much from such treaties. We not only have the evidence of history indicating that when national interests demand, international treaties become less worthwhile than the paper on which they are written. More to the point, just four days after the President addressed a joint session of Congress to extoll his peace-keeping missions, his then Secretary of Defense, Melvin R. Laird, testified to the House Appropriations Committee:

> This is no time for complacency. This is no time to cut back on those programs which are designed to maintain and preserve essential U.S. strength. We must continue such existing deployment programs as MIRV and SRAM, and those development programs we have in our fiscal 1973 budget such as Trident and the B-1 bomber . . . (Knoll, 1972b:14).

Underlying the defense secretary's testimony is the idea that weapon—and especially nuclear weapon—superiority leads to national security. This notion has been undermined with devastating effectiveness by Phillip Green's *Deadly Logic: The Theory of Nuclear Deterrence* (1966). In this work, he shows with utter clarity that every weapons development by any given great power is followed with an answering development by another power. Thus, there is a never-ending cycle so that Russia and the United States now have so much power at their disposal that any further arming can have only the purpose of "making the rubble bounce." Even with the SALT "disarmament" agreements, the United States can build 9,800 strategic warheads by 1977; thus armed, if just half the activated warheads reached their planned targets the nation could exterminate, twenty-two times over, the 219 major cities in the Soviet Union (*Sane World*, October 1972:4).

It is logical to ask: Why has the goal of national security led American government officials to be so aggressive, to commit so many blunders, diplomatic and military, to engender so much fear? There are three major explanatory factors: nationalism, belief that there is an international communist conspiracy, and misunderstanding the global revolution of the deprived. As for *nationalism*, it can be defined as belief on the part of the citizenry of a given nation–state that it is extraordinarily deserving and, therefore, should be a totally independent, sovereign entity whose inhabitants treat it with unquestioning loyalty. No doubt this belief was functionally useful during the time when territorial integrity was important for survival. But the belief has now become maladaptive to such a degree that it threatens humankind's very existence. The notion of "my country, right or wrong" can result only in international aggression and, given the nature of modern weapons, this could mean the end of animate life. Yet nationalism is systematically fostered. In the socialization process of every country, including the United States, there is a deliberate attempt to propagandize the idea that one's nation is better than all others. Usually, only the most liberally educated manage to escape the hold of this dangerous ethnocentric notion; it is therefore not surprising that national leaders often become suspicious of higher education.

A second factor underlying the international blunders made by the American government during the past few decades is the belief that communism is a unified international force that, if not blocked at every juncture, will take over the world. Theoretically, communism is a collectivist ideology that appeals to the disadvantaged because it promises to redistribute the goods of the earth. Within this framework, therefore, it is no menace at all. What *is* a menace is fear and exploitation leading people to respond positively to left and right extremist political proposals. Such response cannot be obtained from people who are content, as Chinese philosopher Lao Tze noted long ago:

> Make the people's food sweet, their clothes beautiful, their houses comfortable, their daily life a source of pleasure. Then the people will look at the country over the border, will hear the cocks crowing and the dogs barking there, but right down to old age and the day of their death, they will not trouble to go there and see what it is like (Rader, 1969:107).

The idea expressed by Lao Tze is so logical, so direct, so noncomplex, one would think even the most simple-minded would understand it. But American leaders in general have not. From all appearances, they do not seem to comprehend the obvious point that the only effective way to counter an *idea* is to come up with a better one; on the other hand, as it has been remarked so often, an idea whose time has come will withstand all the military force in the world. Not comprehending this, ever since

Russia's 1917 October Revolution, American officialdom, generally speaking, has viewed communism as something to be countered by force, and that must be so countered, because it can take over even among the prosperous.

It is difficult to explain America's compulsive anxiety about communism and about the nations committed to it as an official policy. Such fear cannot be accounted for by referring to Russia's invasions of Czechoslovakia in 1968 and Hungary twelve years earlier, and the Chinese takeover in Tibet; although sickeningly deplorable, these were typical great power sphere-of-influence moves, much like the American march into the Dominican Republic in 1965 and the April 1961 attempt at the Bay of Pigs. Nor is it logical to assert that mobilized Russian forces were a threat to Europe immediately following World War II. The Soviet Union came out of the war with a large part of its productive land devastated, its agricultural and industrial potential seriously depleted, and its air force decimated. Most significantly, Russia possessed no atomic weapons. In contrast, the United States was at the peak of its power and world influence. Despite such "security," it began a policy, that still continues, of ringing Russia and China with armed bases and observation posts in Germany, Greece, Turkey, Iran, Pakistan, South Vietnam, Taiwan, the Philippines, Japan, Okinawa, Korea, Iceland, and Norway. It is little wonder that Soviet and Chinese leaders became defensive.

Closely related to belief in the communist menace has been the American misunderstanding of the revolution that has been occurring in many parts of the world since the end of World War I. Henry Steele Commager describes this revolution as:

> . . . the emergence of the forgotten, the neglected, the disparaged, the impoverished, the exploited, and the desperate; one-half of the human race came out of the long dust that hid it from our view and into the bright light of history. Here is not only the greatest revolution of our time but by almost any test, the greatest revolution since the discovery of America and the shift in the center of gravity from the Mediterranean to the Atlantic and beyond. "The peoples of Europe," said Woodrow Wilson at the close of the first war, "are in a revolutionary state of mind. They do not believe in the things that have been practiced upon them in the past, and they mean to have new things practiced. . . ." Now they are determined to close, in a single generation, that gap of centuries which separated them from the peoples of the West—to close it peacefully if that is possible, otherwise through revolution and violence (1968:2).

Instead of understanding and sympathizing with this revolution, American military and governmental authorities have, too many times, cast our lot with exploitive right-wing governments that have attempted to maintain the special privileges of the advantaged. For example, we did this with the French in Indochina, with a number of South American governments, with the Batista government in Cuba, with the most reactionary forces in the Dominican Republic, with the Greek colonels against the Greek people, with the French government against the Algerians, with Franco against the far more liberal loyalist government, with Pakistan against the Bangladesh, with England against India, and with Chiang Kai-shek who led the warlords and monopolists whose like had been exploiting the Chinese masses for centuries. The roll of dishonor could go on and on, but it is sufficient to say that the United States has become ". . . the world's leading *status quo* power" (Miles, 1971:293). Our controlling forces have allied the country with governments representing the dead hand of the past. Effective long-term security has thus been undermined; as Commager phrased it, a half-century after the war that was to end war (World War I) so as to safeguard democracy, the world is not safer for anything.

Our most monumental and recent blunder in support of right-wing extremism was of course our entry into Vietnam. We know now, with little doubt, that the South Vietnam governments we supported were made up of a collection of largely corrupt mercenaries who were once sponsored by the French against the Vietnam masses. These Quislings were maintained by our military might alone. Yet, for years we drafted our young men to fight and die or be captured or injured in a senseless cause whose immediate result was the maintenance of the special privileges of a mandarin class, and whose long-term results will probably be an extension of doctrines we have always professed to despise. This is the essential message of Thick Nhat Hanh, a Vietnamese Buddhist scholar–monk, in his *Vietnam: Lotus in a Sea of Fire*: "The longer you continue to do what you are doing now, the more communists you will create not only in Vietnam but in all of Asia, Africa, and Latin America. Be worried in time!" (1967:x).

Law and Order   Prohibiting and punishing antisocial acts on the part of citizens is another keep-the-peace function of government. It is in this connection that we see the police power of the state in its most active form. It is a power that enjoys general support so long as most community members feel safeguarded.

As embodied in the Fourteenth Amendment, the American Constitution states that all citizens, including those accused of crime, should have equal protection of the law. The reality is a depressing catalogue of horrors, as indicated by former U.S. Attorney General Ramsey Clark in his book, *Crime in America* (1970). In essence, the system Clark was called on to administer provides justice for the rich and jail for the poor. This disparity in treatment exists despite the fact that "respectable" white collar crooks obtain more ill-gotten gain by far than all the pushers, prostitutes, and street bandits put together. Even so, two-thirds of all arrests occur in areas where disease, hunger, and mental retardation rates are the highest. In contrast, there are judicial districts where there has never been a tax fraud conviction. Thus, says Clark, the U.S. system of criminal "justice," having been set up by established forces, takes care of its own.

Clark's recitation of the story of young Ronny Brown is representative (1970:298). In 1969, having been indicted by a grand jury, Brown was held in a New York jail without being advised by a lawyer. On the nineteenth day, tired of dodging other prisoners who wanted to molest him, and despairing of holding himself together so he could "get out and work and do something good" (as he had written to his mother), he used his belt to hang himself from a light fixture. This kind of tragedy is multiplied by hundreds all over the country. And yet, as Clark indicates, "Ronny Brown, dead at seventeen, is still presumed innocent."

It is the tragedies represented by the Ronny Browns of the world that finally led famed defense lawyer William Kunstler to declare, in a public debate, "I hate the law." He went on, "I know the law. It is used to oppress those who threaten the ruling class. The judicial decree has replaced the assassin. . . . I remain a lawyer, I stay with the law, only because the law is maneuverable. It can be manipulated. But in the future?" (as quoted by syndicated columnist James Kilpatrick, February 2, 1971).

Realistic perspective is gained if one contrasts what happens to the "Ronny Browns" with what happens to establishment figures when they are accused of a crime—except when unavoidable public scandal occasionally forces the conviction of members of the power elite; even so, they have the option of executive clemency. For example, in 1969, five drug companies were convicted of price fixing that cheated customers of a minimum of $120 million. The court's sentence said nothing about the responsible executives of the guilty companies; it simply provided that the money was to be returned to those customers affected. However, to get the money, the customers first had to become aware of an announcement printed in small type in selected newspapers. Then they had to submit, by an early date, an itemized year-by-year account of how much money they paid for specific products between 1954 and 1966. Each product had to be listed separately by name even though patients are rarely told the names of drugs prescribed for them. They had to list the name and address of each pharmacy where each purchase was made, and be prepared to show written proof of purchase such as the original prescription. For those who could not fulfill all of these requirements, there was no reimbursement.

Another typical example is suggested by what happened to General Motors executives in the late 1960s when that company tried to devise an elaborate coverup to hide the fact that millions of dangerously defective motor mounts had been installed in their automobiles. Were General Motors executives brought to trial for attempted fraud? No. The government simply put polite pressure on the company to install replacement mounts.

Role of the Court System   It would be difficult for a clear-sighted person to paint too gloomy a picture of our court system. A number of recent appointees to the Supreme Court are symptomatic of the basic problem—namely, that the courts largely function to protect the strong and attack the weak. It is in political cases that the weaknesses of the court system are most apparent. Ms. Angela Davis was incarcerated for months before her lawyers and public pressure finally secured bail for her. Since she was later found innocent, it was obvious that she was forced to pay a severe penalty for offenses that were never attributed to her. Such cases demonstrate why civil libertarians are so concerned with proposals to legalize for the entire nation the pretrial detention that Congress has already authorized for the District of Columbia. The legislation provides that a judge can keep an accused person in prison if the judge merely guesses that the defendant may subsequently commit a crime.

The probable consequences of putting such additional power in the hands of judges was demonstrated in one Black Panther case where the presiding jurist set bail so high ($100,000 each) that the defendants could not possibly raise the sum. The result was that by the time the Panthers were brought to trial *and found innocent*, they had served two years, or about the same time served by a person who has been convicted and received a five-year sentence.

Part of the difficulty with both the court system and police forces is the continued existence of laws proscribing certain forms of purely personal behavior, thus making crimes of actions where there are no victims. Examples include prostitution, addiction, gambling, marijuana possession and use, pornography purveyed to interested adults only, and various forms of nonexploitative sexual deviancy. To many youths and thoughtful adults, such legal provisions make "the law" look arbitrary, ineffectual, and unworthy of respect. Furthermore, there is no evidence that laws of this type actually do any real good. There *is* evidence that "crimes without victims" do not increase when they are not proscribed. In Britain, for example, one can be medically certified as a legal addict; yet, there are fewer than 3,000 narcotics addicts in Britain. However, American officials often like to disparage the British system. A United States government drug pamphlet, issued in 1971, observed that the British approach to drugs is considered a failure and has been modified to meet the increasing problem of addiction; this is simply untrue.

Indeed, since 1969 the monthly additions to the number of British heroin addicts have been falling (May, 1971:60). In contrast, addiction rates in the United States seem to rise steadily, providing ever more fertile opportunity for organized crime. The resulting high price of drugs motivates American addicts to become pushers themselves. The British addict, getting needed supplies by prescription, has little incentive to have others take up the use of the "needle of death."

American Jails and Prisons Jails and prisons both compound and symbolize the limitations of the American criminal justice system. The basic shortcomings of the system are revealed in a single observation: The population of American prisons is drawn, with a minimum of exceptions, from one social stratum—the poor. This does not seem unreasonable to many observers; they feel it is logical since it is the poor who commit the greatest number of crimes. Such a view is not supported by any systematic studies; they show that the predominance of the poor in prison populations is the end product of a long-term and complex system of discriminatory treatment. The prison is thus a reflection of the worst aspects of society, including bureaucratic callousness, racism, and violence.

CONSTITUTIONAL GOVERNMENT

Ideal vs. Real The government ideals of the United States were expressed in the most succinct form in the Declaration of Independence and the first ten Amendments to the Constitution. The Declaration proclaimed that the proper goal of government is preservation of the natural and inalienable rights of all people—life, liberty, and the pursuit of happiness. The rights are secure, according to the Declaration, to the degree that government is by consent of the governed; hence, people at large have the right and duty to alter oppressive authority.

The Amendments concentrate on the importance of freedom from government oppression in general, with special reference to the preservation of free speech, free press, freedom of assembly, freedom from arbitrary search and seizure, and freedom to petition the government for redress of grievances. All these rights were written so that they could be secured within a governmental structure where the three major branches—judiciary, legislative, and executive—would be limited and balanced in their powers so that none could become dictatorial over another.

Some cynics have justification for observing that the American government ideals have been largely verbal exercises in rhetoric and oratory. Certainly, most governmental officials in general, as well as a large portion of the citizenry at large, have paid the ideals little more than lip service. In recent decades, the executive branch of the government has steadily, and extralegally, undermined the power and influence of the legislative branch, and has demeaned and weakened the judicial. In the realm of civil liberties, even the most flagrant violations— for example, when the government incarcerated Americans of Japanese descent in concentration camps during World War II—do not arouse general opposition or indignation. Numerous polls have shown that when Americans are questioned about the Bill of Rights (the first ten Amendments), large numbers reject the application of it, almost out of hand (Andrews, 1971:122; Novak, 1972:260). In a spot poll conducted in St. Louis by the American Civil Liberties Union during the 1960s, 90 percent of the people questioned did not even recognize the Bill of Rights when it was read to them. When they were told what it was, 60 percent said they did not agree with its principles. A recent national study conducted by CBS television indicated that the majority of Americans are opposed to at least five of the ten basic tenets of the Bill of Rights. Members of the majority said they are against allowing "extremist" groups to demonstrate even if there are no clear dangers involved; they are against the right of individuals to criticize the government if such criticism is authoritatively declared "contrary to the national interest." They also indicated they favored the government's having the right to hold suspects in jail, without evidence, long enough for the police to dig up evidence, and they felt that the state should be free to prosecute an individual more than once for the same offense.

As for the responsibility of government officials, one might think they "would know better," but they do not seem to; hence, the American Civil Liberties Union must engage in a continuous battle to prevent government agencies from encroaching on the Bill of Rights. The guiding principle of the ACLU is that where individual freedoms are concerned, the government, any government, is likely to be up to no good (Andrews, 1971:122). This conclusion has been reached on the basis of evidence like the following.

Civil Liberties   It is a fundamental principle that social organizations fail to survive if they are not flexible enough to respond adequately to change and challenge. One important aspect of such flexibility is an arrangement that permits, or, even better, encourages, observers and participants to identify the shortcomings and misdirections of the organization. The importance of such criticism to viable social organization is the ultimate justification for civil liberties. Therefore, to the degree that a society gags its critics, or deports them, or declares them mentally incompetent, to somewhat the same degree does the society become vulnerable to the inexorable forces of change.

It was with the need of flexibility in mind that the Bill of Rights was added to the Constitution. As Thomas Jefferson put it, the strong society is the open society, the free society, the one where people do not fear to speak out. In such a society, even the most bizarre advocacy can be tolerated because in a truly free marketplace of ideas, the truth will out. Error need not be feared, Jefferson said when founding the University of Virginia, ". . . so long as reason is left free to combat it." On the other hand, said Jefferson, since entrenched authority has a strong tendency to become tyrannical, a revolution every twenty years or so would not be a bad idea. Poet Walt Whitman later agreed with him when he warned of "the never-ending audacity of elected persons."

Despite the inspiring advice and example set by the founding fathers, in the United States *meaningful* civil liberties are and have been granted to the members of two groups almost exclusively: the dominant elite and the politically impotent. Whenever dissenters have threatened to become effective, their civil liberties have been abrogated, usually under cover of a manufactured political hysteria, the prototype of which is the "Red Scare" of the early 1920s (Levin, 1971).

The undermining of civil liberties by government officials is not unique to the United States. It seems to be a part of government everywhere. Quebec separatist Pierre Vallieres has described his experience:

> As long as you only preach your utopia, the established order is content to take note of your "dissent" with contempt or indifference. But as soon as you begin to act, the old system hastens to turn you into a public menace and a criminal . . . (1971:60).

The typical cover of those wishing to interfere with the civil liberties of others is to charge that they are not acting or speaking responsibly. However, if free speech is restricted to those defined as responsible, a dangerous principle is established because those in power at any given time almost always view serious challenge as irresponsible. For example, even under Stalin, Russians had extensive freedom as long as they acted "responsibly" (as officially defined).

American government interference with civil liberties is sometimes subtle and sometimes openly evident. A typical example of the subtle approach is the request by the head of the Federal Communications Commission for transcripts of network commentaries on President Nixon's Vietnam speeches in 1972. The implication was that station owners and managers should remember that federal officials hold the power to grant or deny licenses. Other tactics are less subtle. A significant recent example was the government attempt to prevent the *New York Times* and three other newspapers from publishing the Pentagon Papers (Ungar, 1972). This case demonstrated two phenomena:

selective enforcement of the law, thus by definition violating the equal protection provision of the Constitution, and censorship in violation of the First Amendment. The four newspapers sued by the government were known for their anti-administration editorial views; no pro-Nixon newspapers were included although some of them also published the top secret documents. It is, therefore, difficult not to conclude that legal processes were used for purely political ends. More importantly, the case was the first direct act of political censorship attempted by the federal government since the founding of the nation. The implications of such action, if established as a principle, would be the creation of an official secrets act, which is a prime feature of a police state. "It would intimidate every newspaper and magazine and television network because the publication of any leak might lead to prosecution" (Schrag, 1972:13).

According to reporter William Pfaff, the reason the government's foreign and military policy makers were so embarrassed by the publication of the Pentagon Papers is because the documents so clearly revealed that the Kennedy, Johnson, and Nixon administrations alike engaged in ". . . a colossal abuse of power in defiance of the Constitution" (*Los Angeles Times*, June 20, 1971). This abuse of power continued without letup to the point where the case was hopelessly compromised by the grossly illegal behavior of a multitude of highly placed federal officials.

In addition to favoring official censorship, the national administration and some members of Congress enthusiastically support other features of the police state. Two such features were embodied in the 1971 District of Columbia Omnibus Crime Bill, which provided for preventive detention (already discussed in connection with the Angela Davis case) and no-knock entry. Pretrial detention abrogates the constitutional provision that an accused person must be considered innocent until proved guilty by testimony under oath in a court of law; "no-knock" permits police, without announcing their presence, to break in and search homes and other public and private places. Most significantly, the national administration considers the District of Columbia crime bill a model to be applied to the rest of the nation. In addition, the present administration has attempted to establish the principle that the executive department has the right, without court review, to eavesdrop secretly on people whom they deem domestic subversives. Efforts along this line ceased only after several important court decisions asserted that the administration was acting unconstitutionally—violating the basic law of the land. One example of this was in 1971 (United States vs. District Court) when the Supreme Court found that the Fourth Amendment is violated when administrative officials wiretap or bug phones of alleged domestic subversives.

There was also an attempt, in 1972, to pass a federal law permitting police officers to obtain court orders requiring individuals to give fingerprints, voice prints, hair, blood, and handwriting samples, and to stand in line-ups, even when there is insufficient evidence to justify an arrest. Giving such power to the police would contravene the Fourth Amendment, which provides that unreasonable search and seizure are prohibited and that no one can be detained except for probable cause. The administration's proposal is that "probable cause" should be amended to read "reasonable cause."

Another feature of the police state is the use of secret agents to spy on private citizens, thus undermining civil liberties by inhibiting free speech, press, and assembly. Such surveillance by Defense Department intelligence operatives, and by the Central Intelligence Agency and the FBI, has become common practice in the United States and has escalated in the last two decades. In 1971–1972 hearings conducted by North Carolina Senator Sam J. Ervin, Jr., it was revealed that military agents with sophisticated electronic devices at their disposal have spied on both Democratic and Republican political conventions without knowledge or consent of party leaders or seemingly appropriate legal authorities. Spies attended the funeral of Martin Luther King, Jr. and recorded the names of mourners. Racial, religious, and student activist groups are routinely infiltrated; the CIA infiltration of the National Student Association became a cause célèbre. The army alone compiled and computerized a master list of the names and personality profiles of hundreds of thousands of people suspected of being less than 100 percent loyal to what military authorities and other police agencies regard as "the American way of life." This process continues unabated.

Another disturbing development is governmental news management, by lying if necessary. A chilling illustration was provided by a Department of Defense briefing session on the 1971 U.S. invasion of Laos. In order to underline the importance of the invasion, Secretary of Defense Melvin Laird showed the assembled newsmen a small piece of pipe and said it was part of a line used to supply oil to North Vietnam forces on the Ho Chi Minh Trail. This was striking at the time. However, a *Washington Post* reporter, pursuing a suspicion, found that the piece of pipe was a fake. He had known it was a fake, the defense secretary later admitted, when he had shown it to the press, implying that it is in the national interest for the public to be selectively misinformed (Cousins, 1971:26). Other news-management incidents come to mind: the initial disavowals that North Vietnam dikes were bombed; the early refusal to acknowledge that crop-killing poisons were used in South Vietnam; the negative response when My Lai atrocities were first mentioned; the high-level Watergate cover-up, and many more typical incidents.

WESTERN ECONOMICS

Free Enterprise   The American economic system depicted in patri-
otic speeches and promotional brochures is usually termed "free
enterprise." A picture is conveyed of a system where entrepreneurs
individualistically decide how to handle their own property, including
means of production. The society thrives, it is said, through a trickle-
down process where the self-interest of each creates results that are in
the best interests of all. In keeping with these notions, people of this
political persuasion assert the best government is that which governs
least; government exists only to protect the individual and his property.

Despite the traditional oratory, there appear to be few professional
economists of note who still believe the American economy is one of
free enterprise. Economists assert that we have, at best, a system of
flawed competition dominated by gigantic firms which have become a
law unto themselves (Green, 1972:15). That is the *optimistic* view. Many
economists agree with historian Theodore Roszak's pessimism:

> We call it "free enterprise." But it is a vastly restrictive system of
> oligopolistic market manipulation, tied by institutionalized corruption to the
> greatest munitions boondoggle in history and dedicated to infantilizing the
> public by turning it into a herd of compulsive consumers (1969:16).

Instead of a free competitive economy, we have one that has been
termed a shared monopoly. This is an economy dominated by a handful
of large firms that, in collusion with government agencies, control all
major aspects of the market. The monetary size of the firms in question
is mind-boggling. If one lists the world's 100 leading economic entities,
fifty-one are businesses and only forty-nine are nations (Green, 1972:16).
The aggregate 1972 sales for General Motors amounted to $30.4 billion;
the 1971 earnings for Standard Oil were $20 billion, and for American
Telephone and Telegraph, $18.5 billion; the list could go on. The
General Motors budget, based on sales, is larger than that of all but two
nations, Russia and the United States. The Procter & Gamble advertising
budget alone is twenty times as large as the appropriation for the
Justice Department's antitrust division!

Current trends are suggested by the fact that while the top 200
industrial firms controlled 47 percent of total assets in 1950, by 1965 this
sum reached 55 percent. The most recent information shows that the
top 200 corporations now control the same share of assets held by the
1000 largest corporations in 1941 (Viorst, 1972:34). In discussing these
points, Mark Green observes, "Imagine a college classroom seating just
200, and there you could sit the rulers of two-thirds of American
industry and more than one-third of all the world's industrial production.
Pharaohs and emperors would be envious" (1972:16). They would be

especially so upon learning that the largest national firms have long been international in their economic diversification, and that there is now a strong trend toward the creation of world firms so powerful they can function largely independent of national authority (see English economist Turner's *Invisible Empires*, 1971).

Although much is made of "the people's capitalism," referring to the large number of stockholders in major firms, there are numerous indicators that stock ownership is highly concentrated. One of these is a 1963 study showing that 1.6 percent of American adults owned 82.4 percent of all publicly held stock (Green, 1972:17); another is economist Robert Heilbroner's later observation (1970:250) that ". . . some 90,000 families own between two-thirds and three-quarters of *all* corporate stock"; still another, a 1967 staff report to the Subcommittee on Domestic Finance of the House Committee on Banking and Currency, indicated that controlling amounts of stock are owned by institutional investors, not individuals. Such institutional investors (for example, insurance companies and trusts) hold $1 trillion worth of corporate stocks, with 60 percent of this amount held by just forty-nine commercial banks (Mintz and Cohen, 1971:41). The practical result of such concentration is that the largest industries can shrug off monetary market restraints. Those that cannot, such as Lockheed or Penn-Central, are partially rescued by government grants and subsidies to continue operation.

Cooperative working relationships between business leaders and members of the federal bureaucracy have become so pervasive that the country is heading rapidly toward what Mintz and Cohen have termed *America Incorporated* (1971:102)—one gigantic industrial–financial complex that is, for all practical purposes, an independent government. A most important element of this independent government is the Pentagon—described in the last several years as the controlling master of the industrial core of the economic system (Melman, 1970). Every year, by exploiting elements of fear and patriotism in the country, the Pentagon renews its control over the richest portion of the nation's resources. These are then dispersed to cooperating units of the industrial complex. To accomplish its purposes, the Pentagon has a lobbying force of 339 men, or one for every two members of Congress.

There are various theories to account for the relationship of the Pentagon to the business world. One rationale used by the Department of Defense is that the military establishment is simply a unit of traditional civilian authority. A second theory is a Marxian one, asserting that the Pentagon is the creation of the business community and has the primary function of maintaining control of that community. An alternate theory, as propounded by Columbia University industrial engineer Seymour Melman in his *Pentagon Capitalism* (1970), is that today's military establishment is a totally new entity capable of imposing its rule on the entire civilian social system. Consequently, the federal government does not serve business or regulate business, but, rather, *is* business. A similar conclusion is reached by Juan Bosch, former president (1962-1963) of the Dominican Republic. Bosch speaks of *Pentagonism* (1968), which he defines as a new form of imperialism that, in effect, "colonizes" its own people. "Pentagonism" is a system in which an overwhelming defense establishment is used ". . . to conquer positions of power in the pentagonist country, not in some far-off land" (Bosch, 1968:21). Thus, although the pentagonist power wages war, it is not usually imperialist in the classic sense: ". . . it does not need colonial territories in order to accumulate profits. It accumulates them at the expense of its own people" (Bosch, 1968:22).

John Kenneth Galbraith (1971) has written at length on the reasons that account for the growth of largescale business enterprise, including the Pentagon. He says that modern industry is so technologically complex and involves such a vast investment of time, money, and knowledge that it can no longer afford the hazards of a free market. Therefore, ". . . we have an economic system which, whatever its formal ideological billing, is in substantial part a planned economy" (1971:6). The only capitalists still functioning, a nostalgic and often romantic minority, are those engaged in some professions, vice, handicrafts, retail trade, repair work, and personal services. This means that if one speaks of "capitalism," the heartland of modern economy is totally missing.

The so-called free market has been superseded by what has been termed *vertical integration*. This means full control over sources of supply and market demand. The latter is manipulated by informal interindustry agreements, advertising, and regulated pricing—". . . industrial planning requires that prices be under control" (Galbraith, 1971:189). Other uncertainties are eliminated by long-term contracts and by industry control of governmental regulatory agencies, a control that only occasionally shows minor slippage as in the long-pending (from the Johnson administration) showcase antitrust action against IBM. The total result is that we have, to a very large degree, an economy quite similar to that prevailing in the Soviet Union. "The modern large corporation and the modern apparatus of socialist planning are variant accommodations to the same need" (Galbraith, 1971:33).

Thus, in contrast to newspaper verbiage, the reality is that capitalism and Soviet socialism have certain basic similarities. Roszak has written:

> . . . Marxism is the mirror image of bourgeois industrialism: an image reversed and yet unmistakably identical. For both traditions, the technocratic

imperative with its attendant conception of life stands unchallenged (1969:100).

Even Marxist philosopher Herbert Marcuse has noted (1958:258) that the two supposedly antagonistic social systems have developed a surprising affinity. He concludes, ". . . the common requirements of industrialization make for a high degree of similarity between the featured values of 'bourgeois' and Soviet ethics. . . ." Wheeler expresses a related thought:

> The basic economic fact that comes across to the poor is that those who are rich in capital tend to act in much the same way regardless of the ideological differences they allege set them apart (1971:283).

The Great Depression of the 1930s was a major factor in destroying many of the remaining remnants of largescale free enterprise. With business and industry practically at a standstill, and with the specter of revolution haunting the land, all Western governments entered full tilt into the economic system. In English-speaking countries, the intellectual and philosophical justification for economic intervention was provided by the theories of John Maynard Keynes, who expressed his views most completely in his classic, *The General Theory of Employment, Interest and Money* (1936).

Keynesian Economics and Beyond   According to Keynesian economics, when unemployment reaches an unacceptable level, the government has the responsibility of stimulating business so that there can be full employment. The major stimulant available to government when this situation occurs is deficit financing—spending more than is collected in taxes and fees. Such spending gives business a source of profit and this is necessary in a "profit economy" where a large business that simply breaks even is regarded as a failure. Therefore, to be a business stimulant in the Keynesian sense, government spending *must be deficit spending*; if the government spends only what it takes in, stagnated business at large cannot take in more than it puts out—the definition of profit. However, if a government engages in too much deficit spending, inflation occurs; inflation can be defined as a time when money buys relatively less per unit expended. When such inflation reaches an unacceptable level, said Keynes, then the government merely has to raise taxes, restrict bank credit, and cut down spending.

The Keynesian approach to handling unemployment and inflation became so well established, at least in theory, that even President Richard Nixon finally announced he had become a convert—a sure sign, according to one observer, that Keynes is obsolete. And indeed, after World War II, Keynesian theory was superseded by a post-Keynesian theoretical synthesis—that prosperity and full employment would be all but guaranteed by a mix of government aid and private endeavor. Events bore out the theory for a number of years.

Now, however, it is clear that both Keynesian and post-Keynesian theory failed to anticipate several important complications. One of these is that with increasing integration between largescale business and government forces, it is no longer possible to distinguish clearly between private and public endeavor. Another complication is that deficit spending has gone on so long and become so extensive that we have created what economist Anatol Murad (1951) termed a warfare–welfare economy. A central feature of that economy is deficit government spending for welfare projects and for "defense" as a major source of business profit. Government deficit is not the only source of profit; another, and far more traditional source, is increasing productivity. But the importance of deficit financing to business profit is revealed by the regularity with which profits considered in toto increase or decrease strictly in proportion to the excess spending of the federal government. Periods during which there is little excess spending are followed by gloomy business reports about declining profit levels; periods involving spending increases are followed by confident reports about "the improving business climate." It is, therefore, ironic to hear businessmen regularly insist the government should have a balanced budget. The model to which they refer is an ordinary business that naturally fails if it pays out more than it takes in; but the government is not an ordinary business; it is not a business at all. To a large degree, it has the power to spend whatever government authorities decide, and much of the resulting national debt is not, definitively speaking, owed to anyone despite the editorial challenges that the present generation is living fat at the expense of future generations who will have to pay the "debt."

However, there is the penalty of inflation if the government deficit-spends during a time when demand is high and supply cannot readily be increased. Such inflation occurs regularly now because there are fixed public obligations that prevail regardless of supply–demand conditions (Heilbroner and Bernstein, 1963:75–78). There are now so many of these obligations—interest on loans, veterans' pensions, social security, the military establishment, politically untouchable business subsidies—that major aspects of the federal budget simply cannot be cut. This is one reason why neither Democrats nor Republicans have been able to stop inflation; the nation has become locked into a system of deficit financing that constantly devalues the mediums of exchange. All inflation is not inherently evil, but since *uncontrolled* inflation is almost certain to be political–economic dynamite, it rightly causes great concern. It can be controlled, but only by massive and rigid price and wage regulations presently regarded as politically unacceptable; the weak controls that are acceptable generally seem to make matters worse.

One of the most important economic realities of our day, therefore, is not simply that free enterprise is for the most part dead; in addition, the government-involved system that developed as a replacement is also in dire trouble.

Along with the larger more general (macro) problems of the total economic system, there are related specific (micro) problems and changes. One of these is the undermining of traditional values and the resultant confusion and conflict. Fathers today, thirty years old and older, for example, were reared to believe that all persons should ultimately be responsible for their own well-being. But what should such fathers teach their children now that even "self-made" businessmen depend on government handouts? What about the hero of classic free enterprise, the entrepreneur who builds and grows and conquers? He means little to many of today's middle class youth who concentrate on doing their own thing rather than on "becoming somebody." Roszak comments:

> So, by way of a dialectic Marx could never have imagined, technocratic America produces a potentially revolutionary element among its own youth. The bourgeoisie, instead of discovering the class enemy in its factories, finds it across the breakfast table in the person of its own pampered children (1969:34).

The new dialectic is not so evident at the moment, but it has had an obvious spin-off effect on the assembly line procedures used in large industry. Management complains that workers increasingly display a cavalier attitude toward the traditional work ethic and precious little tolerance for the discipline needed to run an assembly line. Part of the problem is that, with modern technology, a multitude of jobs entail deadly monotony, leading directly to high absentee rates and to what has been termed "blue collar blues"—an amalgam of boredom, lessened faith in the economic order, and loss of pride in work. The attitude of many workers was summed up by one worker who habitually works only four days a week and disappears on the fifth. When asked why he only worked four days, he answered, "Because I can't make enough money in three" (*Newsweek*, February 7, 1972:65).

Even though free enterprise no longer exists in major elements of the economy, the individualistic materialism that was its philosophic base still causes problems. The core of this philosophy, as worked out practically, is "make the quick buck and let the future take care of itself." Some recent examples have been provided by the cosmetic industry fiercely opposing any restrictions on the indiscriminate killing of whales even though whales are on the threatened species list; by cigarette industry tactics to get around the ban on TV advertising; by banking industry attempts to circumvent inflation control; by the aircraft industry (including labor) in pushing ahead on the SST (supersonic transport) regardless of the possible increased danger of skin cancer and other hazards; by the chemical industry's continuing to produce countless environment-destroying substances; by the reluctance of the mining industry to establish emission control; by weapons manufacturers hiding defective parts from government inspectors. The list is almost endless.

Distribution of Income In the United States, as in so many nations, distribution of the means to well-being is such that Oliver Goldsmith's observation penned in 1770 is appropriate:

> Ill fares the land, to hastening ills a prey,
> Where wealth accumulates, and men decay.

Although it is common to observe that even the poorest of the American poor live relatively better than the vast majority of Indians, Bangladesh, or Biafrans, the prosperity of Americans has little practical significance when it comes to feelings of dissatisfaction among some Americans. What does have significance is suggested by two related concepts, *relative deprivation* and *rising expectations*, described below.

The concept *relative deprivation* is based on the idea that people seldom feel maltreated in an absolute sense. What is crucial is what people think about their "equals"—if those who are "equal" appear to be much better off, then deprivation feelings are high. In societies with a hierarchical tradition, people seriously deprived in a physical sense frequently do not feel aggrieved; they do not consider themselves worthy of having more. But in societies with an egalitarian ideology, such as the United States, many feel deprived—*relatively* deprived, that is—and under these conditions, inequalities can become a serious social problem. As black psychologist Kenneth Keniston has put it, when prosperity is generally evident, then ". . . to be poor shifts from being an unfortunate fact of life to being an outrage" (1969:126).

Harvard political scientist Edward Banfield has observed:

> The poor today are not "objectively" any more deprived relative to the nonpoor than they were a decade ago. Few will doubt, however, that they *feel* more deprived—that they perceive the gap to be wider and that, this being the case, it *is* wider in the sense that matters most. By constantly calling attention to income differences, the war on poverty has probably engendered and strengthened feelings of relative deprivation (1970:124).

Banfield's observation suggests that partial relief of feelings of relative deprivation sometimes creates a new problem. This often occurs because of *rising expectations*. Such expectations are experienced by deprived or exploited people whose life situation has improved to a degree; the relief obtained creates an impatient desire for more of the same. Hence, *rising expectations* can be defined as the increasing hope for further betterment that takes hold of the downtrodden once their living conditions are somewhat improved.

The monetary income differentials mentioned by Banfield are the most obvious inequalities in American life; they are also among the most important because so many life chances are related to income. Despite this basic importance, it is not possible to be up to date when discussing specific income differentials; precise amounts change from year to year. However, general relationships do not change so readily; hence, the dollar and percentage amounts included in the material that follows have a long-run significance in a *relative* sense.

As reported by the Cambridge Institute in the summer of 1972 (UPI, June 4, 1972; *The Progressive*, August 19, 1972:9–10), the poorest 20 percent of Americans received less than 4 percent of the nation's annual income; the amount received by this large group is almost exactly the same as the after-tax income of the 1 percent of Americans with the highest incomes. The second poorest 20 percent of the population got only 11 percent of the income received by all Americans. In contrast, the top 20 percent of the population received 45 percent of the total, with the 5 percent at the peak receiving over 20 percent. Another cogent comparison is between the poorest 40 percent and the richest: The former received 14 percent of the nation's income, the latter almost 69 percent.

Trends are suggested when 1958 to 1968 percentage figures are expressed in terms of 1970 dollars. In 1958, according to the United States Census Bureau, the dollar gap between the most and least prosperous fifths of the nation was approximately $13,750. In 1968, it was more than $20,000. In the latter year, the ten and a half million families constituting the richest fifth of the nation had an average yearly income of $23,100. For those making up the poorest fifth of the nation, the average was $3,054. Families with such a low income, at a time when prices are constantly inflated, are not likely to take refuge in reports that more than half of America's families received over $10,000 during 1972; nor are they comforted, it would seem, by the fact that in the same year more than 320,000 families had incomes over $50,000.

For those who claim that America is a mass middle-class society, and, therefore, the vast majority of people must be affluent, sociologist Richard Parker in *The Myth of the Middle Class* (1972) provides some explanation. He points out that the upper boundary of the middle class is usually set at or between the $25,000 and $50,000 income levels, while the lower boundary is $5,000. Thus, being middle class can mean comfort bordering on opulence; but it can also mean outright poverty or deprivation depending on how many members there are in a given family. The latter part of the observation applies to nearly half of the American people (not including the hardcore poor). In Michael Schneider's words, "The truth is, the majority of the people who work for a living are not part of affluent America" (1970:5).

The people with the least income of all are obviously the poverty stricken. According to 'the U.S. Labor Department's 1973 "poverty cut-off" (in nonfarm areas, $4,275 for four-person families and $2,100 for single individuals; for those living on farms, $3,575 for four-person families and $1,800 for single persons), almost twenty-six million out of a total population of 210 million Americans are presently classified as living in poverty. Such people frequently have a diet that is so poor, so laden with starch, that they give a false impression of being well-fed. Such "fat of poverty" connotes the opposite of good health. The worst effects of poverty can be seen in embryos and on infants. According to President Nixon's Committee on Mental Retardation, chronic food deprivation spanning more than one generation produces increasingly serious effects in reduction of learning ability. Even when diet deficiencies are corrected, some retardation is still not curable.

Some welfare measures intended to help the poor have been attacked by persons such as Governor Ronald Reagan of California. He and others speak of "welfare cheats." However, 75–80 percent of all welfare recipients are either dependent children, the totally disabled, or the aged. The ability of such people to do much chiseling would seem doubtful. Welfare workers point to what appears to them as the far more significant problem of subsidies given to many businesses. Individual farmers can receive $55,000 each year on price support programs for wheat, cotton, and feed grains. Such payments are less than those previously permitted. However, the $55,000 can be paid on each crop up to a maximum of $115,000. Hundreds of the country's richest "farmers" simply reshuffle their businesses to avoid the effects of the limitations imposed by the legislation passed in 1970. One United States Senator, for example, is alleged to have circumvented the $55,000 maximum by creating eight new businesses to farm the family's 5,200 acre plantation in the rich Mississippi delta. A number of others shared in the bonanza—13,751 farmers received $20,000 or more during 1971. In Arizona alone, 887 farm operators received 1972 subsidy payments of $20,000 and up. Most of the recipients are large businesses; relatively few are family farmers. In 1970, six California corporations received more than a million dollars in agricultural subsidy payments; two got more than four million (*Los Angeles Times* Service, August 13, 1972).

It is not just the farmer who receives subsidies. Other recipients are listed in a 220-page study, *The Economics of Federal Subsidy Programs*, published by the U.S. Government Printing Office. This study indicates that during 1970 at least $63 billion were spent on subsidies. Benefits such as welfare and aid to the blind were not included in the total. Subsidies included payments to dairymen and those who raise beef cattle, special depletion allowances for major corporations, cash payments to particular industries, tax subsidies to investors, homeowners, and life insurance companies, credit subsidies for farming, hospital construction, and the like (Knoll, 1972a).

Writer-philanthropist Phillip M. Stern has called the internal revenue code the rich man's most important welfare bill (1973:Ch. 1). In testifying to the Congressional Joint Economic Committee, he indicated that each of the nation's wealthiest families—that is, those with incomes over a million dollars a year—has its taxes reduced $14,000 *each week* as a result of deductions written into tax regulations (Knoll, 1972a:25). Comparable savings for the nation's poorest families—those earning less than $3,000 a year—are 40 cents per week. Stern points out that families having incomes of more than $100,000 a year receive "tax welfare benefits" totaling more than $11 billion each year. This is four times the amount the government spends for food stamps to feed the poor; it is 1,000 times the amount spent for federal health programs serving migrant workers.

Senator William Proxmire from Wisconsin is quoted, "How is it that the average citizen puts up with such an unfair system?" The answer: "The average citizen has no idea what is going on. He staggers under his tax burden, grumbling about pathetically small 'giveaways' to the poor and totally unaware of the generous giveaways to the rich" (Knoll, 1972a:26).

Tax "subsidies" are indeed maddening. In 1969, people with annual incomes under $2,000 paid 27.2 percent of their income for state and local taxes; those earning $50,000 yearly paid only 6.7 percent of their income for such taxes (*The Progressive*, August 1972:9). According to the census bureau, when other taxes are included, poor families with incomes of $2,000 or less pay fully 50 percent of their earnings in taxes. A bureau report indicates that because of deduction possibilities for the prosperous, the tax bite steadily *declines* as income rises. Thus the *progressive income tax* has become even more regressive than the sales tax or the value-added tax that is applied at each stage of a production process. The latter two are obviously inequitable since they hit the low income worker relatively harder than the affluent, but at least they hit comparatively lightly, and they do not insult one's intelligence by being labeled "progressive."

Syndicated columnist Sylvia Porter has asked, "Whatever happened to the 154 Americans who had incomes of $200,000 to one million and

more in 1966 on which they paid not a penny in federal income taxes—
and who thereby kicked off what was to become the historic tax reform
act of 1969?" Her answer: They grew. In 1969, there were 301 families
earning $200,000 and up who paid no federal income tax whatsoever.
The 1969 act called for at least a 10 percent minimum tax, but the most
popular tax shelters—the oil depletion allowance and tax-exempt
municipal bonds—were not even touched by the "reform" law.

In 1972, Rep. Henry S. Reuss from Wisconsin reported that 18,646
Americans earning more than $100,000 each used special tax loopholes
so that they had to pay less than 7 percent in federal income tax for
1970. The 18,646 people did not include the 394 Americans with 1970
incomes of over $100,000 who paid no federal tax at all. Rep. Reuss
pointed out that a 7 percent tax is the same percentage paid by a wage
earner making $6,500 a year. Tax loopholes also include lower taxes on
investments. Thus, if in 1971 a family of four had an income of $10,000
from wages only, they paid $905 in federal income tax; if the $10,000
were derived solely from investments, the tax was only $98.

SUMMARY AND COMMENTARY

When the various themes explored in this chapter are considered in
toto, the overall implications that emerge are clear even though the
materials presented were a selective sample of a vast array of related
and similar data. The message is that the political–economic system of
the world, with particular reference to the industrialized aspects, has
produced a relatively few advantaged "units" and multitudes of disadvantaged ones. The units in question are, in some cases, individuals; they
are also groups such as races or classes; in other cases, they are entire
nations. Wheeler has written:

> If, like Toynbee, we see the world as a single political community, the poor
> nations within that community are the contemporary counterparts of the
> exploited working classes within the nation–states of 19th century Europe. In
> short, all of today's capital-rich nations confront the poor in the stance of
> ruling classes (1971:284).

No doubt, division of the world politically and economically into the
haves and the have-nots goes back before the beginnings of recorded
history. But the division did not assume vast proportions until about 400
years ago when Western peoples, due to the interplay of unique values
and technological developments, embarked on a systematic exploitation
of all aspects of nature including humankind itself. This process has been
expressed in its most extreme form in the United States, the country that
became a haven for the Europeans and Eastern peoples whose value

system glorified hard-driving performance above all else. The value system preached, "God gave you the world; use it." These people landed on the shores of a vast area that for all practical purposes was free for exploitation. True, it was occupied by indigenous Indians whose basic orientation was generally to simply integrate harmoniously with nature. Therefore, when the American Indian met the Puritan, the Puritan drive for land and success was bound to prevail—and prevail it did. With the aid of slave labor, and with the riches of the resources wrested from the Indians, the Puritan settlers and their descendants created an unprecedentedly prosperous life in a material sense.

One important element of the prosperity was the development of an economic system known as "free enterprise," the theoretical basis of which was the belief that if every individual seeks his own good, the total result will serve the common good. In practice, however, there were only two truly free elements in "free enterprise": one, that the system gave powerful entrepreneurs unhampered opportunity to exploit the weak; the other, that when such entrepreneurs accumulated enough resources, they could ignore the laws that applied to them. The most successful of these entrepreneurs became known as Robber Barons, who founded the great American fortunes in the latter part of the nineteenth century and the early part of the twentieth century. Every one of these fortunes, sociologist Robert Cook has pointed out, was the product of organized crime since each was accumulated in violation of the laws set up to regulate monopolies, trusts, stock manipulation, and conspiracy in restraint of trade.

But nothing much could be done about this form of organized crime, because it gave its perpetrators such power that they also controlled the government, including the police, hired by those in power to maintain the status quo. The court system is similarly used by those in power. Therefore, law and order, in reality, means maintaining the prevailing set of political–economic and general social relationships. Thus, in turn, civil liberties are *meaningfully* extended only to those agreeing with the existing order. For those who disagree and propose to engage in action for change, various tactics are used to undermine their right to speak freely, to assemble, and to allow effective action. A closely related watering down of the constitutional ideals is embodied in the growth of the federal executive branch. In some respects, this growth has made a mockery of the slogan, "government of the people, by the people, for the people."

Despite the great power of those who dominate the American and other units of Western society, a crisis point has been reached because the foundation of the society, *exploitation*, is seriously eroded. We have, to a large degree, come to the end of major exploitation possibilities. Energy sources are badly depleted and people everywhere are resisting shoddy treatment, whether in Vietnam, Watts, Selma, Alabama, Algeria, Bangladesh, or on the Navaho reservation. They have decided they will no longer be the compliant victims of ". . . the hypocrisy of self-serving, hymn-chanting haves. . ." (Tobin, 1972). Furthermore, as shown in Chapter 11, environmental realities are such that world resources cannot stand much more exploitation. For this reason, among others, the Western world has become postindustrial. That is, the earlier goals of industrial society—mass production and widespread consumption—have been achieved to the point that they have become self-defeating. Although distribution problems are not solved, production/consumption has become so massive, so overwhelming, that the world's delicate ecosystem is in serious danger. At the same time, people living in most of the poor areas of the world are anxiously attempting to emulate the living standards of our society and parts of the Western world. Thus the potential for environmental and/or political upheaval is multiplied exponentially.

REFERENCES AND FURTHER SOURCES

Andrews, Peter
    1971   "A.C.L.U.—let there be law." Playboy 18 (October): 119, 122, 222–224, 228.

Banfield, Edward C.
    1970   The Unheavenly City: The Nature and Future of Our Urban Crisis. Boston: Little, Brown.

Bosch, Juan
    1968   Pentagonism: A Substitute for Imperialism. Translated by Helen R. Lane. New York: Grove Press.

Brzezinski, Zbigniew
    1971   "Imperial dilemmas." Newsweek 78 (November 22): 62.

Clark, Ramsey
    1970   Crime in America: Observations on Its Nature, Causes, Prevention and Control. New York: Simon and Schuster.

Commager, Henry Steele
    1968   "1918–1968: Is the world safer for anything?" Promoting Enduring Peace, Inc., pamphlet reprinted from Saturday Review by PEP, Woodmont, Connecticut.

Cousins, Norman
    1971   "Toward a military welfare state?" Saturday Review 54 (March 27): 26–27.

D'Antonio, William V. and William H. Form
    1965   Influentials in Two Border Cities. Notre Dame: University of Notre Dame Press.

Dahl, Robert A.
    1961   Who Governs: Democracy and Power in an American City. New Haven, Conn.: Yale University Press.

Domhoff, G. William
    1967   Who Rules America? Englewood Cliffs, N.J.: Spectrum.

    1970   The Higher Circles: The Governing Class in America. New York: Random House.

Feis, Herbert
    1966   The Atomic Bomb and the End of World War II. Princeton, N.J.: Princeton University Press. Revised edition.

Friedenberg, Edgar Z.
    1969   "The revolt against democracy." Change Magazine 1 (May–June): 11–17.

Galbraith, John Kenneth
1971   The New Industrial State. Boston: Houghton Mifflin. Second edition, revised.

Green, Mark J.
1972   "The high cost of monopoly." The Progressive 36 (March): 15–19.

Green, Phillip
1966   Deadly Logic: The Theory of Nuclear Deterrence. Columbus: Ohio State University Press.

Hanh, Thick Nhat
1967   Vietnam: Lotus in a Sea of Fire. New York: Hill and Wang.

Heilbroner, Robert L.
1970   Between Capitalism and Socialism: Essays in Political Economics. New York: Random House.

Heilbroner, Robert L. and Peter L. Bernstein
1963   A Primer on Government Spending. New York: Random House.

Hunter, Floyd
1953   Community Power Structure. Chapel Hill: University of North Carolina Press.

1959   Top Leadership, U.S.A. Chapel Hill: University of North Carolina Press.

Kaufman, Arnold S.
1968   The Radical Liberal: New Man in American Politics. New York: Atherton Press.

Keniston, Kenneth
1969   "You have to grow up in Scarsdale to know how bad things really are." New York Times Magazine (April 27): 27–28, 122–130.

Key, V. O.
1958   Politics, Parties and Pressure Groups. New York: Crowell.

Keynes, John Maynard
1936   The General Theory of Employment, Interest and Money. New York: Harcourt, Brace.

Knoll, Erwin
1972a   "It's only money." The Progressive 36 (March): 23–26.

1972b   "More weapons for the 'generation of peace.' " The Progressive 36 (August): 14–16.

Kornhauser, William
1959   The Politics of Mass Society. New York: Free Press.

Lemon, Richard
1970   The Troubled American. New York: Simon and Schuster.

Lens, Sidney
1971   The Forging of the American Empire. New York: Crowell.

Levin, Murray B.
1971   Political Hysteria in America: The Democratic Capacity for Repression. New York: Basic Books.

Lipset, Seymour M.
1963   Political Man: The Social Bases of Politics. Garden City, N.Y.: Anchor.

Lowenstein, Karl
1959   Political Power and the Governmental Process. Chicago: University of Chicago Press.

MacIver, R. M.
1965   The Web of Government. New York: Free Press. Revised edition.

Marcuse, Herbert
1958   Soviet Marxism: A Critical Analysis. New York: Columbia University Press.

May, Edgar
1971   "Drugs without crime: A report on the British success with heroin addiction." Harper's Magazine 243 (July): 60–65.

Mead, Margaret and James Baldwin
1971   A Rap on Race. Philadelphia: Lippincott.

Melman, Seymour
1970   Pentagon Capitalism: The Political Economy of War. New York: McGraw-Hill.

Michels, Robert
1962   Political Parties: A Sociological Study of the Oligarchical Tendencies of Modern Democracy. Translated by Eden and Ceder Paul. New York: Collier. Originally published in 1915.

Miles, Michael W.
1971   The Radical Probe: The Logic of Student Rebellion. New York: Atheneum.

Mills, C. Wright
1956   The Power Elite. New York: Oxford University Press.

Mintz, Morton and Jerry S. Cohen
1971   America, Inc.: Who Owns and Operates the United States. New York: Dell.

Murad, Anatol
1951   "The sources of profit and the economic revolution of our time." Southwestern Social Science Quarterly 32 (December): 150–170.

Novak, Michael
1972   The Rise of the Unmeltable Ethnics: Politics and Culture in the Seventies. New York: Macmillan.

Parker, Richard
  1972   The Myth of the Middle Class: Notes on Affluence and Equality. New York: Liveright.

Rader, Melvin
  1969   False Witness. Seattle: University of Washington Press.

Rose, Arnold M.
  1967   The Power Structure: Political Process in American Society. New York: Oxford University Press.

Roszak, Theodore
  1969   The Making of a Counter Culture: Reflections on the Technocratic Society and Its Youthful Opposition. Garden City, N.Y.: Anchor.

Saposs, David J.
  1935   "The role of the middle class in social development: Fascism, populism, communism, socialism." Pp. 393–424 in Economic Essays in Honor of Wesley Clair Mitchell. Freeport, N.Y.: Books for Libraries Press. Reprinted in 1968.

Schneider, Michael M.
  1970   "Middle America: Study in frustration." The Center Magazine 3 (November–December): 2–9.

Schrag, Peter
  1972   "Criminal case 9373." Saturday Review 55 (July 15): 12–14.

Stern, Philip M.
  1973   The Rape of the Taxpayer. New York: Random House.

Tobin, Richard L.
  1972   "The Puritan ethic today." Saturday Review 55 (January 1): 16.

Tuccille, Jerome
  1971   Radical Libertarianism: A New Political Alternative. New York: Perennial Library.

Turner, Louis
  1971   Invisible Empires: Multinational Companies and the Modern World. New York: Harcourt Brace Jovanovich.

Ungar, Sanford J.
  1972   The Papers and the Papers: An Account of the Legal and Political Battle Over the Pentagon Papers. New York: Dutton.

Vallières, Pierre
  1971   White Niggers of America: The Precocious Autobiography of a Quebec "Terrorist." New York and London: Monthly Review Press.

Viorst, Milton
  1972   "Gentlemen prefer monopoly." Harper's Magazine 245 (November): 32, 34, 36, 38.

Wheeler, Harvey
   1971   The Politics of Revolution. Berkeley, Calif.: Glendessary Press.

Williams, William Appleman
   1966   The Contours of American History. Chicago: Quadrangle.

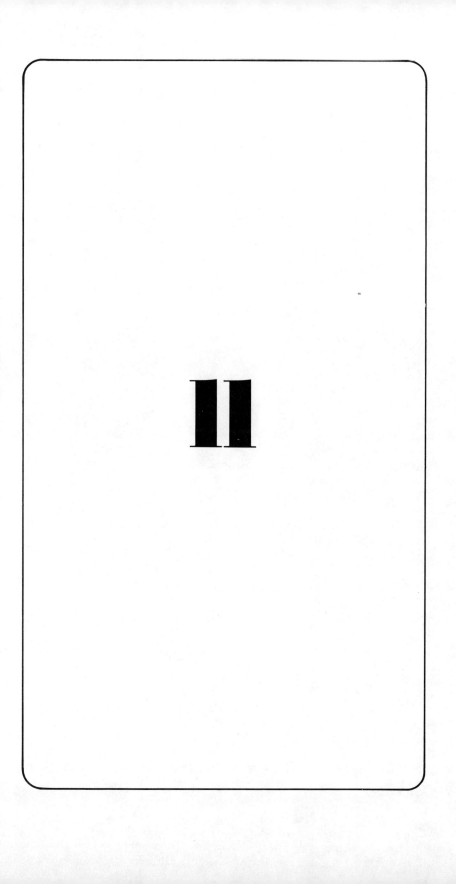

Ecology, Demography, and Humanity's Home

Borrowing the term ecology from the biological sciences, sociologists during the 1920s and 1930s developed a specialty known as *human ecology*. Its concern is the relationship of humans to their physical surroundings. One aspect of the surroundings is the human species itself; hence, ecologists are often grouped with the statistician–sociologists known as *demographers* who specialize in the study of continuing phenomena that alter the size and composition of populations.

In the early years, human ecologists concentrated primarily on the city scene, with particular reference to such things as urbanization, segregation, zoning, natural areas (territorial units with boundaries determined solely by movement and communication barriers), invasion (entry of new units into an area), and suburbanization; there was also some concern with larger areas termed regions. At the same time, demographers focused on highly abstract analyses of migration, marriage and mortality trends, sex ratios (number of males to a given number—usually 100—of females), and fertility (reproductive performance) and fecundity (reproductive capacity).* Such ecological and demographic studies are still very important; but those who, at the present time, concentrate on them alone give an impression of picnicking in a forest afire.

The prime concern of a multitude of ecologists and demographers

---

* These definitions generally apply among social scientists in English-speaking countries; in the Romance languages, the definitions are reversed; in the biological sciences, the terms sometimes appear as in the Romance languages and sometimes as exact synonyms for one another.

today is to find an answer to the following question: *How can we divert or stop the processes that threaten to end all forms of organic life?* The doomsday implications of this question make the early concerns of demography–ecology seem trivial. However, they were not trivial, nor are they now, since they pertain to phenomena continuing to have a great impact on personality development and on practically all institutionalized aspects of life. But, since there obviously would be no personality at all, or institutions, if organic life were to cease, many ecologists and demographers have at least temporarily put aside their earlier concerns. Those who have not done so sometimes speak with scorn about "irresponsible" scaremongers and devotees of "pseudoscience" and "polemical fiction" (*Psychology Today*, September 1972:12–13). Despite evidence of lack of unanimous expert opinion, the worried, often frightened, ecologists and demographers make an impressive case. The unworried ones sometimes appear to be victims of the short-sightedness common among those with comfortable status.

THE RADICALISM OF MODERN ECOLOGY

The present concern of many human and biological ecologists with *evocide*—the destruction of the earth—is potentially the most radical social movement of our time. It does not simply question existing political or economic arrangements, threatening to displace and reconstruct them. It implies that the most fundamental philosophical assumptions on which the whole superstructure of industrialized society is built are completely faulty and must be discarded. The most damaging assumption of all, according to historian Lynn White, Jr. (1967), is the central idea of both Judaism and Christianity: God created nature so humans might exploit it.

White traces the unique "marriage" of Western science and technology back to the Judaic and Christian conception of the beginnings of humans and their world:

> . . . Christianity inherited from Judaism not only a concept of time as nonrepetitive and linear but also a striking story of creation. By gradual stages a loving and all-powerful God had created light and darkness, the heavenly bodies, the earth and all its plants, animals, birds, and fishes. Finally, God had created Adam and, as an afterthought, Eve to keep man from being lonely. Man named all the animals, thus establishing his dominance over them. God planned all of this explicitly for man's benefit and rule: no item in the physical creation had any purpose save to serve man's purposes. And, although man's body is made of clay, he is not simply part of nature: he is made in God's image (1967:1205).

Belief in this story makes Christianity the most man-focused of all major religions, because it asserts, in effect, that "Man shares, in great measure, God's transcendence of nature." The same idea was expressed in ancient Hebrew literature addressed to the Almighty, expressing gratitude for the godlike character of humans:

> . . . thou has made him little short of Divine—Everything hast thou placed under his feet (Eban, 1972:51).

In sharp contrast, the prevailing idea of other ancient societies and some cultures even today—such as the many varieties of American Indians—was that every rock and tree and stream had its guardian spirit to be placated before ground was dug, a tree cut, a mountain mined. This animistic vision of a living nature, including humans, was replaced by Christianity which preached that animism—belief that practically all physical things have an indwelling spiritual being—is a forbidden form of pagan belief. Thus, "Christianity made it possible to exploit nature in a mood of indifference to the feelings of natural objects. . . . The spirits *in* natural objects, which formerly had protected nature from man, evaporated. Man's effective monopoly on spirit in this world was confirmed, and the old inhibitions to the exploitation of nature crumbled" (White, 1967:1205). This was particularly true in the Western world; it was not so true in ancient Greece where Orthodox faith preached that salvation could be found in clear thinking. In Western Europe, salvation was seen in right conduct—in *works*, in doing, in striving. These views subsequently culminated in the Puritan belief that every human has a "calling," a worldly task set by God, and it is every individual's duty to tend to that assignment.

With Western Christian ideas about man and nature as a foundation, man developed science as the most efficient and thorough method of *knowing* nature; technology was continually improved so nature could be *exploited* with ever greater facility. It is conceivable that nature could have survived these assaults if either effort (knowledge and exploitation) were made separately. But they did not remain apart. About 150 years ago they were merged as the core of the Industrial Revolution, and the result was the precipitate growth of Western society exploiting nature so completely and swiftly that even some conservative ecologists are now ringing the death knell. "For whom doth the bell toll?" asks humankind; and the ecologist answers, "It tolls for thee."

The practical political and economic implications of modern ecology and demography have been spelled out by John Fischer in a piece titled "How I Got Radicalized" (1970). The significance of Fischer's view is that he is a long-time "traditionalist," a contributing editor to *Harper's Magazine*. But the ecological crisis has radicalized him so that he no longer believes in three central aspects of American life: growth, the idea that technology can fix anything, and private property. He writes, "To my astonishment, the political convictions that I had cherished for most of my life have suddenly deserted me" (p. 18). Their place has been taken by ideas so radical that Fischer is alarmed: ". . . I seem to be a lot more radical than the children. Those SDS youngsters who go around breaking windows and clubbing policemen now merely depress me with their frivolous irrelevance" (p. 18). He also feels out of tune with vintage socialists and communists. From an ecological point of view, there are no significant differences between ordinary capitalist and collectivist orders; they all seem dedicated to the type of growth and industrial technology that the world, as a closed ecosystem, will not be able to survive.

The turning point for Fischer was his appointment to a committee assigned to work out an environmental policy for the state of Connecticut. Information brought to the committee's attention was such that within a few months Fischer concluded, ". . . the Democratic party, and most of our institutions of government, and even the American Way of Life are no damned good. In their present form, at least, they will have to go. Either that, or everybody goes—and sooner than we think" (p. 18). Fischer and his fellow committee members found that growth, as embodied in an expanding gross national product, leads to suicide rather than to the salvation described by men in business circles:

> The most important lesson of my life—learned shamefully late—was that nonstop growth just isn't possible, for Americans or anybody else. For we live in what I've learned to recognize as a tight ecological system: a smallish planet with a strictly limited supply of everything, including air, water, and places to dump sewage (Fischer, 1970:18).

Therefore, the prime national goal should be Zero Population Growth— the name of a new social movement dedicated to the proposition that the only hope of preventing utter deterioration of our environment is to decrease the population growth as well as the consumption of literally everything. This is, of course, a subversive notion from the point of view of the capitalist; it is profoundly un-American. It is also un-Marxian to the communist bureaucrats who boast of outdoing the productive capacity of the United States and other industrialized societies.

Is the technological know-how of private enterprise the answer? Fischer answers negatively, asserting that unrestrained use of property is the root cause of the impending ecological disaster. In the "Survivable Society," if we can create one, a landowner cannot be permitted to pave a pasture for a landing strip or parking lot just because to do so would bring more income: "He will have to understand that his quick profit may, quite literally, take the bread out of his grandchildren's mouths, and the oxygen from their lungs" (Fischer, 1970:28). As for technology itself, Fischer is skeptical because, although technologists often solve given problems, in the process they frequently create new ones. Even if this were not true, historian Lynn White concludes, it is doubtful that a technology resting on a base of exploitation is a trustworthy vehicle for reform. He asserts that the current prevailing attitude is well symbolized by the present Governor of California, Ronald Reagan, who said, "When you've seen one redwood tree, you've seen them all." White could also have mentioned the Governor of Arizona, whose answer to a concerned environmental group was, "The only grass I'm interested in is on the golf course."

Such expressions lead White to the idea that ecological salvation can be achieved only if there is a new prevailing philosophy. "What we do about ecology depends on our ideas of the man–nature relationship. More science and more technology are not going to get us out of the present ecologic crisis until we find a new religion, or rethink our old one" (White, 1967:1206). By "religion," White does not refer to specific theological ideas. He means, rather, convictions about what is transient (temporary) and what is transcendent (going beyond purely material existence); it is only by concentrating on the latter, in a most profound and all-encompassing sense, that we will find a solution.

> The beatniks, who are the basic revolutionaries of our time, show a sound instinct in their affinity for Zen Buddhism, which conceives of the man–nature relationship as very nearly the mirror image of the Christian view (White, 1967:1206).

However, White does not suggest Zen is the ultimate answer; the philosophy has already been too infiltrated by Western ideas. Rather, he attempts to make the more profound point that a problem basically religious is not going to be solved by purely secular efforts:

> . . . we shall continue to have a worsening ecologic crisis until we reject the Christian axiom that nature has no reason for existence save to serve man.
>
> The greatest spiritual revolutionary in Western history, Saint Francis, proposed what he thought was an alternative Christian view of nature and man's relation to it: he tried to substitute the idea of the equality of all creatures, including man, for the idea of man's limitless rule of creation. He failed. Both our present science and our present technology are so tinctured with orthodox Christian arrogance toward nature that no solution for our ecologic crisis can be expected from them alone. Since the roots of our trouble are so largely religious, the remedy must also be essentially religious, whether we call it that or not. We must rethink and refeel our nature and destiny. The profoundly religious, but heretical, sense of the primitive Franciscans for the spiritual autonomy of all parts of nature may point a direction. I propose Francis as a patron saint for ecologists (White, 1967:1207).

THE POPULATION PROBLEM

The apocalyptic flavor of the writings of Fischer and White is well-supported by the findings and views of biologists such as Paul Ehrlich (1969; 1971; 1972) and Barry Commoner (1971); biochemists, zoologists, and botanists such as J. B. Neilands and his colleagues (1972); and social scientists such as Richard Falk (1971). These observers do not agree on every particular point—Ehrlich and Commoner argue about population growth or technology as the prime danger, for example—but they are in complete agreement in warning that the Western way of life as we know it is, in a manner of speaking, the way of death. Ehrlich's article, "Eco-Catastrophe!" (*Ramparts,* 1969) is typical of this point of view, although deliberately overstated to illustrate his ideas. The article was written in science-fiction form, as if completed in 1980; the commentator notes the day, in 1979, when the ocean died—that is, the time when the ocean's life-sustaining and oxygen-producing functions came to a total end. He recounts the many warnings issued throughout the 1960s and 1970s: the cautions about pesticides, the prophetic signs when some species such as whales failed to maintain their numbers, the oil slicks, the "red tide" attacks by micro-organisms that destroy ocean fish, the debris found floating far at sea, the declining fishing industry, the satellite photos indicating that in the early 1970s many large bodies of water were already in the dying state known as eutrophication.

He comments on the various feeble efforts of government to make reforms, efforts that are consistently too little and too late because they are opposed by various business interests staffed by bureaucrats or executives prized for their concentration on today's profits. When it was found that pesticides in rain runoff were having a serious effect on fish,

> The United Nations attempted to get all chlorinated hydrocarbon insecticides banned on a worldwide basis, but the move was defeated by the United States. This opposition was generated primarily by the American petrochemical industry, operating hand in glove with its subsidiary, the United States Department of Agriculture. Together they persuaded the government to oppose the U.N. move (Ehrlich, 1969:24).

This description, although fictional in its details, accurately expresses underlying meaning and trends, particularly since many of the conditions Ehrlich thought would not prevail until the mid- and late-1970s are already evident in 1973: the red tide moving north from Florida, its destructive micro-organisms flourishing on pollution; the fast dwindling Peruvian anchoveta beds; the crisis in the Iceland fishing industry; the serious shortages in various important sources of energy; tuna catches ruined by unacceptable levels of DDT; all but elimination of the great whale species; salmon blocked from their spawning areas by dams and polluted runoff; dying and dead bays and lakes; shellfish coastal breeding grounds ruined by oil spills (central California crab catch: 1957– 9,000,000 lbs.; 1972–300,000 lbs.); a "harvest of death" from chemical warfare in Vietnam (Neilands, et al., 1972); fishing equipment suppliers boasting in advertisements that their electronic devices will keep fishermen in business until the "final kill." Examples are endless.

Ehrlich feels that population pressure is the basic difficulty. Thus, he speaks about *The Population Bomb* (1971) and gives population the first priority in his recent *Population–Resources–Environment* (1972). But he gives no serious attention to horror stories based on simplistic projections from current trends—for example, the purely mathematical prediction that since the last doubling of world population took only thirty-five years, therefore, in just 1,000 years there will be 1,700 persons per square yard of the earth's surface, including water as well as land. However, Ehrlich is serious indeed about United Nations predictions based on the best available demographic and social data. These show that the world population—approximately 3,700 million in 1971—will, by the year 2000, be somewhere between a low of 5,449 million and a high of 6,994 million, with a medium estimate of 6,130 million people. Ehrlich concludes that the high and medium projections are probably excessive because ". . . we predict a drastic rise in the death rate will either slow or terminate the population explosion, unless efforts to avoid such a tragic eventuality are immediately mounted" (1972:51). The predicted increase in the death rate, particularly in so-called underdeveloped areas (India, Africa), is likely to occur because of new diseases caused by pollution, serious interferences with vital food chains, and famine. Our ability to deal effectively with such phenomena is questionable, since we are already far outstripping the ability of nature to adjust and recoup.

Even the most sophisticated technology, says Ehrlich, cannot, in the long run, compensate for population pressures that use up limited supplies of all available resources:

> Both worldwide plague and thermonuclear war are made probable as population growth continues. These, along with famine, make up the trio of potential "death rate solutions" to the population problem. . . . Make no mistake about it, *the imbalance will be redressed.* The shape of the population growth curve is one familiar to the biologist. It is the outbreak part of an outbreak–crash sequence. A population grows rapidly in the presence of abundant resources, finally runs out of food or some other necessity, and crashes to a low level or extinction. Man is not only running out of food, he is also destroying the life support systems of the Spaceship Earth. The situation was recently summarized very succinctly: "It is the top of the ninth inning. Man, always a threat at the plate, has been hitting Nature hard. It is important to remember, however, that NATURE BATS LAST" (Ehrlich, 1969:28).

As for the comfortable pollyannas who assert it is not numbers that count, but distribution, Ehrlich retorts that age and other distributions of the population are important but not vital. An aging population creates a multitude of problems, among them health care, school support, and retirement systems. But even the most bizarre distributions are benign in the face of totals that use up total resources. It is conceivable that advanced technology will provide new sources of energy, perhaps from controlled atomic fusion (which, in comparison with atomic fission, is potentially far safer and pollution-free), or maybe in the form of artificial satellites on which the sun's light is converted into nuclear energy that can safely be transmitted to the earth. But many techniques, touted as ways to accommodate the population growth, will be sadly disappointing—for example, "farming" the sea, considered an inexhaustible future food supplier in the form of fish meal. The sea, not to speak of the organisms it sustains, is in imminent danger. For example, the decline of the Peruvian fishing industry is a significant omen. To the surprise of many, Peru has ranked among the top five fishing nations because the anchovetas (a small fish resembling a cross between an anchovy and a sardine) living in its territorial waters permitted it to become the chief world supplier of fishmeal for animal feed. But, during the summer and fall of 1972, pollution and other factors raised the temperature of coastal waters, causing the anchoveta beds to move or decline so that production was sharply curtailed and never fully restored. The resulting shortage in the supply of fishmeal has sent a shock wave around the globe.*

Some have suggested colonizing other planets as a possible solution to population pressures. It has been proposed that the planets could be made physically tolerable by enclosing them in plastic domes. Those who think in terms of such "solutions" are not motivated to face up to the realities of current trends; therefore, it is important to make the point that we are in all likelihood confined for the foreseeable future to one small planet, Earth. We are so confined because—even if other planets were made habitable (which seems unlikely)—we would have to export seventy million people per year just to keep a stable world population (presuming no major change in current vital statistics). To do this ". . . would require the launching of very nearly 2,000 spaceships each day, year in and year out. The cost, not counting the expense of

---

* The shortage is only in part a function of a cyclical process. Each year in late December, warm currents drive the anchovetas from their feeding grounds; the cold Humboldt Current generally restores favorable conditions by March. Every seven years, however, unfavorable conditions have lasted longer than usual. In 1972, which was supposed to be normal, the Humboldt Current was so weak that by June the anchoveta catch was only 10 percent of that expected; even after another year had passed, only Peru's needs could be supplied.

recruiting and training migrants, would exceed $300 billion daily" (Ehrlich, 1972:60). In just three days, the cost of launching would almost equal the entire U.S. annual gross national product.

But even if economic problems were not a factor, the Earth's atmosphere probably could not survive the heat pollution that would result from a multitude of spaceship launchings; "Earth's atmosphere can absorb only so much thermal pollution before life is extinguished" (Ehrlich and Holdren, 1971). Further, present population growth rates are such that within fifty years colonized Mars, Venus, Mercury, and all the moons of Jupiter and Saturn would have the same population density as the Earth. In another 200 years, the same density would apply to the larger planets—Jupiter, Neptune, Saturn, Uranus—if they too could be colonized. Thus, in 250 years, humanity would be faced with the population problems we face today, but on a scale so immense it is difficult to comprehend.

THE PROBLEM OF TECHNOLOGY

Those who assert that the ecological crisis is primarily due to population growth are often bitterly criticized as "neo-Malthusian crusaders" (Ridgeway, 1970:181), an appellation derived from the name of Thomas Malthus, a British clergyman who asserted, early in the nineteenth century, that population increases always tend to outstrip subsistence methods. Neo-Malthusianism is said to be both dangerous and suspicious—dangerous because it sidetracks efforts to cope with pollution, and suspicious because population control has long been a concern of well-to-do whites who are basically motivated by fear of "teeming masses."

Among those stressing technology rather than population as the primary ecological threat, biologist Barry Commoner is one of the most responsible and persuasive. His *The Closing Circle* (1971) has received wide publicity; substantial portions of it have appeared in a number of magazines and books. Commoner feels that the most thorough solution to ecological problems would combine control of population with safe technological innovation. But, he says, since voluntary population control does not seem likely in many areas for a long time to come, the only alternative is technological reform to support a growing population. *Involuntary* population control means "political repression," because it would involve government control of aspects of life that have heretofore been regarded as purely private concerns.

Commoner mentions the credibility gap that has arisen because some ecologists have escalated their warnings that catastrophe is imminent. Are such warnings realistic? Commoner observes, "The issue of survival can be put into the form of a fairly rigorous question: Are present ecological stresses so strong that—if not relieved—they will sufficiently degrade the ecosystem to make the earth uninhabitable by man?" (Commoner, 1971:217). The answer to such a question is largely a matter of judgment; Commoner's judgment, after considering the totality of current information, is:

> . . . the present course of environmental degradation, at least in industrialized countries, represents a challenge to essential ecological systems that is so serious that, if continued, it will destroy the capability of the environment to support a reasonably civilized human society. Some number of human beings might well survive such a catastrophe, for the collapse of civilization would reduce the pace of environmental degradation. What would then remain would be a kind of neobarbarism with a highly uncertain future (1971:217–218).

Commoner stresses the need to be cautious about interpreting too literally from present trends. He quotes Mark Twain's comment that the Mississippi River is shortening at a rate such that, in 742 years, New Orleans, Louisiana and Cairo, Illinois will be grouped together as twin cities. One is also reminded of the late nineteenth century prophets who warned that in a hundred years cities would be buried beneath mountains of horse manure. "There is something fascinating about science," Twain noted. "One gets such wholesale returns of conjecture out of such a trifling investment of fact" (Commoner, 1971:218). Commoner feels this is a useful warning; only a few accurate extrapolations can be made from current conditions. One of these is the depletion rate of oxygen in United States surface waters. According to a National Academy of Sciences study, by the year 2000, the nation's rivers, lakes, and coastal waters will have insufficient oxygen to degrade the organic wastes washed into them (Commoner, 1971:219). Some people might say, "So what? We could get used to the smell." But offensive odors would be the least of the resultant problems. Indeed, the odors in themselves might not be a worry at all: ". . . the predicted quantitative change in surface waters will probably generate qualitative changes in the ecosystem, which could gravely threaten human survival" (Commoner, 1971:220).

The most immediate threat would be from diseases caused by microorganisms that multiply most rapidly in organic-rich water. Some of this disease threat has already become evident and real: meningioencephalitis (the new brain disease) that attacks swimmers in Florida waters; increased bacterial count in New York harbor despite a considerable decline in the number of bacteria discharged into the water; soil molds that are normally harmless but become cancer causes or infectious when released from the soil by polluted water; the accelerating rate of deterioration in European coastal waters, to name but a few. In addition, organic pollution intensifies the hazards from dangerous metals—mercury, lead, nickel, and cadmium—that industrial producers commonly dump into rivers and discharge as "smoke" that eventually becomes rain runoff. Metallic mercury, for example, is relatively harmless until bacterial action converts it into methyl mercury, which is very toxic to the food chain involving ocean life.

> As a result of such interactions, we must anticipate that new *kinds* of environmental hazards may suddenly emerge as the levels of organic matter in surface waters gradually increase (Commoner, 1971:225).

Air pollution containing oxides of sulfur is a related danger. Regular measurements made in Sweden demonstrate that the acidity of rain and snow has gradually increased and has spread geographically (Swedish Preparatory Committee, 1971). Time series maps of Scandinavia show that the resulting unnatural influx of acid into the soil has been creeping northward at a frightening rate. This is significant on two grounds. First, it has a deleterious effect on plant growth and has apparently already cut into timber yields; when plant life is threatened, oxygen production through photosynthesis may also become endangered. Second, it indicates that pollution control would be relatively useless if it were not international in scope.

Commoner and others describe numerous additional technological hazards: nuclear fallout, insecticide and chemical fertilizer runoff, smog attacks, increased nitrogen oxides resulting from efforts to control smog, largescale inadvertent bird kills resulting from seed dressed with alkyl mercury compounds, cancer-causing asbestos particles from building materials and automotive brake linings, deleterious food additives, predator control measures damaging the "web of life," oil spills, sewage sludge, clearcutting (that is, timber industry removal of all growth in cutting areas), dams that alter basic ecological processes and needs, flood control techniques that lower water tables, irrigation practices that dangerously increase the salinity of important river systems. All these, and more, have a most serious effect on the closed and limited ecosystem. In addition, nonrenewable mineral resources are being used at a growing rate. A fundamental paradox of human life is, therefore, suggested:

> . . . human civilization involves a series of cyclically interdependent processes, most of which have a built-in tendency to grow, except one—the natural irreplaceable, absolutely essential resources represented by the earth's minerals and the ecosphere. A clash between the propensity of the man-dependent sectors of the cycle to grow and the intractable limits of the natural sector of the cycle is inevitable (Commoner, 1971:122).

Among the growth factors mentioned by Commoner (1971:Ch. 12), he names as the most important the productivity emphasis of today's large-scale socialist countries (such as Red China) and the profit search of industrialists in the Western nations. In pointing to private enterprise as particularly harmful because of its stress on individualism, Commoner registers his agreement with such perceptive economist-analysts as Robert L. Heilbroner (1968) and K. W. Kapp (1963), not to speak here of Karl Marx. These and other qualified observers conclude that only with constant growth of supply and demand can an economy produce the profit that is the touchstone of private enterprise. And, since the end of World War II, industry has found that more assured profits lie in the development and use of synthetic products; such products are ecologically very costly. With the mass development of these products, private enterprise is, in effect, digging its own grave:

> The course of environmental deterioration shows that as conventional capital has accumulated, for example in the United States since 1946, the value of the biological capital has *declined*. Indeed, if the process continues, the biological capital may eventually be driven to the point of total destruction. . . . Thus despite its apparent prosperity, in reality the system is being driven into bankruptcy. Environmental degradation represents a crucial, potentially fatal, *hidden* factor in the operation of the economic system (Commoner, 1971:273).

THE LIMITS TO GROWTH

This section is titled the same as a widely noted recent publication sponsored by the Club of Rome, a prestigious group of problem-conscious businessmen and scholars. Club members, concerned with environmental trends, commissioned a Massachusetts Institute of Technology group to conduct a suitable study. The published result (Meadows, et al., 1972) indicated how the MIT team used a high-powered computer to simulate models of the environment in which five critical variables—food supply, industrial production, natural resources, pollution, and population—were systematically altered.

The study has been criticized on a number of grounds; primary among these is the observation that "Population, capital and pollution grow exponentially in all models, but technologies for expanding resources and controlling pollution are permitted to grow, if at all, only in discrete increments" (*Newsweek*, March 13, 1972:103). Similarly, a specially commissioned report on the "Limits" study asserted, "Any model that assumes that certain things will grow at exponential rates and others will not, is inherently unstable" (World Bank Task Force, 1972:16). These are serious rebukes; however, it would be unwise to ignore three related points. First, the quoted criticisms have been formulated by personnel who essentially obtain their income from associations (such as the World Bank and Resources for the Future, Inc.) dedicated to the proposition that planned growth must continue. Second, the "Limits" authors point out:

> There is no single variable called "technology" in the world model. We have not found it possible to aggregate and generalize the dynamic implications of technological development because different technologies arise from and influence quite different sectors of the model (Meadows, et al., 1972:130).

Therefore, each proposed technology is handled separately in the model, ". . . considering carefully how it might affect each of the assumptions we have made about the model elements" (Meadows, p. 131). Third, even assuming that technologic optimists are correct and, therefore, resource problems are solved, the Limits authors concluded after careful study, "The application of technological solutions alone has prolonged the period of population and industrial growth, but it has not removed the ultimate limits to that growth" (Meadows, p. 141).

The Limits scholars found that no matter how they altered the variables and technological innovations—even when they were combined in the most benign way reasonably possible (for example, by doubling assumed reserves of natural resources)—the resulting models showed that within one hundred years, system breakdown is the inevitable result. Given this finding, the MIT scholars were conservative in stating their central result:

> If the present growth trends in world population, industrialization, pollution, food production, and resource depletion continue unchanged, the limits to growth on this planet will be reached sometime within the next one hundred years. The most probable result will be a rather sudden and uncontrollable decline in both population and industrial capacity (Meadows, et al., 1972:23).

They repeatedly caution that not one of their computer outputs should be considered a prediction because "The model contains dynamic statements about only the physical aspects of man's activities" (p. 142). Social variables were not included as part of the model and can be assumed to change as they have in the past: "We have ample evidence of mankind's ingenuity and social flexibility" (p. 128). Even so,

> The basic behavior mode of the world system is exponential growth of population and capital, followed by collapse (p. 142).

Those who may feel skeptical about predictions as discussed above might find it instructive to consider present trends in the GWP (gross world product). In 1950, when environmental stress was little noticed, the GWP was approximately $1.25 trillion. By 1970, about $2 trillion had been added to the GWP, and environmental difficulties were much in evidence. If the established GWP 5 percent growth rate continues to the year 2000, so that the GWP is $13 trillion, what will the environmental conditions be?

Even such trends do not impress some observers who fault the Club of Rome study for not giving sufficient weight to advancing knowledge and also for failing to note recent evidences of a downward turn in birth–death growth rates. Several countries, including the United States, have, in the last few years, achieved zero growth in terms of these birth–death ratios, and the most productive countries (like Japan, West Germany, and the United States) are becoming environmentally conscious to a point where they may well slow down their economic activity. But, environmental deterioration has advanced to such a degree that deleterious trends are likely to occur even if all growth ceases. Further, such growth will not cease, at least for a long time: even with a birth-death ratio that merely provides for population maintenance, the United States population will continue to expand for *seventy* more years because of previously established age distributions; and almost all poorer countries (such as India) are deeply determined to emulate the productive capacity and consumption style of the West. As for technological advances, they usually engender ecological costs. These were not significant in the day of Malthus, but now they are often potentially lethal. For example, the Green Revolution which makes land so productive is dependent on chemical fertilizers and pesticides that, in the long run, deplete further production possibilities. Similarly, the nuclear energy touted as a solution to the problem of disappearing fossil fuels produces radioactive waste and thermal pollution that can become more dangerous than anything yet known. Russia's proposal to obtain irrigation water by reversing the flow of four rivers now draining into the Arctic Ocean threatens to alter the balance of nature so seriously that meteorologists throughout the world have protested.

CRITICS OF ZERO GROWTH

The authors of The Limits to Growth believe that the only realistic way to avoid an environmental Armageddon is to level off all the world's significant economic and population growth rates to the point where a steady-state economy can be achieved. This proposal has generated protest from all sectors of the ideological spectrum. At the Denver hearings on the 1972 Democratic party platform, a Colorado state

Senator—a black—denounced environmentalists for diverting attention from pressing poverty problems (*Environmental Action*, August 5, 1972). Almost at the same time, Yale economist Henry Wallich wrote, "Growth is a substitute for equality of income. So long as there is growth, there is hope, and that makes large income differentials tolerable" (*Newsweek*, January 24, 1972:62). Wallich went on to criticize the Limits study as "irresponsible nonsense." He was offended when the publishers presented the study findings at a Smithsonian Institution press conference; he wrote, "Growth is made to sound scary by words like 'exponential'. . . ." And he concluded, "Considering the unbelievable difficulties of halting growth and equalizing the world's income . . . there can be no doubt which way the decision should go" (*Newsweek*, March 13, 1972). Among the "unbelievable difficulties of halting growth," a few have abiding significance: increasing political and economic power for the elderly; relative decline for youth-oriented businesses and for educational establishments accustomed to continuous expansion; smaller-scale living and traveling accommodations; and, most important, abandonment of the "bigger means better" philosophy that has for so long been a basic American tenet.

India's prime minister, Indira Gandhi (1972), has expressed criticism of Western environmentalists on the grounds that, in effect, they condemn the less developed nations to an unfinished revolution. Madam Gandhi fully admits that India, along with other nations, has been "guilty of wanton disregard for the sources of our sustenance" (1972:35). But she feels that present gross disparities in national living levels are largely due to the ruthlessness of developed nations which, undisturbed by any thoughts of compassion or environmental safety, have plundered the weaker nations. Therefore, the prosperity of the West is in large part built on the labor and raw materials of less developed areas. Further, Westerners today consume far more than their proportionate share of natural resources. Therefore, Madam Gandhi asserts, it is an oversimplification to say that the basic environmental problem is population. Rather, it is the maldistribution of the world's goods and services. To the degree that this is so, it is unseemly for Westerners to warn that the environment will be injured if less developed nations use modern methods for combating poverty. "Are not poverty and need the greatest polluters?" Madam Gandhi inquires (p. 36). How can we decently ask the poor, living for the most part in rural and urban slums, to refrain from polluting rivers when their own lives are contaminated? Madam Gandhi concludes that the environment cannot be protected until poverty is eliminated, and poverty can be controlled only through social and technological innovation.

TWO SCENARIOS

Given the sharp differences of opinion among environmental specialists and powerful political leaders, it is not possible to predict our ecological future with a great degree of confidence. However, we can indicate a range of likely possibilities, thus emulating demographers who customarily make several predictions both high and low, any one of which will apply depending on intervening variables. This is what Richard Falk has done in presenting his "Two Images of the Future" (1971:Chapter 9).

Falk begins by quoting one-time United Nations Secretary-General U Thant: "I do not wish to seem overdramatic, but I can only conclude . . . that the members of the United Nations have perhaps ten years left in which to subordinate their ancient quarrels and launch a global partnership to curb the arms race, to improve the human environment, to defuse the population explosion, and to supply the required momentum to world development efforts" (Falk, 1971:415). Suppose, Falk continues, the United States elects a president who decides to check on the accuracy of U Thant's gloomy time-schedule. Expert opinion confirms U Thant, prompting the president to arrange secret meetings of leaders from the ten most powerful nations. After study, they conclude the situation is desperate. What then? Falk sketches two possible consequences. One sketch is based on the assumption that the various nations do relatively little to alter their present course; the other sketch assumes that world leaders cooperate to do what is necessary to save humanity from annihilation.

In the first sketch, governments continue to concentrate on competitive rivalry—large states maintaining their traditional armed power and smaller ones developing their ability to wage mass war with nuclear weapons. Poorer countries attempt to modernize, contributing to increasingly severe ecological crises. Alarmist predictions are heard, but technological experts counsel that ways to solve problems can be developed. Thus, no lasting serious attention is given to the smog attacks, famine, and radioactive-waste accidents that kill hundreds of thousands; even less concern is expressed as millions press onto previously unoccupied areas, causing the disappearance of marine and wildlife. Finally, though, the inability of governments to cope with the mass problems of the day generates a "Politics of Despair." During the late 1970s, *"People will increasingly doubt whether life is worth living"* (Falk, 1971:421). To counter the resulting reform and revolutionary social movements, right-wing politics is increasingly apparent and popular; governments establish control over the mass media lest they "mislead the public."

By the 1980s, the "Politics of Desperation" prevails. Those who have hoped to make needed changes gradually disappear from the scene. Cynics abound, predicting that nothing can or will be done—"Eat, drink, and be merry, for tomorrow you will be vaporized or die of asphyxiation." The few who continue to counsel reform become threats to those in power. And, since nothing is more important to the powerful than power itself—even the possibility of death cannot move those for whom power is an addiction as compelling as light to the moth—the still hopeful, the potential leaders for new directions, are harried, hounded, and sequestered as a menace to the public order. The methods of repression, using the most up-to-date technology, become very sophisticated and all-pervasive. By 1984, it can be interjected, governments will be ". . . able to ignore the grievances and disaffection of despairing masses of men and women" (Falk, 1971:424).

But domestic control in the traditionally dominant nations does not seriously affect the Third World (the less developed and nonindustrialized nations) residents, whose rage becomes almost uncontrollable. To pacify them, their governments rail against the "haves" and prepare for the "final battle." This leads to a frenzied realignment of powers, combining the relatively rich U.S.S.R., Western Europe, and the United States into an alliance whose basic aim is to keep poor Asians, Africans, and Latin Americans from "stealing what is rightfully ours."

By 1990, perhaps, the "Politics of Catastrophe" will take over. The specific date is not important—what is vital is that ". . . throughout the period of the future there will exist at every moment some risk of catastrophe, perhaps gradually increased by the steady buildup of a danger of ecological collapse" (Falk, 1971:428). Even if government leaders, at long last, attempt to do something, basement H-bombs make it likely that a cataclysm will occur. Mounting pressure on the environment will lead to a complete breakdown of the world system. At that point, attention will be given to reform measures that were previously defined as unreal, visionary, or impractical. But it is too late, Falk speculates, so there is no avoiding the debacle. With the oxygen supply seriously depleted, with a rise in temperature such that the polar caps melt, causing massive flooding and catastrophic weather changes, with governments impotent and economic systems collapsed—". . . the capacity for spontaneous adjustment is likely to be minimal, if not negative" (Falk, 1971:430).

> It seems almost certain that the compulsions of the power-wielders will lead to a surge of repressive political energy reinforced by the super-technologies that lie ahead. Such a system cannot be peacefully transformed: It is taken over or it crashes down in ruin, leaving the entire system in disarray, perhaps irretrievably so. For this reason, we would suppose that the twenty-first century will inaugurate the Era of Annihilation (Falk, 1971:430–431).

But what if the far less believable comes to pass? Let us imagine that the recommendations of the United Nations Conference on the Human Environment, held in Stockholm during June 1972, are adopted by the U.N. General Assembly. The result would be the creation of a world-wide set of monitoring stations that would provide ample warning of impending environmental danger. This could make the 1970s a "Decade of Awareness," says Falk. With sufficient public awareness, the élite groups and their political allies who, because of vested interests, try to block real progress, can be overcome. A general arousal would also spark a global demand for adequate change. The result could well make the 1980s a "Decade of Mobilization" leading to a world political movement. Of course, those committed to the old ways would fight bitterly, but they would be overwhelmed by the momentum toward an international order.

By 1990, a "Decade of Transformation" would prevail. Such a decade would be characterized by the appearance of several versions of ecological humanism. These would make it possible to stabilize popula-tion, recycle wastes creatively, and use resources harmoniously. Al-though conflicts, reactions, and disaffections would no doubt continue, the strength of ecological humanism would be too great; it would bring such satisfaction to almost everyone that a twenty-first century of "World Harmony" would be irresistible. This would be the time when ecological humanism would be accepted on a worldwide scale. The consequence would be the establishment of optimum levels of popula-tion and resource use. Pollution problems would be handled by cooper-ative international agencies. Human energy would be concentrated on community activities, with special reference to crafts and creative arts.

> The applications of science and other branches of knowledge will be guided by service to the maintenance of harmony on the planet. A less homocentric scale of values will underlie political decision. The welfare of plants, animals, and machines will all be considered benevolent in this kind of humanism. It is a humanism only because the whole process is conceived of and worked out by man, as if man were hired as an architect to rehabilitate the ecosphere inhabited by all that exists on earth (Falk, 1971:436).

OUR ECOLOGICAL FUTURE

Which of Falk's two scenarios is the more accurate prediction of future events? It is clear that he naturally hopes for the second but despond-ently concludes that the first is the most likely because national leaders are almost always trapped by their social systems. Even those well aware of the dangers of an anarchic world ". . . refrain from taking crucial steps for fear of losing support in the arena of internal politics. . ." (Harold Lasswell, quoted in Falk, 1971:417). One cannot even count on clear and certain ruin to sway many people from action that can bring them short-term gain only; whalers are a sobering example. They develop ever more sophisticated fishing techniques, the success of which are such that very quickly whalers knowingly destroy the very foundation of their own livelihood.

Does all this mean that the destiny of organic life is quick extinction? Not necessarily. I take what comfort I can from the fact that the prophets of doom, in their desire to generate needed action, almost always overstate their case. But even if future conditions become only half as bad as those predicted by ecological alarmists, the possibilities are frightening. Therefore, appropriate action is imperative. Whether or not it will occur, and what its exact form would be if it did occur, remains an open question. We are already seeing the first evidences of what is needed—namely, a worldwide radical movement dedicated to creating harmony with nature everywhere. To be effective, the movement must be radical because stopping the rape of nature before the victim perishes will necessitate altering fundamentally the principle governing the use of the world's resources. This principle has been "to the victor belong the spoils"; the new principle must be *global-cooperative-sharing*. This would, of course, mean the end of the nation–state (independent country) as it has existed. It would mean that all socioeconomic systems entailing private control of major forms of property would be discarded. It would also mean that the presently privileged—be they individuals or nations—would have to divide their resources with the less privileged. Such apportionment would no doubt require the affluent to lower their level of living.

It will seem to some unbelievably idealistic to imagine the privileged ever sharing to the point that their own living level would decline. But it is conceivable that even the most selfish will be carried along—may be converted, as it were—by the religious-like nature of the ecological movement. The need is so universal, so transcendent, that the movement already partakes, and will probably increasingly do so, of some of the ennobling elements of religion: mercy, love, trust, and self-sacrifice. But if the privileged are not converted spiritually, even the most myopic of them may become "idealistic" when they learn that the ecological state of the world is such that the alternative to sharing is not simply that given livelihoods will be undermined. The *sole* alternative, sooner or later, is total system breakdown, eliminating the possibility of any livelihood whatsoever. As the late Lester Pearson put it, what has been true for individual nations now applies to the planet: It cannot long survive half in misery and half engulfed in self-indulgent consumerism. Neither the ecological order nor morality can stand such contrast:

In short, we face an essential need and an unprecedented opportunity. International development is a great challenge of our age. Our response to it will show whether we understand the implications of interdependence or whether we prefer to delude ourselves that poverty and deprivation of the great majority of mankind can be ignored without tragic consequences for all (Pearson, 1969:11).

One may ask, how can the needed ecological reform movement be further enhanced? How can desired social change be implemented? The answers to these vital questions—to the degree that one can provide these answers—will be considered in the final chapter.

REFERENCES AND FURTHER SOURCES

Commoner, Barry
1971   The Closing Circle: Nature, Man, and Technology. New York: Knopf.

Eban, Abba
1972   "No way back to Eden." Bulletin of the Atomic Scientists 28 (September): 49–51.

Ehrlich, Paul
1969   "Eco-catastrophe!" Ramparts 8 (September): 24–28.

1971   The Population Bomb. New York: Ballantine. Second edition.

Ehrlich, Paul R. and Anne H. Ehrlich
1972   Population–Resources–Environment: Issues in Human Ecology. San Francisco: Freeman.

Ehrlich, Paul R. and John P. Holdren
1971   "The heat barrier." Saturday Review 54 (April 3): 61.

Falk, Richard A.
1971   This Endangered Planet: Prospects and Proposals for Human Survival. New York: Random House.

Fischer, John
1970   "How I got radicalized; the making of an agitator for zero." Harper's Magazine 240 (April): 18–29, *passim.*

Gandhi, Indira
1972   "The unfinished revolution." Bulletin of the Atomic Scientists 28 (September): 35–38.

Heilbroner, Robert L.
1968   Understanding Macroeconomics. Englewood Cliffs, New Jersey: Prentice-Hall. Second edition.

Kapp, K. William
1963   Social Costs of Business Enterprise. New York: Asia Publishing House.

Meadows, Donella H., Dennis L. Meadows, Jørgen Randers, and William W. Behrens III
1972   The Limits to Growth: A Report for the Club of Rome's Project on the Predicament of Mankind. New York: Universe Books, A Potomac Associates Book.

Neilands, J. B., Gordon H. Orians, E. W. Pfeiffer, Alje Vennema, and Arthur H. Westing
1972   Harvest of Death: Chemical Warfare in Vietnam and Cambodia. New York: Free Press.

Pearson, Lester B.
1969   Partners in Development: Report of the Commission on International Development. New York: Praeger.

Ridgeway, James
1970   The Politics of Ecology. New York: Dutton.

Swedish Preparatory Committee
1971   Air Pollution Across National Boundaries: Sweden's Case Study for the United Nations Conference on the Human Environment. Stockholm: Kungl. Boktryckeriet P.A. Norstedt & Söner.

White, Lynn, Jr.
1967   "The historical roots of our ecologic crisis." Science 155 (March 10): 1203–1207.

World Bank Task Force
1972   Report on the Limits to Growth.

12

Collective Behavior and Sociocultural Change

I. COLLECTIVE BEHAVIOR

For four days in March of 1970, the Urbana campus of the University of Illinois became an occupied and scarred battleground. The conflict was sparked by a Radical Union rally called to protest oncampus recruiting by General Electric, one of the nation's prime military contractors. Following the rally, several hundred students marched to the electrical engineering building where GE interviewers were conducting their business. Finding all entrances blocked by police, fifty students climbed up a fire escape and entered by a window; once inside the building, they scuffled with guards and officials.

The university board of trustees responded immediately. Directly following the news that protesting students had gained entry into the building, the board voted to cancel a planned speech by a radical lawyer, William Kunstler. He would, the board said, be a clear and present danger to the campus.

At 7 P.M. the same day, 5,000 angry students gathered at the student union, then charged through the campus and city of Urbana attacking selected targets. Hardest hit was the Armory housing the university R.O.T.C. program. Windows were broken in the administration building as well as in the chancellor's office and the mathematics department. Four hundred police were unable to contain the student mob. The following day, the campus was swarming with national guard troops augmented by the police force. Two thousand students countered with retaliating measures; 300 sat down in the third floor hallway of the Illini

Union Building where General Motors, Lockheed, Standard Oil, and U.S. Steel were trying to conduct employment interviews.

This little-publicized riot has been described in some detail here because it illustrates important aspects of what is known as *collective behavior.* All *social* action is, of course, essentially collective by definition. But collective behavior, as the term is generally used in the social sciences, has a narrower referent. In this more restricted sense, *collective behavior* is defined as group action that is not guided by established patterns or norms. Hence, *collective behavior* is the very opposite of *institutional behavior.* The former either is unorganized and unsystematic, or is an attempt (perhaps organized) to challenge one or more aspects of the existing order; the latter is the organized and systematic expression of established situations.

Two Forms of Collective Behavior   There are two basic forms of collective behavior: one, *elementary collective behavior,* the emotionalized, spontaneous variety; and the *social movement,* the more developed type. The former is characterized by erratic, often wild behavior: riots, panics, stampedes, fads, crazes, and manias. The latter is exemplified by behavior that is at least minimally predictable in terms of general direction. The importance of both types of collective behavior is that they constitute a foundation out of which new forms of sociocultural order can arise. They suggest impending social change, often giving specific dimension and direction to such change. Therefore, despite its sometimes transitory nature, collective behavior has an enduring significance. This aspect of the phenomenon prompted sociologist Herbert Blumer (1969) to outline a description of it that has achieved classic status within sociology. Most of the following discussion of collective behavior is inspired by Blumer's work; but deficiencies in what is said should not be ascribed to Blumer. The major weakness lies in the specialty of collective behavior. It is long on theory and short on empirical data. Further, the presumed inner feelings of collective behavior participants can only be inferred from overt actions. But even if alleged feelings are mistakenly attributed to given individuals or groups, no real harm is necessarily done because the significant question for sociology is not inner states as such, but: Under what *sociocultural* conditions are people prompted to engage in particular behaviors?

Elementary Collective Behavior   The genesis of collective behavior appears to be unrest or dissatisfaction with an existing situation. Structural strain, such as interest conflict, value difference, malintegration, or perceived deprivation, generates uneasiness (Smelser, 1963:Ch. 3). People experiencing such feelings, but unable to resolve them, tend to move about restlessly. Aimless movement often relieves individual tension; but a number of people stirring about in a relatively restricted area may well feel heightened arousal rather than relief—"milling" is the cause.

Milling is defined as a situation where a number of people or animals, engaging in random movement, increasingly excite one another. For example, this often happens with a large herd of cattle. On a sunlit prairie, a peacefully grazing herd is startled by the bellow of a steer, Elmer; Elsie calls an anxious query; Elmer roars back; Ferdinand sounds his response; the cattle stop eating; they are restless; there are increased bellows and responses; the chorus grows in a circular fashion; the noise becomes greater; the herd moves closer and unease multiplies; there is shoving, bumping, kicking; excitement rises; Ferdinand has had it; he takes off; look out! It's a stampede!

Similarly, humans milling develop increased awareness of one another, sometimes to the exclusion of all else. They become very suggestible, responding quickly and thoughtlessly to one another, almost as if hypnotized. If, in a milling group, one person yells excitedly, "Let's storm the jail!" everyone else may shout "Let's go!" thinking little of the immediate motives or consequences. The arousal may be so great that a stage known as *collective excitement* develops. This more intense form of milling speeds up the circular reactions of the group members. Attention concentrates inward, dimming standard ideas and values. Thus, "good citizens" can become so aroused that they will join a destructive mob, engaging in behavior they would ordinarily regard as unacceptable. The most stoic conservative can be equally affected, as was illustrated by historian E. Herbert Norman's description of religious pilgrimages in feudal Japan. These became known as *nuke-mairi*—that is, secret visits to a shrine—because:

> . . . so many participants, often women of good family who ordinarily would never venture out unattended, are seized with a sudden impulse to join the jostling crowd of pilgrims as it passes through the streets of their town, slipping off quietly without telling anyone of their departure (Norman, 1945:68).

Collective excitement that reaches an almost unbearable state results in a condition known as *social contagion.** An analogy would be an epidemic that swept across an entire population affecting nearly

* Psychologist Roger Brown is sharply critical of terms such as circular reaction, rapport, and contagion. He says they lead to pseudoexplanations that are exercises in circular reasoning. For example, it is said that contagion occurs in a mob, and a mob is defined as a collectivity in which there is a high degree of contagion (Brown, 1954:843).

everyone. This occurred during the Middle Ages when a "dance" mania gripped northwestern Europeans. For weeks on end, particularly in the German states, young and old, sick and well, swayed and leaped wildly through the streets, screaming and often foaming with fury. Falling from exhaustion, they would rest just long enough to gather their strength for a renewed burst of frenzy. Such compulsive behavior often grips almost all members of select populations. Schuler and Parenton, both sociologists, have described several examples (1943). One occurred in a large French convent where a nun began mewing like a cat. Other nuns also began "mewing." Finally, all the nuns met regularly every day and mewed for several hours without stop. Another case reported was a "nun-biting" mania that began in a fifteenth-century German nunnery when one nun bit several of her companions. Soon all the nuns in the convent were biting one another. The news spread; nuns in other convents began to bite one another. The mania did not subside until it reached to the very doors of the Vatican. More recently, a number of girls in a Louisiana high school were gripped by an apparently involuntary convulsive jerking of the muscles controlling the diaphragm, chest, neck, and legs. Several weeks passed before the hysteria ran its course and the behavior subsided.

Elementary Collective Groups   Four varieties of elementary collective groups have been identified: *acting crowds, expressive crowds,* the *mass,* and the *public.* These are termed elementary because, like their behavioral counterparts, they arise spontaneously and are not guided by established conventions or norms. The crowd groupings, acting and expressive, are just two of four types of crowds and the only ones termed elementary. The other two are called *casual* and *conventionalized.* A casual crowd is a momentary gathering without form or sense of oneness; a "sidewalk supervisor" grouping is an example. People assembling on a more formal basis, perhaps for a dramatic performance, constitute a conventionalized crowd. Casual and conventionalized crowds are not *elementary* collective groups because their actions are regulated by societal norms. Not so the acting or expressive crowd! The former is an aggressive grouping exemplified by the erratic, rioting mob; the latter group engages in nonpurposive, often rhythmic, movement.

The acting crowd is frequently spectacular: the wildcat strike, the mutiny, the lynching vigilante committee, the revolt, the craze. Acting crowds often form when a milling process builds rapport among the members of a contiguous collectivity to such a degree that most participants become possessed by a fever of anticipation. Such crowds are most likely to form when large numbers of people congregate, especially if they are lower status young men who may be generally violence-prone, have a minimal attachment to the status quo, and substantial periods of free, uncommitted time. The presence of such persons was the most important element in almost all of the riots that occurred during the 1960s (Banfield, 1970:Ch. 9; McPhail, 1971:1070). Discrimination, lack of equal job opportunity, racism, depressed living conditions—all the factors one would think ought to precipitate a riot—apparently do not, in *themselves*, generate acting crowds. However, such conditions are not irrelevant to rioting, since the conditions are products of the same causal factors producing the aimless milling numbers necessary for the acting crowd.

The expressive crowd, unlike the acting crowd, is not goal-oriented. It is made up of people who gather together, mill about, and finally express themselves in some nonpurposive manner. The prototype of such a crowd can be seen in a saturnalia—a primitive sect whose members wail and dance in unrestrained revelry. Many a religious group has begun with such behavior, perhaps in response to a wandering evangelist who is able to whip his audience into fever pitch so that speaking in "tongues" might be the expected thing to do. It was doubtless at just such a meeting, that the Holy Rollers began—one person, overcome with emotion and tension, falls to the ground and rolls about seeking relief and release; others note the sign of grace and also begin to roll; eventually, it is the nonrollers who stand out as a conspicuous minority. A similar process apparently started the Holy Jumpers. These are the Molokans who, when they lived in the Caucasus Mountains of southern Russia, often became frenzied in their practice of the Orthodox faith. At some point, one or more members began leaping during a religious service. After a while, entire congregations would leap. Very quickly, leaping in place again and again was interpreted as a sign of possession by the Holy Ghost; nonleapers then became suspect. This interpretation prevailed even after the group, persecuted by Russian authorities, moved to Los Angeles in the late nineteenth century.

The term "mass" denotes a third type of elementary collective group. Attributes of the mass, writ large, are seen in the "mass society" as described in Chapter 10. Thus, a *mass* is a relatively extensive group whose members participate jointly in some event, perhaps a land boom, yet remain largely anonymous to one another. Since the mass has no organization or history, it sustains no norms and has no established authority. Therefore, its members have no guides for individual action relative to the mass; lacking these behavioral guides, they are easily confused. As such, they are manipulable in a way similar to the excited crowd. Hence, a mass has vast potential influence if mobilized and given direction. This is a fairly easy task for a skilled demagogue whose frenzied presentations, appealing to common denominators of fear, anger, and disenchantment, can weld a fractured mass into an irresistible unity. If such a mass is the population of an entire nation or a substantial part thereof, the totalitarian threat assumes gigantic proportions and can become a reality. Post-World War I Italy is a classic example. The nation became a setting for a variety of socialist groups attempting to implement a number of basic reforms. No one group had enough of a following to dominate politically, but socialism as a doctrine was so popular that few observers felt any idea could challenge it successfully. Then Benito Mussolini and his fascist revolution burst on the scene. With their flags, uniforms, and colorful ceremonies, the fascists captured the imagination and hopes of the Italian masses. Their leader, Mussolini, once a socialist himself,

> . . . became the new Caesar, the strong, fearless man destined to restore order and prosperity to a weary nation. He promised to place Italy in her proper place, a leader in European affairs. Rome was to be born again. Glory and a New Order! For the first time in decades, Italy turned her eyes toward the future (Paget, 1929:443–444).

A fourth type of elementary collective group has been identified as the public. A *public* is a group of people who, being confronted with an issue, engage in a discussion of it. Thus, the members of a public, unlike those of a mass, interact, at least to the extent of communicating with one another. It should be noted that, as defined, a public does not refer to the devotees of a well-known individual, although the term is sometimes used that way.

A public is an elementary grouping because it arises spontaneously as issues develop; the very fact that there is uncertainty relative to what must be done about an issue implies that existing values, organizations, and norms do not, in themselves, settle the problem. If they did, there would be no issue and, thus, no public. Discussion about an unresolved issue means that one can speak of *public opinion*—the central tendency of the variety of opinions existing in a given public relative to a given issue. Defined this way, public opinion does not denote the ideas of all members of a particular public; indeed, it may express the feelings of a small minority alone if the minority is especially influential, an influence that may rest on control of propaganda instruments. For present purposes *propaganda* can be defined as any covert technique to manipulate public opinion for the selfish purposes of those who employ the technique. Thus, propagandists attempt to make biased statements seem unbiased; in contrast, educators—unless they are simply propagandists who adopt a more socially acceptable title—openly label biases, including their own.

Social Movements   Some of the unfortunate elements humankind has been able to count on are injustice, greed, intolerance, and exploitation. But we have also been able to depend on the appearance of social movements to challenge the injustice and those who perpetrate it. The question arises: From whence come the movements that give us hope? The answer is that they arise from the elementary collective behaviors and groupings that are the first manifestations of uneasiness, fear, or dissatisfaction.

Social movements are formally defined as collective attempts to establish new sociocultural forms. In the earlier stages, such movements are loose groupings. However, with time, given movements may become more stable, organized, and systematic, manifesting the characteristics of institutionalized phenomena. "Organization," Michels pointed out, ". . . is the weapon of the weak in their struggle with the strong (1962:61).

Three types of social movements can be identified: general, specific, and expressive. A *general social movement* is simultaneously an indicator of a broad drift in cultural values and a relatively uncoordinated, widespread attempt to see that the values become well established. The women's liberation movement is one typical example— representing a trend in values toward that day when male dominance has ceased, at the same time, it is an attempt on the part of those with vested interest in the trend to see that it accelerates and its base widens. These attempts often generate specific social movements such as NOW, the National Organization for Women.

In a *specific social movement*, general directions are supplanted by carefully defined goals, and uncoordinated efforts are organized for greater efficiency and stability within the organization. Two important types of specific social movements are *reform* and *revolutionary*. A *reform movement's* aim is to change aspects of a system by using methods generally accepted by system participants; a *revolutionary movement* attempts, by any means necessary, to overturn the existing social system. A third significant variety of specific social movement can be termed the *retreatist*. It attempts neither to reform nor to overturn the existing order; rather, it counsels withdrawal in one form or another. The Marcus Garvey back-to-Africa movement of the 1920s is an example. One of the Garvey movement's current "descendants," the Nation of Islam (Black Muslims), urges black Americans to live and work totally apart from white America.

Success for any of these movements depends, of course, upon effective tactics. Blumer mentions four additional success variables, all of which, along with tactics, he terms "mechanisms": agitation, *esprit de corps*, high morale, and a compelling ideology. The special role of *agitation* was recently described by the editor of the periodical

Chemical and Engineering News in answer to complaints about "environmental alarmists":

> If real and steady progress is to be made in improving the quality of the environment then, perhaps, continuous and steady, albeit modest, inputs of alarm, panic and hysteria are required of interested citizens. Otherwise, progress comes haltingly, if at all. . . . Only when the complaints of the citizenry have become strident, when measured alarm, panic, and hysteria come on the environmental scene, has any real action toward general pollution abatement taken place. A rational, systematic, scientific approach seems to work better with a healthy dollop of emotion added (*Arizona Republic*, October 28, 1970).

Frederick Douglass, once a slave, put it very well:

> . . . Those who profess to favor freedom, and yet depreciate agitation, are men who want crops without plowing up the ground. They want rain without thunder and lightning. They want the ocean without the awful roar of its waters. This struggle may be moral; or it may be physical; or both moral and physical; but it must be a struggle. Power concedes nothing without a demand. It never did, and it never will (Goodman, 1970:135).

While agitation serves to obtain recruits to a movement, *esprit de corps* gives movement participants a sense of oneness in their endeavors. It builds a feeling of unity, closeness, and camaraderie that inspires and strengthens. It is engendered by cultivation of the idea that movement members are *in* and everyone else is *out*. Such feelings are enhanced by informal fellowship gatherings and ceremonial observances extolling the virtues of movement membership. The TOPS (Taking Off Pounds Sensibly) meeting procedure is one example. Each gathering begins with this dialogue:

> *Leader:* Who pounds at our door?
> *Recorder:* Not who pounds. What pounds?
> *All:* Surplus Pounds!
> *Leader:* Pounds Off! (Toch, 1965:73).

This exchange is followed by a procession during which members join hands and sing:

> The more we get together,
> Together, together—
> The more we get together,
> The slimmer we'll be.
> For your loss is my loss;

And my loss is your loss;
The more we get together
The slimmer we'll be.

Clever leaders of embattled social movements are particularly concerned with maintaining *esprit de corps*. One way of doing this, even under stress, is to minimize differences between leaders and followers, especially during periods of hardship. Thus does Jules Roy explain the late Ho Chi Minh's uncanny ability to survive as a leader of his people despite more than a quarter century of unending war and total opposition by three powerful nations (France, Japan, and the United States):

> There is nothing to distinguish their generals from their private soldiers except the star they wear on their collars. Their uniform is cut out of the same wretched material, they wear the same boots, their cork helmets are identical and their colonels go on foot like privates. They live on the rice they carry on them, on the tubers they pull out of the forest earth, on the fish they catch and on the water of the mountain streams. No beautiful secretaries, no prepackaged rations, no cars or fluttering pennants . . . no military bands. But victory, damn it, victory! (Roy: 1965:304).

Relative to any given social movement, *high morale* is defined as a widely felt and deeply experienced conviction that the ideals of the movement will eventually triumph. This conviction is enhanced by stressing the idea that the movement is "in tune with the infinite." It represents reality as it must be, as it shall be, as it will be. "I present to you the next President of the United States" is often the phrase of those who introduce presidential candidates. By assuming that sure victory is imminent, leadership attempts to create and maintain high morale, knowing that a lowered morale would only cause despair and decline in effort. It was with such ideas in mind that Susan B. Anthony, women's liberation pioneer during the nineteenth century, said upon retiring from active campaigning (Kern, 1971:44), "I have never lost my faith, not for a moment in 50 years." And, although only four states had adopted woman suffrage by the time Mrs. Anthony died in 1906, her last words to her followers were, "Failure is impossible!" Similarly, Marxists are sustained, even in the darkest hours, by the belief Karl Marx himself first expressed: The triumph of the proletariat is inevitable.

The role of *ideology* in social movements is to present to movement participants and potential recruits a coherent statement describing the nature of reality while indicating how it should be changed. Thus, an ideology is a body of doctrine giving both direction and hope. It specifies the range of effective weapons that may be used, while stimulating believers to expend their greatest efforts to achieve common goals. Among the ingredients of effective ideology are inspiring myths, stories about hero pioneers, and symbolism that has wide appeal.

Finally, we come to the *expressive social movement*. Such movements generally seem less important than reform and revolutionary movements; nevertheless, they are no less fascinating. There are two basic types: *religious movements* and *fashion movements*. The characteristic feature encompassing both is that they embody largely nonpurposive behavior, at least from an ordinary practical point of view. Thus, unlike reform and revolutionary movements, expressive movements do not aim to change the world in any fundamental way; instead, they give their participants opportunities for engaging in ceremonial and related behavior so that inner feelings can be satisfactorily expressed. Religious examples of this kind of movement have previously been mentioned— the Holy Rollers, the Holy Jumpers, the Methodists, the Quakers, to name but a few.

Fashion movements, too, provide opportunity for expressive behavior. Fashion can be defined as a relatively short-lived folkway evoking rather widespread conformity because of the status value involved. Thus, fashion does not prevail in the small, equalitarian society. It is uniquely a feature of a stratified society made up of groups having differential status. Select behavior of those having high status is often emulated, especially such overt expressions as clothing. But almost anything can become fashionable, as noted during the 1960s when students on some campuses were heard to say, "They're having riots all over. What's wrong with us? Maybe we should start one."

The aim of *new* fashions is to set the initiators apart from the mainstream. Young male counterculture advocates during the 1960s wore their hair long to symbolize the rejection of traditional norms. However, the symbolic value of wearing long hair lost its significance when older men began emulating the young. The result is that long hair on males today is solely a fashion and, therefore, purely a temporary phenomenon, no more significant than high heels or wide lapels.

The Importance of Collective Behavior   Although some aspects of collective behavior may strike the casual observer as trivial, it is clear that when considered in toto collective behavior has a fundamental importance. It is such behavior, in one form or another, that underlies the seemingly more important sociocultural order. On the other hand, collective behavior is often a prime ingredient in a breakdown of order; the Russian Revolution is one example. Collective behavior, thus, is a harbinger of change as well as a cause of it. This may be true even when the collective behavior involved is nothing more than fashion initially— that "nothing more" may lead to a riot that subsequently may be instrumental in the fall of a major government.

II. SOCIOCULTURAL CHANGE

Systematic study of sociocultural changes brought about by collective behavior and other forces (such as cultural trends, natural disasters, inventions, and so forth) has become a sociological specialty. This would seem to imply that change, like collective behavior, has definite characteristics setting it apart from other aspects of human life. But this is not the case. Instead, as sociologist Neil Smelser has pointed out (1967:674), sociocultural change as a focus of study lies uneasily on the borderline between history and sociology, threatening constantly to engulf the parent disciplines—or to be engulfed by them.

Theories of Change   The difficulty of delineating the boundaries of sociocultural change has not prevented the development of numerous theories intending to explain the nature of change. These theories can be grouped into five general categories: *evolutionist, accretionary, Marxian, functionalist,* and *cyclical.* The essence of the evolutionary approach is the belief that sociocultural systems, or aspects of them, grow just as organisms do, each stage of growth having inherent in it the necessary elements for subsequent stages. An example of such a theory was presented earlier in Chapter 3—the description of Auguste Comte's belief that the scientific outlook in various fields is the end product of a three-stage growth process. Another evolutionary theorist, Sir James Frazer (1951), asserted that modern religion is simply an outgrowth of magic that is a primitive form of science.

The evolutionary perspective also appears in the more recent works of those who stress the "natural history" of various phenomena. Historian Crane Brinton's *The Anatomy of Revolution* (1965) is one example. Brinton found that the typical revolution proceeds through stages characterized by economic difficulties, government weakness, defection on the part of intellectuals, replacement of traditional authority by moderate new authority, replacement of moderates by extremists, gradual moderation of the extremists, institutionalization of some of the revolutionary aims, and, finally, reestablishment of most of the prerevolutionary norms and social structures. In short, as the French put it, *Plus ça change, plus c'est la même chose* (that is, the more things change, the more they are the same).

Accretionary theories of change stress the fact that in most societies there is a gradual accumulation of sociocultural elements. These accumulations, resulting from culture borrowing and evolutionary development, are important because they constitute a broadening of the culture base which, in turn, expands the possibilities for new combinations of sociocultural elements. The phrase "new combinations of sociocultural elements" is the sociological definition of *invention;* it is inventions that are most emphasized by accretion theorists. Inventions are termed prime, perhaps *the* prime, agents or instruments of change (Herman, 1949:58). According to one theorist, William Fielding Ogburn, it is material inventions in particular that accumulate (1950:73–79; 103–118); nonmaterial things are simply replaced. Therefore, Ogburn concluded, material culture tends to change rapidly in comparison with related nonmaterial changes; the lag of the latter leads to strain, said Ogburn, causing social problems. This theory, although provocative, has been disparaged on the grounds that priority of material change neglects the fact that such change is necessarily preceded by relevant value and knowledge (that is, nonmaterial) change.

The Marxian theory of change holds that the only significant determining factor in society is the relationship of individuals and groups to the means of production. Those who control production, said Marx, control humanity; sociocultural change of consequence occurs only when there is a fundamental alteration in the ownership or control of production. This enormously influential theory of order and change has been severely criticized by sociologist Max Weber and others, who point out that although economic factors are vastly significant, they are often consequences of other aspects of life such as education or religion. Weber's chief example was the important part played by Protestantism in the creation of capitalism, as detailed earlier in Chapter 9.

The functionalist school of thought has given rise to change theory focusing on the dissolution of order. Functionalism stresses the contributions that sociocultural traits and complexes make to an integrated system:

> The *function* of any recurrent activity, such as the punishment of a crime, or a funeral ceremony, is the part it plays in the social life as a whole and therefore the contribution it makes to the maintenance of the structural continuity (Radcliffe-Brown, 1952:180).

With the emphasis on sociocultural order, functionalists have generally thought of change primarily in terms of a breakdown in system maintenance; hence, they speak of dysfunction and strain as making a system susceptible to change. One variation on this theme is the *social disorganization* theory of problems; the disorganization theorist asserts that problems arise or are aggravated when a social system loses control over its parts. This stress on control, order, and strain has given rise to intense criticism of the functionalist viewpoint. It is a view that almost invariably favors the status quo since it uses the established order as the base for measurement. In terms of such a base, almost all variations are deviant, disruptive, and contentious.

Finally, there are the cyclical theories of change which have been widely popular. Two of the best known were developed by historian

Arnold Toynbee and sociologist Pitirim Sorokin. Toynbee's theory, as explicated at length in his twelve-volume *A Study of History* (1934–1961), asserts that change occurs depending upon how challenge is handled. Change is "progressive" if the response to challenge is creative; if it is not, change is regressive to the point where a civilization may withdraw and finally die. To Toynbee, the pattern of challenge-response-withdrawal recurs throughout history and can be discerned in the lifestory of twenty-six civilizations including Greece, Rome, and Egypt.

A somewhat similar cyclical theory of historical change was described in Sorokin's *Social and Cultural Dynamics* (1957). Sorokin felt that change is an inherent part of any sociocultural system, a fundamental point that he termed "the principle of immanent causation" (1957:18; 254–255). The specific nature of change, and of given sociocultural systems, said Sorokin, is a function of the degree to which a system is *sensate* (emphasizes material phenomena) or *ideational* (emphasizes spiritual concerns), or is a mixture of the two *(idealistic)* (1957:Ch. 2). Sorokin's use of such categories aroused a criticism that applies to all-encompassing historical theories in general: They typically involve the use of data that are classified according to an individual's ideas; hence, there is no sure way of testing the value of the theory as an explanation.

Induced Change   The fundamental task of philosophy, said Marx, is not to study change; it is to create it in a progressive sense. Sentiments of this type generate reactions from sociologists such that the critical difference between "old" and "new" sociology is thrown into sharp relief. The difference is not necessarily chronological as one might assume from the adjectives; nor from the writer's point of view is it primarily methodological (that is, the best of both the "new" and "old" sociologists are scientists in the sense that they are thoroughly committed to obtaining representative data and analyzing it carefully). The difference is a fundamental clash in values that prompts "old" sociologists to disagree with Marx. These sociologists prefer to divorce themselves from ideological battles; their prime concern is to be technically accurate in making abstract analyses. In contrast, advocates of "new" sociology, concurring with Marx, do not try to remain free of ideological involvement. In the first place, they feel that "value-free" scientists, whether intentionally or not, give tacit support to the existing order, so it is an illusion that one can divorce oneself from ideological contests. Secondly, new sociologists perceive that both they and their discipline would be the first to go if a totalitarian regime were to prevail. So, unabashedly and unapologetically they throw themselves into political affairs, attempting always to help forces that are the most humanistic—that is, democratic, equalitarian, nonexploitive, civil libertarian, and ecologically sensitive.

The differences between traditional sociology and humanistic sociology intended for a new day are most apparent when students and citizens in general become concerned about social problems. They so often ask, "What can we do? How can we help? How can we work to change the situation for the better?" A traditional sociologist might likely answer, "I cannot give advice. But if you tell me your goals, I'll try to indicate all the costs of the various ways given goals can be achieved." The traditional sociologist would not presume to comment on goals or make value judgments on the ethical nature of means to achieve them.

Not so the new sociologist! The humanistic sociologist is inclined to say, "I am glad to give advice on matters for which I am qualified; but my help is available only to those pledged to humanistic values and methods." Further, he would feel the need to participate fully in political, economic, and educational contests. Even more than that, a pressing professional and personal obligation to participate is felt. Of course, the particular form of participation varies with personality and political needs of the moment.

Despite the important differences between representatives of the old and the new sociology ideologically, they commonly answer in unison to purely factual or benign instrumental questions such as, "How fast can sociocultural change occur?" or "How can change be induced?" Their answer to the first question is, in general, "Very slowly." Any full-fledged sociocultural system is best compared to a gigantic gyroscope; it resists sharp changes in direction and orientation. It *can* be changed, but only with relatively smallscale nudges. The same is true of sociocultural systems; they change very slowly, barring most unusual circumstances such as a national catastrophe. This is why, with small exception, the characteristic last step in the revolutionary process is "return to most of the . . . interactions in the old network" (Brinton, 1965:258).*

When queried about how change can be induced, social scientists in general can provide an accurate answer in one word:

ORGANIZATION

---

* It is too early to tell at the time of writing if this generalization will apply to Communist China; however, past experience would lead a gambler concerned with favorable odds to rely on it. In addition, there is the complication that the communist message was highly compatible to a number of important aspects of traditional Chinese culture; this compatibility purportedly led Max Weber to predict, as early as 1918, that China would be "next" (after Russia) to become communistic. Such compatibility suggests that recent changes in China are not, in a strict sense, revolutionary.

This answer is a disappointment for many. Either it seems too simple to be believable, or it implies too much work and delay. But historical experience suggests there is no other logical way. There are no shortcuts to solving complex problems; there is no magical answer, no mystical road to salvation. There is just:

ORGANIZATION

As indicated earlier in the quotation from Michels, it is *organization* that is "the weapon of the weak in their struggle with the strong" (1962:61).

Skeptics can be referred to the innumerable historical examples showing that aroused citizens, when organized, can do remarkable things. For example, consider black Americans in southern states; during countless decades they have been victims of discriminatory practices in education, hiring and firing, voter registration, and the like. But when sufficiently mobilized during the 1960s, they *organized* marches, confrontations, and voter registration drives that have radically and perhaps permanently altered the political balance of power in the South. Much more improvement is obviously needed, but few still speak of "hapless darkies."

Other examples come to mind: When American pioneers *organized* as a new nation, they successfully carried out a war of national liberation. As another example, once *organized*, auto workers ceased to be ready victims for greedy entrepreneurs. Unionized (that is, *organized*) teachers have similarly begun to exercise some control over their economic destiny. The contrary principle is similarly instructive, as illustrated in Alexander and Beringer's description of the Confederate Congress which sat from 1861 to 1865. Confederate officials spurned the idea of formal party organizations on the grounds that parties are divisive. But those who rejected the party system also unwittingly killed any realistic hopes of establishing effective alternatives to executive decisions. Therefore, when some Southerners attempted during 1864 to counter the measures of President Jefferson Davis and bring the war to a quick end, they were powerless: "The structure was not just faulty; it was fatally deficient" (Alexander and Beringer, 1972:342).

"People's Organizations" can achieve remarkable results even under the most depressing circumstances. This is the message of social activist Saul Alinsky's *Reveille for Radicals* (1969). During the 1940s and 1950s, Alinsky went into the most deprived neighborhoods in Chicago's "back of the yards" district in an attempt to help residents find some relief for living conditions described as "Intolerable—but what can you do?" Alinsky's answer was to act as a catalytic agent:

> This has always been the prime task of the organizer—the transformation of the plight into the problem (1969:209; original italicized).

The resulting "people's organization" that was set up was based on the idea that, to be successful, it must: 1) concentrate solely on practically achievable goals desired by members, not outsiders, 2) be led by indigenous people who are "natural leaders" in the sense that others look up to them without question, 3) utilize, not challenge, local traditions, and 4) involve the people at large—"It is impossible to overemphasize the enormous importance of people's doing things themselves" (1969:174). Alinsky does not apply these principles to local scenes alone:

> The program of a real People's Organization calmly accepts the overwhelming fact that all problems are related and that they are all the progeny of certain fundamental causes, that ultimate success in conquering these evils can be achieved only by victory over all evils. For that reason a people's program is limited only by the horizon of humanity itself (1969:59-60).

Occasionally the question arises, "Shall we go to the barricades?" The new sociology counsels: Recall the historical reality that truly basic changes in sociocultural systems are almost always realized only in the long run. Note, too, the historical experience that armed revolt (except wars of national liberation) has typically degenerated into simply a substitution of one band of exploitive thieves for another (for example, Napoleonic France, Stalinist Russia, and China in the 1920s). One should also not be misled by those who cry out against all authority. In truth, civil society shorn of authority is a contradiction; it is properly designated a jungle.

But if those in power are *sufficiently* arbitrary, then it is reasonable to ask about going to the barricades. However, such revolutionary action is not sensible unless three conditions prevail: 1) the existing order is genuinely intolerable, 2) there is no peaceful way to improve the situation from within, and 3) there is widespread support for fundamental change (Berger and Neuhaus, 1970:esp. 50-63; 190-214). Such cautions are necessary because resorting to revolution is most serious and should occur only in situations of extreme despair. It cannot be indulged in "for the hell of it"; it, and the answering counterrevolution, shatters families, separates friends and lovers, and almost always generates the most vicious kind of violence, terrorism, and elimination of those who advise moderation.

> The "best" of the reformers must be ranked with the regime itself as enemies of the revolution. Second-phase armed revolution in the United States at present requires the effective elimination of persons such as Galbraith, McGovern, McCarthy, Randolph, Harrington, Goodwin, Chávez, and, if

someone had not already seen to it, Martin Luther King (Neuhaus, in Berger and Neuhaus, 1970:221).

Revolution is, furthermore, a lifetime commitment, not something from which one withdraws when weary. If successful, it must be followed by a tremendous organizational effort to insure even a minimal achievement of the desired goals; if unsuccessful, its proponents are defined as traitors, maligned, and eliminated.

Despite the serious limitations and difficulties inherent in revolt, many of those who guide their behavior by humanistic values as described in this text agree that under certain circumstances various acts of disobedience to established authority become a sad duty for all humanitarians; of course, this includes new-day sociologists. In the words of the Declaration of Independence,

> . . . all Experience hath shewn, that Mankind are more disposed to suffer, while Evils are sufferable, than to right themselves by abolishing the Forms to which they are accustomed. But when a long Train of Abuses and Usurpations, pursuing invariably the same Object, evinces a Design to reduce them under absolute Despotism, it is their Right, it is their Duty, to throw off such Government, and to provide new Guards for their future Security.

Or, as the point was phrased by Abraham Lincoln at his first inaugural in 1861: "This country . . . belongs to the people who inhabit it. Whenever they shall grow weary of the existing government, they can exercise their constitutional right to amend it, or their revolutionary right to dismember or overthrow it." The humanistic principle, underlying both the Declaration and President Lincoln's observation, is this: Government must be resisted if it persists in actions that are grossly inhumane, particularly when those actions involve matters of life and death. Examples include drafting men to fight indefensible wars, using weapons that damage indiscriminately, incarcerating people solely on the basis of race or national origin, conniving in genocidal ecological action or in discriminatory treatment that condemns whole groups to lives of degradation (for example, blacks in the United States). Opposition to such programs has to be very subtle if reformists are particularly weak. But tactical needs of the moment may necessitate open confrontation, various forms of which range from nonviolent resistance to fullscale revolution.

Violence on the part of an aggrieved populace is, of course, roundly condemned by officials threatened to the point where they speak in accusatory tones about the evil of those who "go outside the system" and use "illegal" means. But those who are historically aware know that, for example, literally nothing was gained in civil rights so long as interested parties confined their efforts and activities to purely legal techniques. And as for the violence that revolutions involve, it is relevant to quote Thomas Paine's answer to a complaint made by English statesman Edmund Burke. It was, said Burke, "barbaric" for Parisian revolutionists during 1789 to impale the heads of several victims on spikes and march triumphantly through the streets. Paine replied,

> . . . examine how men came by the idea of punishing in this manner.
> They learn it from the Governments they live under, and retaliate the punishments they have been accustomed to behold. . . .
> Lay then the axe to the root, and teach Governments humanity. It is their sanguinary punishments which corrupt mankind (1915:31–32).

To bring the point into a modern perspective, government officials today are in a morally indefensible position to condemn violence when they have, to name but a few: dropped napalm on noncombatant village farmers and children in "free fire zones"; used A-bombs to kill hundreds of thousands; ecologically damaged a whole country (Vietnam), probably permanently, for military reasons; engaged in the obscene hypocrisy of toasting "peace" in Moscow while the United States and Russia busily contributed to genocide in the Far East.

If what has been said above implies radicalism, that was intended. Radical action is often the only way to achieve humanistic goals. So, the humanistic new sociologist is in many respects a radical. The radical— *not* the leftist extremist whose excesses simply provide an excuse for rightwing extremists to use wholesale repression—adheres to the promise of the democratic ideal:

> He is angry with and hates those parts of the body politic that have broken faith with the future, with the dreams and hopes of a free way of life.
> His is a quest for a future . . . a world where all the revolutionary slogans of the past would come to life: "Love your neighbor as you would love yourself"; "You are your brother's keeper"; "Liberty, Fraternity, Equality"; "All men are created equal"; "Peace and bread"; "For the general welfare"; a world where the Judeo-Christian values and the promise of the American Constitution would be made real (Alinsky, 1969:xvii).

The above quote suggests that the true radical is paradoxically conservative, wanting to regain and preserve the most fundamental values. In America, these are freedom of expression, freedom to challenge the prevailing order and change it when necessary, and freedom from arbitrary economic, governmental, and business decisions. In contrast, we have—riding high, as spokesmen for the establishment— those un-American extremists who support special tax and marketing privileges for the rich alone, business interests that have exploited nature to the degree that worldwide ecological disaster is a likely long-term result, and armament policies that promise megadeath (from atomic fallout) for all. These are the programs supported by those who describe themselves as "realists," and "practical, hardheaded business-men." With such "realism," given the nature of modern technology and speed of change, it seems obvious that the forces of darkness will win the impending battle of Armageddon.

Unless. Unless. There is still hope that the unrealistic, meek, imprac-tical, sentimental humanists can coalesce into a force of light. As Nathan Wright, Jr., a black activist, has put it: "Our times call for men, women, and perhaps especially young people who will work to chart a new day by firmly setting aside the shibboleths of the past and by looking openly toward the future sure of but one thing: Those whose eyes are cast backward are lost (1968:257). Looking back, we see that the past has been characterized by war, racism, sexism, exploitation, disease, and disaster. The future need not be. In the words of a favorite hymn:

> Earth might be fair and all men glad and wise.
> Age after age their tragic empires rise,
> Built while they dream, and in that dreaming
>   weep;
> Would man but wake from out his haunted
>   sleep,
> Earth might be fair and all men glad and wise.*

---

* The phraseology of part of my last two paragraphs is adapted from a piece done originally for *Phi Kappa Phi Journal* (Hoult, 1971); the hymn is from *Hymns for the Celebration of Life* (Boston: The Beacon Press, 1964), No. 196.

REFERENCES AND FURTHER SOURCES

Alexander, Thomas B. and Richard E. Beringer
1972   The Anatomy of the Confederate Congress: A Study of the Influence of Member Characteristics on Legislative Voting Behavior, 1861–1865. Nashville, Tenn.: Vanderbilt University Press.

Alinsky, Saul D.
1969   Reveille for Radicals. New York: Vintage.

Banfield, Edward C.
1970   The Unheavenly City: The Nature and Future of Our Urban Crisis. Boston: Little, Brown.

Berger, Peter L. and Richard John Neuhaus
1970   Movement and Revolution. Garden City, N.Y.: Doubleday.

Blumer, Herbert
1969   "Collective Behavior." Pp. 65–121 in Alfred McClung Lee (ed.), Principles of Sociology. New York: Barnes & Noble. Third edition.

Brinton, Crane
1965   The Anatomy of Revolution. New York: Vintage. Revised and expanded edition.

Brown, Roger W.
1954   "Mass phenomena." Pp. 833–873 in Gardner Lindzey (ed.), Handbook of Social Psychology. Reading, Mass.: Addison-Wesley.

Frazer, Sir James George
1951   The Golden Bough: A Study in Magic and Religion. New York: Macmillan. One volume, abridged, new-plate edition of the 1922 original.

Goodman, Mitchell (ed.)
1970   The Movement Toward a New America: The Beginnings of a Long Revolution. New York: Knopf.

Herman, Abbott P.
1949   An Approach to Social Problems. Boston: Ginn.

Hoult, Thomas Ford
1971   "The radicalization of intellectuals and the quality of life." Phi Kappa Phi Journal 51 (Spring): 55–65.

Kern, Edward
1971   "Women's fight for the vote." Life 71 (August 20): 40–50a.

McPhail, Clark
1971   "Civil disorder participation: A critical examination of recent research." American Sociological Review 36 (December): 1058–1073.

Michels, Robert
  1962   Political Parties: A Sociological Study of the Oligarchical Tendencies of Modern Democracy. Translated by Eden and Ceder Paul. New York: Collier. Originally published in 1915.

Norman, E. Herbert
  1945   "Mass hysteria in Japan." Far Eastern Survey 14 (May 28): 65–70.

Ogburn, William Fielding
  1950   Social Change: With Respect to Culture and Original Nature. New York: Viking Press. New 1950 edition with supplementary chapter.

Paget, Edwin H.
  1929   "Sudden changes in group opinion." Social Forces 7 (March): 438–444.

Paine, Thomas
  1915   Rights of Man: Being an Answer to Mr. Burke's Attack on the French Revolution. London: Dent. Originally published in 1791.

Radcliffe-Brown, A. R.
  1952   Structure and Function in Primitive Society: Essays and Addresses. Glencoe, Ill.: Free Press.

Roy, Jules
  1965   The Battle of Dienbienphu. Translated by Robert Baldick. New York: Harper & Row.

Schuler, Edgar A. and Vernon J. Parenton
  1943   "A recent epidemic of hysteria in a Louisiana high school." Journal of Social Psychology 17 (n.d.): 221–235.

Smelser, Neil J.
  1963   Theory of Collective Behavior. New York: Free Press of Glencoe.

Smelser, Neil J. (ed.)
  1967   Sociology: An Introduction. New York: Wiley.

Sorokin, Pitirim
  1957   Social and Cultural Dynamics: A Study of Change in Major Systems of Art, Truth, Ethics, Law and Social Relationships. Boston: Sargent. Revised and abridged in one volume by the author.

Toch, Hans
  1965   The Social Psychology of Social Movements. Indianapolis: Bobbs-Merrill.

Toynbee, Arnold
  1934–1961   A Study of History. New York: Oxford University Press. 12 volumes.

Wright, Nathan, Jr.
  1968   Let's Work Together. New York: Hawthorn.

Glossary *

* These terms are defined in greater detail, and usually are illustrated with appropriate quotations from the literature, in Thomas Ford Hoult (compiler), *Dictionary of Modern Sociology* (Totowa, New Jersey: Littlefield, Adams and Co., 1969).

accommodation A social process such as arbitration that reduces conflict between groups or individuals.

acculturation An anthropological concept denoting the process whereby people adopt aspects of cultures that are not their native one; equivalent to the sociological concept *assimilation*.**

achieved status See *status*.

ascribed status See *status*.

assimilation A fusion process wherein immigrants lose visibility as they adopt the culture of their new area; equivalent to the anthropological concept *acculturation*.

association An organized *group*.

associational society The relatively largescale society that is highly urbanized and industrialized, and characterized by a complex *division of labor* and a predominance of *secondary group* relationships; sometimes termed *secular society*. See *communal society*.

attitude An individual's learned tendency to react positively or negatively to given stimuli.

authority A special form of *power* that is based on *legitimacy*.

* These terms are defined in greater detail, and usually are illustrated with appropriate quotations from the literature, in Thomas Ford Hoult (compiler), *Dictionary of Modern Sociology* (Totowa, New Jersey: Littlefield, Adams and Co., 1969).

** Italicized terms are separately defined in the glossary.

berdache   An American Indian male who wore women's clothes and did women's work.

bureaucracy   A group of people who are formally organized so that there is a clearly defined *division of labor* and chain of command.

caste   A major *social stratum* in a system of *social stratification* in which stratum membership is directly inherited and relatively immutable. See *class*.

clan   A group of people who, counting descent from a common ancestor, think of themselves as a kin group whose members have family-type rights and responsibilities relative to one another; sometimes termed "sib."

class   A major *social stratum* in a system of *social stratification* in which stratum membership is relatively acquirable. See *caste*.

classless society   The utopia of classical Marxists, characterized by universal brotherhood, fair distribution of privilege and power, and a subsequent withering away of government.

closed class system   The most rigid *class* system of *social stratification*.

collective behavior   Group action that is not guided by established patterns or norms. See *elementary collective behavior* and *social movement*.

collective excitement   An intense form of *milling*.

common law   Law that is based on custom rather than on written statute; thus distinguished from *statutory law*.

communal society   A relatively small, homogeneous society characterized by the predominance of *primary group* relationships, attachment to tradition, and minimal *division of labor*. See *associational society*.

communist   A social philosophy stressing that in the ideal society a general commitment to the welfare of all societal participants makes private property undesirable; loosely used by Westerners to designate countries that are officially committed to a collectivist economy administered by an authoritarian government.

community   Interdependent grouping of relatively like-minded persons living somewhat permanently in a geographically limited area that serves as a focus for a major portion of the residents' daily life.

competition   A *social process* wherein two or more people or groups make a regulated attempt to achieve a goal that is such that goal achievement by one party precludes full goal achievement by the others.

concept   An idea about a class of phenomena (in contrast to "percept," which is an idea about a single phenomenon) denoted by a technical term peculiar to a learned discipline.

conflict   A *social process* wherein two or more persons or groups seek to block one another in reaching a goal or to injure, defeat, or annihilate one another.

consciousness of kind The tendency of people to be favorably inclined toward those perceived as having similar *values*.

conservative The political outlook that traditional social arrangements are in accordance with reason and justice.

cooperation A *social process* wherein two or more individuals or groups work together to achieve a shared goal.

correlation The degree to which related phenomena change relative to each other in response to some influence.

crescive institution Well-established organization or process that has no specific, traceable beginning.

cultural relativism The philosophic position that there is no scientific basis for making ultimate judgments about society and culture.

culture All the things that humans acquire purely as an aspect of social life; the total way of life unique to a people and the associated meanings passed on from generation to generation.

culture base The total array of *culture traits* in a sociocultural system.

culture complex One of the interrelated sets of *culture traits* in a sociocultural system.

culture pattern One of the enduring organizations of *culture traits* and *culture complexes* in a sociocultural system.

culture trait One of the functionally simplest elements in a sociocultural system—analogous to a separate part of an automobile engine.

demography The statistical study of continuing factors that alter the size and composition of populations.

determinism The philosophic position that phenomena are best explained in terms of the most immediate factors antecedent to them.

deviant In the broadest sense, an individual who engages in behavior that is noticeably different from the average; usually denotes the person who engages in disapproved behavior that goes beyond community tolerance limits.

division of labor Separation of a total work process into interdependent tasks.

Down's syndrome The condition affecting individuals who, being born with an extra chromosome, suffer from various metabolic imbalances that cause degrees of brain damage and facial deformation; commonly termed "mongolism."

economy All the components involved in the production, distribution, and consumption of goods and services in a society.

education Any dissemination of knowledge, or knowledge that people acquire; the relatively formal *socialization* processes involved in systematic instruction.

elementary collective behavior   Emotion-charged, spontaneous group behavior; the least organized form of *collective behavior.*

empiricism   The philosophic position that only sense impressions are a reliable source of scientific knowledge.

enacted institution   A well-established organization or process that is consciously developed by people with a specific purpose in mind.

endogamy   Relative to a social group, mate selection within the group. See *exogamy.*

esprit de corps   Feeling of unity within a social group or movement.

estate   A major *social stratum* in a relatively rigid *social stratification* system wherein stratum membership, together with duties, powers, and privileges of membership, is defined by law as well as by custom. See *caste.*

ethnic   Pertaining to a particular sociocultural group; in the United States often refers to characteristics of immigrant groups; usually denotes lower-middle-class and upper-lower-class Americans who are in general the Catholic descendants of immigrants from southern and eastern Europe, plus many of those of Irish descent.

ethnocentrism   The attitude that one's own sociocultural system is superior to all others.

cthnomethodology   Primarily by means of participant observation, systematic study of the hidden formal factors underlying informal interaction patterns.

exogamy   Relative to a social group, mate selection outside the group. See *endogamy.*

extended family   Either (a) a kinship group consisting of a married couple, their children, and a number of other relatives, all sharing a common domicile, or (b) a set of marital groupings living in close association and related through the male line ("patrilineal extended") or the female line ("matrilineal extended").

extremist   A person whose apparent major need is to be caught up in a vigorous social movement to gain a sense of being larger than self; distinguished from a *radical* by the nonintellectual nature of his tie to a group.

family   A group of closely related people, especially when the nucleus of the group is a married couple and their children.

fascist   An extreme *rightwing* government, highly centralized, autocratic, and military-based, that puts special stress on protecting the power and privilege of the middle class.

fecundity   Reproductive capacity. See *fertility.*

feral   A form of *isolate;* a human who has allegedly been reared by animals other than humans.

fertility   Reproductive performance. See *fecundity.*

folk society   A small, intimate society in which all members tend to think of one another as "one of the folks."

folkway   A *norm;* in a society, a customary way of behaving, nonobservance of which is punished by only minor inconvenience; thus distinguished from *mos.*

formal social organization   Carefully specified behavioral rules and relationship regulations governing a grouping of people.

free will   See *indeterminism.*

functional-structuralism   See *structural-functionalism.*

Gemeinschaft   German word meaning *community;* in modern sociology, used to designate social groups or relationships wherein participants treat one another as whole persons, as ends, as important in themselves—for example, the *ideal type* mother-child relationship.

gene   An element of the germ plasm that transmits hereditary characteristics.

general social movement   A more-or-less uncoordinated, widespread attempt to see that particular values become better established.

Gesellschaft   A German word meaning *society;* in modern sociology, used to designate social situations where relationships among participants are segmented and specialized and where people therefore treat one another as means, not ends—for example, the *ideal type* buyer-seller relationship.

government   In an area, either the institutionalized system of political administration or the people controlling such a system. See *politics.*

group   Any aggregate of units; in sociology, usually applied to sets of two or more people who are interacting.

horizontal mobility   Geographical movement or job alteration that does not involve a change in *status;* thus distinguished from *vertical mobility.*

human ecology   The systematic study of the various factors involved in the relationships between humans and their physical surroundings.

humanism   Belief that all humans have potential worth and should have the opportunity to develop to the greatest extent possible consistent with the development of others.

humanistic sociology   Sociology that plays an active part in helping to develop society so that all humans will have maximum opportunity to develop their potential to the greatest extent possible consistent with the development of others.

ideal type   A hypothetical conception of a phenomenon that, for the purpose of providing a standard for the measurement of other phenomena, stresses the phenomenon's most characteristic features.

ideational   A term used by P. Sorokin to denote a sociocultural system wherein spiritual concerns are particularly emphasized. See *sensate.*

ideology The philosophic underpinnings of a *social movement.*

incest Sexual relations forbidden to those defined as too closely related.

indeterminism The philosophic position that some phenomena are not the result of antecedent factors; when applied to human behavior, often termed "free will."

indigenous Native to an area.

individualism The philosophic position that each individual is an independent entity who should be responsible for his or her own welfare and should not be hampered by others.

in-group See *we-group.*

instinct A biologically inherited predisposition to react to particular stimuli in a particular way.

institution A standardized way of responding to basic needs; a long-term, organized group or procedure.

institutionalization The process whereby human groups and procedures are organized, systematized, and stabilized.

instrumental Stressing purely practical results; equivalent to "utilitarian."

intelligence A broad coping ability, including the capacity to adapt to new situations, to perceive and understand relationships, and to acquire and retain knowledge.

intelligence quotient See *I.Q.*

intergenerational mobility In a family, achievement by particular individuals or subgroups of a social *status* that is higher or lower than that associated with recent ancestors.

internalization Adoption by individuals of their society's *norm* system as their personal *value* orientation.

intragenerational mobility The process of a family going "from rags to riches," or vice versa, in a single generation.

invention A new arrangement of existing sociocultural elements.

I.Q. Initials commonly used to denote the so-called *intelligence quotient,* which is the numerical indicator of a person's supposed mental age (derived from a *standardized* test) divided by his chronological age and multiplied by 100 to produce a whole number.

isolate A child who has been reared under conditions where there was no, or little, exposure to human influences.

law A *norm* that is enforced by *government.*

Law of Karma The traditional Hindu belief that everything a person does, thinks, and believes is entered into a cosmic balance sheet that determines his ultimate fate.

law of three stages   In the works of sociological pioneer Auguste Comte, the supposed necessity for intellectual disciplines to progress through three developmental periods.

learning theory   Any attempt to state the general principles of how and under what conditions learning occurs.

leftwing (or left)   That group of people and doctrines—ranging from the *radical-liberal* position, through the *socialist*, to the most doctrinaire *communist*—opposed to the traditional distribution of power and privilege, especially with regard to control over the means of production.

legitimacy   The state or quality of conforming to generally accepted standards.

liberal   A person unhampered by arbitrary dogma or authority; a centrist political position that stresses individual liberty along with social responsibility, hence a position somewhat *leftwing* as well as somewhat *rightwing*.

looking-glass self   As suggested by Charles Horton Cooley, an individual's idea of what he or she is like, developed as a consequence of the apparent reactions of others to him.

lower class   In a *class* system of *social stratification*, the broad *social stratum*—ranging from irregular workers to *working class*—whose members have relatively little power, privilege, and prestige.

marriage   The institutional process wherein particular males and females ceremonially establish and pursue a relationship, usually intended to be long-term, appropriate for the satisfaction of sexual and affectional needs and, in general, for founding and sustaining a family.

mass society   A largescale, modern society characterized by the predominance of *secondary group* relationships, and by participants who are highly mobile, specialized in terms of *role* and *status*, and indifferent to traditional values—hence a society made up of units with so little attachment to one another that the whole is a ready victim for the demagogue who can play all against all.

matrilineal extended   See *extended family*.

mechanical solidarity   The sociocultural bond, based on kinship, religion, and communal ties, prevailing among the members of a traditional society.

middle America   In the American *social stratification* system, the broad *social stratum* consisting of members of the *working class* and the less privileged members of the *middle class*.

middle class   In a *class* system of *social stratification*, the broadest *social stratum*, characterized by members who have power, privilege, and prestige that ranges from very modest to very abundant.

milling   A situation in which a number of people or animals, engaging in random movement, excite one another increasingly.

mongolism   See *Down's syndrome.*

monogamy   A *marriage* form in which each adult is permitted only one mate at a time.

mores   Plural of *mos.*

mos   In a society, a *norm* that is thought to be essential to the group's welfare, hence a norm that is regarded as a "must behavior"; singular of *mores.*

nationalism   Belief on the part of citizens of a nation-state that it is especially deserving and therefore should be a totally independent, sovereign entity whose inhabitants should rightly accord it unswerving loyalty.

negative reinforcement   Any factor in a situation that discourages a given behavior.

negative sanction   See *sanction.*

noblesse oblige   The "obligation" of the privileged to be generous to the underprivileged; the special social responsibilities incumbent on those who have an abundance of power and privilege.

norm   In a society, the behavior expected of people in a particular situation; distinguished from "normal," which denotes the average of a range of behavior.

nouveau riche   "New rich," as distinguished from the established rich.

nuclear family   A married couple and their dependent, unmarried children, if any.

open class system   A *social stratification* system in which *vertical mobility* from one stratum to another is possible with relatively little difficulty. See *closed class system.*

organic solidarity   The sociocultural bond, based on a *division of labor* that makes people interdependent, prevailing among the members of a heterogeneous, *secular society.*

out-group   See *they-group.*

paramarriage   An informal *marriage;* a stable relationship maintained by a man and woman who live intimately together for a time and who consider themselves married for all practical purposes.

Parkinson's law   A satirical statement that in a typical formal social organization, work expands to fill available time; hence there is no realistic relationship between an amount of work to be done and the size of the staff needed to do it.

participant observation   Research in which the researcher becomes directly involved in the situation being studied.

participatory democracy   Continuous involvement of every adult member of a society in the decisions, processes, and workings of government.

patrilineal extended See *extended family*.

personality The more-or-less organized totality of personal traits peculiar to an individual.

Peter Principle A satirical statement that in a hierarchically organized work situation, employees tend to be promoted until they reach a point where they do not demonstrate competence; hence almost every job is handled by an incompetent person.

petite bourgeoisie That group of lower-middle-class white-collar workers, shopkeepers, farmers, and so on that supports the established distribution of power and privilege.

phenomenological sociology Sociological analysis and research that attempts to ascertain the complete meaning of social phenomena, in contrast to the superficial knowledge achieved when readily perceivable actions alone are studied—hence, that stresses intent aspects of human action.

politics The entire process of obtaining the power to set government policy, as distinguished from administering it; thus distinguished from *government*.

polyandry The form of *polygamy* that permits a woman to have two or more husbands at the same time.

polygamy Any form of marriage permitting a person to have more than one spouse at a time. See *polygyny* and *polyandry*.

polygyny The form of *polygamy* that permits a husband to have two or more wives at the same time.

positive reinforcement Any factor in a situation that encourages a given behavior.

positive sanction See *sanction*.

positivism Either (a) Auguste Comte's conclusion that an intellectual discipline contributes to knowledge only to the degree that it is scientific (i.e., is grounded on facts about which one can reasonably make positive statements), or (b) the contemporary philosophic view that the sole job of science is to state the nature of relationships between sets of phenomena.

power The control, based on force or *legitimacy*, that people or groups can exert on any aspect of their environment.

prejudice An opinion that is assumed irrespective of the nature of possibly relevant information.

prestige Public regard or honor.

primary group A relatively intimate group, such as a family, which typically has a basic influence on *personality* development.

principle of sociocultural compatibility A *concept* to denote the fact that since the constituent parts of a society are typically products of the same general social forces and cultural norms, they tend to be consistent with one another and thus to uphold complimentary beliefs and practices.

privilege   Advantage available only to selected persons or groups.

process   A series of steps or changes leading toward a particular end.

propaganda   Any technique to manipulate public opinion for selfish purposes.

public   The group of people before whom an issue is brought.

public opinion   The central tendency of the variety of opinions existing in a given *public* relative to a given issue.

radical   A social outlook that advocates fundamental re-understanding and re-ordering of social conditions; distinguished from *extremism* by its emphasis on rational processes over emotionalism.

radical-liberal   A moderate *leftwing* political position that blends democratic *socialism* with the individual freedom stressed by the classic *liberal* position.

radical libertarianism   A far *rightwing* political position that asserts that a government's only proper role, if any, is to protect the freedom of individuals to own and control as much private property as they can rightfully obtain; often called "social Darwinism."

reference group   Sets of persons used negatively or positively by individuals as points of reference for evaluating important aspects of life.

reflexive sociology   Commitment to the idea that sociology is properly a liberating discipline that ideally embodies both a critical analysis of society and an obligation to act on the basis of the results of the analysis.

reform movement   A *social movement* that aims to change aspects of a system with methods generally accepted by system participants.

reincarnation   Transmigration of souls (for example, a spiritual movement) among bodily hosts.

reinforcement   See *positive reinforcement* and *negative reinforcement.*

relative deprivation   In an individual, a feeling of being maltreated based on the assumed better condition of others perceived as no more deserving.

religion   Doctrines and practices associated with belief in, and attempts to relate favorably to, ultimate spiritual forces or transcendental values.

revolutionary movement   A *social movement* with a goal of making—by any means necessary, including violence—a complete and swift change in a total social system or in some major part of such a system.

rightwing (or right)   That group of people and doctrines—ranging from moderate *conservative,* through the *fascist* position, to *radical libertarianism*—who favor the traditional distribution of power and privilege and the private ownership and control of property, including the means of production.

rising expectations   The quickened hopes for further betterment that grip the downtrodden once their living conditions are somewhat improved.

role   The constellation of behaviors generally expected of individuals in particular social situations.

sanction   A reward or penalty for approved or disapproved behavior, rewards often being termed "positive sanctions" and penalties "negative sanctions."

science   A relatively standardized, systematic procedure for developing reliable, verifiable knowledge about phenomena.

secondary group   A human grouping whose members have no more than a formal, limited relationship with one another, and who therefore tend to use one another as means rather than as ends.

secular   Worldly, hence nonspiritual or nonreligious; of or pertaining to that which is purely rational or utilitarian.

secular society   A society dominated by *secular* values; similar to *associational society*.

self   An individual's awareness of, and attitudes toward, his or her own psychic and biologic person.

self-fulfilling prophecy   A prediction based on false premises but that, through acceptance by a number of people, evokes behavior from them such that the prediction comes true.

sensate   Term used by P. Sorokin to denote a sociocultural system wherein material concerns are particularly emphasized. See *ideational*.

sib   See *clan*.

social (and **social interaction**)   Pertaining to relationships among organisms; among humans, having to do with mutual awareness and expectations and the effect each person has upon others.

social contagion   Collective excitement reaching an almost unbearable state.

social control   Any process directing the actions of individuals or groups.

social Darwinism   See *radical libertarianism*.

social differentiation   Processes whereby people and groups acquire characteristics that set them off from one another.

social interaction   See *social*.

socialism   A theory or system of social organization which advocates the vesting of the ownership and control of the means of production, capital, land, etc., in the community as a whole.

socialist   A *leftwing* political position that favors public ownership and control of the means of production, particularly the more pervasive aspects of the economy such as heavy industry, transportation, and banking.

socialization The entire process whereby people are taught to behave in particular ways.

social movement A collective attempt to establish new sociocultural forms.

social order See *social organization.*

social organization (and **social order; social system**) The totality of relationships prevailing among the elements of a group, including the array of roles, statuses, norms, values, and subgroups.

social process Any type of social interaction, such as *accommodation, assimilation, conflict, cooperation,* or *competition.*

social stratification The process whereby a society is divided into a broad spectrum of *status groups* and/or social strata (see *social stratum).*

social stratum In a *social stratification* system, one of the widely inclusive groups—termed *class, caste,* or *estate*—each of which is made up of people of both sexes and all ages who have roughly similar access to power and privilege.

social structure An arrangement of group or individual statuses.

social system See *social organization.*

society Either (a) the totality of human beings, together with all the social relationships and values existing among them, or (b) any one of a number of relatively independent, self-perpetuating human groups, each of which has its own territory and unique *culture.*

sociocultural A coined word that combines the two terms *society* and *culture* so that attention is called to the inseparability of these two critical aspects of human existence.

sociology The academic discipline concerned with the systematic study of human social relationships in general.

standardized test A test that has been applied in a sufficient number of cases under controlled conditions to build up a set of data which can act as a basis for legitimate comparison.

status The relevant rank of a person in a group, such rank being either ascribed (assigned, frequently at birth, regardless of individual inclination) or achieved (open to persons who meet the requirements).

status group In the sociology of Max Weber particularly, a set of people who recognize each other as social equals and interact with one another regularly; thus distinguished from *social stratum.*

statutory law *Law* that is formally enacted by *government;* thus distinguished from *common law.*

stereotype A group-shared idea about the supposed basic nature of all members of a particular category of persons, with the most important of such ideas typically being emotion-charged negative evaluations.

structural-functionalism   A type of social analysis, often termed simply "functional," that stresses the contributions, negative or positive, that social entities make to the system to which they belong.

subculture   The distinctive values and ways characteristic of the members of a subgroup in a society.

symbolic interaction   The uniquely human mode of influencing others by means of conventionalized signs that become organized into languages.

system   Any set of interrelated elements that may be regarded as a single entity.

taking the role of the generalized other   In G. H. Mead's account of self-development, the process whereby mature people mentally assume the *role* of numerous others and, looking back on their own person, make judgments about that person from a variety of standpoints.

taking the role of the other   As described by G. H. Mead, the process whereby an individual develops a *self* by assuming another's *role* and, assuming the other's *values* as he understands them, looks "back" on his or her own person and comes to negative or positive conclusions about it.

talent   The ability to do something particularly well.

technicway   A *folkway* that arises out of technological innovation.

they-group   All persons who are not members of a group designated when the term *we-group* is used; equivalent to "out-group."

Thomas theorem   A statement by W. I. Thomas to the effect, "If men define situations as real, they are real in their consequences."

trait   See *culture trait.*

universal culture pattern   Elements of culture, such as family life, that are found in all known human societies.

unobtrusive measurement   Social and psychological research methods that retain as much as possible of the precision of traditional methods, yet avoid the contaminating effects produced when study subjects know they are objects of attention, hence methods other than interviews and questionnaires, but methods that do not ignore the moral obligation not to manipulate people or invade their privacy.

upper class   In a *class* system of *social stratification*, the relatively small *social stratum* whose members have extensive amounts of power, privilege, and prestige.

utilitarian   See *instrumental.*

value   The special positive or negative meaning of any phenomenon to the members of a group.

variable   In scientific study, any factor that may influence the results of research.

vertical mobility   An individual's or group's more-or-less permanent alteration of *status;* thus distinguished from *horizontal mobility.*

WASP   White, Anglo-Saxon Protestant.

we-group   Any group designated when a person uses the pronoun "we"; equivalent to "in-group."

working class   In a *class* system of *social stratification,* a *social stratum* whose wage-earning members regularly engage in manual occupations.

Index

Academic freedom, 205–213
Accommodation, interaction and, 98
Accretionary change theory, 299–300
Achieved statuses, 129–130
Acting crowds, 292–293
Adam, Heribert, 125
Agitation, 295–296
Agnew, Spiro, 228
Air pollution, 275
American Civil Liberties Union, 240
American economic system, 244–256; growth of business, 244–245; Pentagon and, 245–246; socialist planning in, 246–247; subsidies in, 252–253; tax subsidies in, 253
American empire, 232–233
American Revolution, 160–161, 162
American Sociological Association, 73
Anarchists, 229–230
Anthropology: culture and, 104; sociology and, 65, 66–67
Asceticism, Protestant ethic and, 155
Ascribed statuses, 129–131
Assimilation, interaction and, 98
Associational society, 100; defined, 311
Associations, institutions and, 172–173
Atomic bomb, 232–233
Attitudes, defined, 60
Authority, governmental power, legitimacy and, 223–225

Banfield, Edward, 156, 250–251
Baxter, Richard, 196
Behavior: collective, 289–298; learning theory, 42–44; norms and, 107; religious beliefs and, 198–201; roles and, 131–132; values

and, 106–107. *See also* Collective behavior
Behaviorism: dangers in, 82–83; defined, 82
Bell, Wendell, 162
Benda, Clemens, 37
Bendix, Reinhard, 4
Bensman, Joseph, 108
Berger, Peter, 50, 112
Bernard, Jessie, 205
Bernard, L.L., 198
Biesanz, John, 140
Bill of Rights, 239–240, 241
Biological relationships, intelligence and, 18–19
Biology: psychology and, 68; sociology and, 12–14
Blacks: caste stratification and, 148–150; social differentiation and, 124–128; vertical mobility and, 157–160
Black–white caste stratification in United States, 148–150
Blau, Peter, 158–159
Blumer, Herbert, 290
Bolton, Charles, 12
Bosch, Juan, 246
Boulding, Kenneth, 64–65
Bredemeier, Harry, 42
Brinton, Crane, 65–66, 299
Britain, drug addiction in, 238–239
Bronfenbrenner, Urie, 127
Brookings Institution, 208
Bureaucracy: institutionalization and, 177–178; organization and, 177; as social organization, 132–133; systematization and, 177
Bureaucrats, 100

Calderone, Mary, 204
Calvinism, 196–197
Cambridge Institute, 251

Capitalism: American, 244–254; American empire, 232–233; religion and development of, 195–197

Caste stratification, 134–136; black–white, 148–150; in United States, 148–150

Censorship, United States government and, 240–242

Central Intelligence Agency, 243

Change. *See* Sociocultural change

Chinoy, Ely, 100

Chomsky, Noam, 82

Christianity: capitalism and, 195–197; ecology and, 266–267, 269

CIA, 243

Civil liberties, 240–243; government interference with, 241. *See also* Bill of Rights

Clans, 202

Clark, Ramsey, 236–237

Class stratification, 137–140

Classes: in United States, 151–156. *See also* Lower classes, Middle classes, Upper classes

Classless society, social stratification and, 140–141

Closed class system, 139

Club of Rome, 276

Coleman, James S., 209–210

Coleman report, 209–210

Collective behavior, 289–298; elementary, 290–294; forms of, 290; importance of, 298; institutional behavior and, 290; milling and, 291; social movements, 295–298. *See also* Behavior

Collective excitement, milling and, 291

Colleges. *See* Universities

Commager, Henry Steele, 162, 235, 236

Committee for Economic Development, 208

Committee on Mental Retardation, 252

Commoner, Barry, 270, 273–274, 275

Communal societies, 100

Communism, 229; American anxiety over, 234–235; class stratification and, 138–139; classless society and, 140–141. *See also* Marxism

Communities, sociological concept of, 98–100

Competition, interaction and, 98

Comte, Auguste, 61–64

Conflict, interaction and, 98

Conflict school in social science, 73

Consciousness of kind, 110

Consensus, power and, 223

Conservatives, 226–227

Constitutional government, ideal vs. real, 239–240

Cooley, Charles Horton, 13, 45–46, 102

Cooperation, interaction and, 98

Counterrevolution: order and, 114–115; sociology and, 113–115

Court system, role of, 238–239

Crescive institutions, defined, 172

Cultural order, 104–112

Cultural relativism, 104–105

Cultural values. *See* Values

Culture: defined, 104; freedom and, 112–113; institutions and, 171; relative nature of, 105; sacred and secular, 199; sociology and, 104; values and, 105–107

Culture base, 106

Culture complexes, 106

Culture of poverty, 151, 159–160. *See also* Vertical mobility

Culture patterns, 106

Culture traits, 106

Cuzzort, R.P., 82

Cyclical change theory, 299, 300–301

Dahl, Robert, 222

Davis, Angela, 238, 242

Davis, Kingsley, 10

de Chardin, Teilhard, 74–75

de Tocqueville, Alexis, 91, 161

Declaration of Independence, 161

Deficit spending: Keynesian economics and, 247, 248; post-

Keynesian economics and, 247–248

Democracy, education and, 207

Demographers, 265–266

Deschooled society, 210–213; defined, 211

Determinism: and humanism, 47–51; sociological commitment to, 47

Deviant behavior: genesis of, 42–44; reactions to, 44–45

Differential casualty rates, social differentiation and, 124–125

Disorder, governmental legitimacy and, 224–225

District of Columbia Omnibus Crime Bill, 242

Domhoff, G. William, 222

Down's syndrome. See Mongolism

Duncan, O.D., 158–159

Ecocide, 266

Ecology: diseases and, 274; economic implications of, 267–269; future, 280–284; Judeo-Christian tradition and, 266–267; political implications of, 267–269; population problem and, 270–273; private enterprise and, 268–269; radicalism of modern, 266–269. See also Human ecology

Economic growth: critics of zero, 278–279; limits of, 276–278

Economic power. See Political–economic power

Economics: American system, 244–245; free enterprise, 244–247; growth limits, 276–278; institutionalized aspects of, 178; Keynesian, 247–250; sociology and, 64–65; western, 244–254, 255, 256. See also Keynesian economics

Education: as big business, 208; busing and, 209–210; democracy and, 207; deschooled society, 210–212; ferment in, 208–209; function of, 205–206; industrialization of, 208; new industrial state and, 208; social problem cures and, 209; sociocultural system and, 205–206, 212

Ehrlich, Paul, 270–273

Elementary collective behavior, 290–295; genesis of, 290–292

Elementary collective groups, types of, 292–294

Élite-dominance theorists, political–economic power and, 222–223

Élites: civil liberties and, 241–242; political–economic power and, 230–231. See also Political–economic élites

Empiricism, 90–91

Enacted institutions, defined, 172

Endogamy, 202

Ertl, John, 27

Ervin, Sam J., Jr., 243

Esprit de corps, 295, 296–297; defined, 314

Establishment sociologists, 73–74

Estate stratification, 136–137

Ethnic, defined, 314

Ethnocentrism, 110–111; defined, 315

Ethnomethodology, 86

Eutrophication, 270

Evolutionist change theory, 299

Exogamy, 202

Exploitation, American system and, 255–256; Judeo-Christian tradition and, 266–267, 269

Expressive crowds, 292, 293

Expressive social movements, 298

Extended families, types of, 202

Extremism, 81–82

Falk, Richard, 270, 280–282, 283

Families: changes in, 203–205; defined, 314; marriage and, 202–203; types of, 202–205

Farm subsidies, 252

Fascism, 226–229; defined, 314; middle-class American, 227–228

Fashion movements, 298

Federal Bureau of Investigation, 243

Federal Communications Commission, 241

Feis, Herbert, 232–233
Feldman, Saul, 131
Feral children, 11–12
Fischer, John, 267–269
Folk societies, 99, 315
Folkways: institutions and, 172; as norms, 107; power of, 107
Food supply, growth limits and, 276–278
Formal social organization, defined, 315
Fox, George, 181–182
Free enterprise, 244–247, 255; vertical integration and, 246
Free market system, vertical integration and, 246
Freedom, sociocultural order and, 112–115
Freire, Paulo, 128
French Revolution, 161
Friedrichs, Robert, 49–50, 59, 71, 72–73
Functional prerequisites of societies, basic list of, 178
Functionalist change theory, 299, 300
Functionalists, 70–71; and status quo, 73–74

Galbraith, John Kenneth, 246
Gandhi, Indira, 279
Gemeinschaft groups, 102–103
General Motors, 244
General social movements, defined, 315. See also Social movements
Genetic interpretation of I.Q., 25–29
Gerth, Hans, 66
Gesellschaft groups, 102–103
Giddings, F.H., 12, 69
Ginsberg, Morris, 100–101
Glass, John, 47, 51
Global-cooperative-sharing, 283–284
Gouldner, Alvin, 72
Government: court system and, 238–239; law and order and, 236–238; power, legitimacy and, 223–225; United States, 239–

240. See also Constitutional government
Governmental legitimacy: disorder and, 224–225; effectiveness and, 224; governmental power and, 223–225; values and, 224
Governmental power, legitimacy and, 223–225
Graham, Billy, 200
Greeley, Andrew, 197
Green, Philip, 233
Groups: defined, 315; elementary collective, 292–294; individuals and, 9–29; primary and secondary, 102–103; sociological concept of, 98–100
Growth. See Economic growth

Hard work, Protestant ethic and, 155
Hartnett, Rodney, 206
Health care, institutionalized aspects of, 178–180
Heber, Rick, 17–18
Heilbroner, Robert, 245
Hertzler, J.O., 157
Hierarchy, social stratification and, 160–162
Hilgard, E.R., 19
Hinduism, caste system of, 135–136
Hiroshima, 232–233
History: narrative, 65; new, 65–66; sociology and, 65–66
Hollingsworth, Leta, 22–23
Holt, John, 211, 212
Homosexuality, 41, 44
Horizontal mobility, defined, 157, 315
Horowitz, Irving Louis, 72
Human ecology: concerns of, 265; defined, 315; ecocide and, 266. See also Ecology
Human welfare: behaviorism and, 82–83; scientific sociology and, 81–84
Humanism, 3–5; defined, 315; determinism and, 47–51; social stratification and, 163–165; sociology and, 74–76, 115

Humanistic sociology, 3–5, 74–76; defined, 315, task of, 115
Humanistic values, institutionalization and, 185–186
Hunter, Floyd, 222
Hutchins, Robert, 212
Huxley, Aldous, 82

Ideational systems, 301, 315
Ideology, social movements and, 297–298
Illich, Ivan, 211, 212
Income: distribution of, 250–254; education and, 159; relative deprivation and, 250–251; rising expectations and, 250–251
Indeterminism, 47
India, caste system in, 135–136
Individualism: group and, 9–29; Protestant ethic and, 154–155
Industrial production, growth limits and, 276–278
Industrial Revolution, 267
Industrial societies, vertical mobility in, 158
Industrialization of education, 208–209
Inflation: control, 248–249; Keynesian economics and, 247–248
In-groups, 102; institutionalization and, 182
Institutional behavior, collective behavior and, 290
Institutionalization, 171–186; bureaucracy and, 177–178; defined, 173; humanistic values and, 185–186; suggested view of, 173–177
Institutionalization process, 181–183
Institutions: associations and, 172–173; characteristics of, 173; crescive, 171–172; defined, 171; enacted, 171–172; interrelationship between, 191–192; MacIver's approach, 172–173; marriage and family, 201–205; processes and, 172; religion as, 192–201; satirizing, 183–185; Sumner's approach to, 171–172
Intelligence, 14–18; genetic view, 14–15; learned aspects of, 17; twin studies, 18–19
Intelligence quotient. See I.Q.
Interaction, Gemeinschaft and Gesellschaft, 102–103
Intergenerational mobility, defined, 157
Inventions, sociocultural change and, 106
I.Q.: genetic interpretation of, 25–29; environment and, 15–18
I.Q. tests, social background and, 15–16
Isolate, 10–11

Jackson, Elton, 89–90
Jacobs, Paul, 4
Jails, American, 239
Jefferson, Thomas, 207, 241
Jencks, Christopher, 159
Jensen, Arthur, 14, 25–29, 68
Jensen–Shockley thesis, 25
Jesus movement, 200
Judeo-Christian tradition, ecology and, 266–267, 269

Keller, Helen, 10–11
Keniston, Kenneth, 250
Kenyon, Dorothy, 164
Key, V.O., 222
Keynes, John Maynard, 247
Keynesian economics, 247–250, deficit spending and, 247–248; inflation and, 247–248; unemployment and, 247–248
Klineberg, Otto, 17
Knoblock, Hilda, 127–128
Kornhauser, William, 223
Kunstler, William, 237, 289
Kurtz, Paul, 3

Laird, Melvin, 233
Landau, Saul, 66
Law and order, 236–238
Law of Karma, 135–136
Law of Three Stages, 62–64
Laws: defined, 109; equal protection and, 236; as norms, 107,

109–110; victimless crimes and, 238–239

Learning, talent and, 19–25

Learning process, culture and, 105

Learning theory, deviance and conformity, 42–44

Leftist, defined, 225

Legitimacy: disorder and, 224–225; effectiveness and, 224; governmental power and, 223–225; values and, 224

Lens, Sidney, 232

Lenski, Gerhard, 122

Liberals, 225–226

Life and death, social differentiation and, 124–128

Lipset, S.M., 163–164

Love, as basis of marriage, 202–203

Lowenstein, Karl, 222

Lower classes: defined, 151; income, 251–252; jails and prisons and, 239; religion and, 194; in United States, 151–152

Lundberg, George, 70

Lynd, Robert S., 71–72

MacIver, Robert, 172–173, 196, 224

Magna Carta, 160

Malnutrition: learning and, 252; social differentiation and, 125–128

Malthus, Thomas, 273

Marcuse, Herbert, 247

Marriage: foundations of, 202–203; paramarriage and, 204–205; romantic love and, 202–203; types of, 201–202

Marsh, Alan, 27

Marx, Karl, 222

Marxian change theory, 299, 300

Marxism: class stratification and, 138–139; classless society, 140–141

Maslow, Abraham, 68, 82, 113

Mass, as elementary grouping, 293–294

Mass society, 222–223, 317

Matrilineal extended families, 202

McReynolds, David, 197

Mead, George Herbert, 45, 46–47

Mead, Margaret, 43, 44

Mechanical solidarity, 102, 317

Melman, Seymour, 245–246

Mercer, Jane R., 15–16

Merton, Robert K.,38, 84

Michels, Robert, 182, 222, 224

Middle classes: fascism and, 227–228; income, 251–252; lower, 152–154; privileged, 154–155; religion, 194; in United States, 152–155; vertical mobility and, 157–158

Miles, Michael W., 206–207, 208

Mill, John Stuart, 20–21, 64

Miller, S.M., 151–152

Milling, collective behavior and, 291

Mills, C. Wright, 72, 122–123, 222

Mobility, kinds of, 157. See also Vertical mobility

Mongolism, society and, 37–40

Monogamy, 201

Monopoly, in United States, 244–245

Moore, Barrington, Jr., 204–205

Mores, as norms, 107, 108–109

Mormons, 193

Murad, Anatol, 248

Murphy, Gardner, 68

Myrdal, Gunnar, 85

Nader, Ralph, 177, 186

Nagasaki, 232–233

National Security, 233–236

Nationalism, 110, 234

Natural resources, growth limits and, 276–278

Negative reinforcement, 22; defined, 318

Negroes. See Blacks

Neilands, J.B., 270

News management, United States government's attempts at, 243

Nixon, Richard, 150, 181, 182, 228, 233, 247; and civil liberties, 241–242

No-knock entry, 242

Normative systems, theories, 107–108

Norms: behavior and, 107; kinds of, 107–110
Nuclear families, 202

Objectivity: biases and, 84–86; humanistic sociology and, 86; problems of, 84–87; scientific method and, 84–87; in sociology, 84–87
Ogburn, W.F., 12
Order: conflict theorists and, 107–108; functional theorists and, 107–108; importance of, 114–115; and law, 236–238; legitimacy and, 223–225
Organic solidarity, 102
Organization: bureaucracy and, 177; humanistic values and, 185–186; induced change and, 302–304; institutions and, 173–177
Orwell, George, 82
Out-groups, 102; institutionalization and, 182–183

Palmer, R.R., 161–162
Paramarriages, society and, 204
Park, Robert E., 13
Parker, Richard, 251–252
Parkinson, C. Northcote, 183–184, 185
Parkinson's Law, 183
Parsons, Talcott, 65
Participant observation, defined, 86
Participatory democracy, 186
Pasamanick, Benjamin, 127–128
Patrilineal extended families, 202
Peace, governments and, 232
Pentagon, business community and, 245–246
Pentagon papers, 225, 241–242
Personality, self and, 45
Personality development: feral children and, 11–12; group and, 9–29; individual and, 9–29; intelligence and, 14–29; isolate and, 10–11; sociology, biology and, 12–14; talent and, 19–25; twins and, 18–19

Peter, Laurence, 183, 184–185
Peter Principle, 184–185
Petite bourgeoisie, 227
Pfaff, William, 242
Phenomenological sociology, defined, 86
Philosophy, ecology and, 269
Platt, John, 49
Pluralist theorists, political–economic power and, 222–224
Police state, United States and, 241–243
Political–economic élites, 230–239
Political–economic power: Elite-dominance theorists, 222–223; legitimacy and, 223–225; pluralist theorists, 222; theories of, 222–223
Political–economic systems, spectrum of, 225–230
Political science, sociology and, 64–65
Pollution, growth limits and, 276–278
Polyandry, 202
Polygyny, 201–202
Population: control, involuntary, 273; ecological problems and, 268, 270–273; economic growth limit and, 276–278; effects of growth, 271
Populism, 228
Porter, Sylvia, 253–254
Positive reinforcement, 22; defined, 319
Power, social differentiation and, 122–124. See also Governmental power, Political–economic power
Prejudice, 111–112
Prestige, social differentiation and, 122–124
Preventive detention, 238, 242
Primary groups, 102–103; ideal type, 103
Prisons, American, 239
Private enterprise, profit, ecology and, 276
Private property, leftist and rightist attitude toward, 225

Privilege, social differentiation and, 122–124

Processes, MacIver's view, 172–173

Profits, government spending and, 248

Progressive income tax, 253–254

Property, Protestant ethic and, 155

Protestant ethic, 154–155, 196–197

Protestantism, 161

Psychology: biology and, 68; social behavior and, 68; sociology and, 67–69

Public, as elementary grouping, 294

Quakerism, 181–183

Radical–liberals, 229

Reference groups, 102–103

Reflexive sociology, defined, 86

Reform movements, 295

Reagan, Ronald, 252

Relative deprivation, concept of, 250–251

Religion, 192–201; behavior and, 198–200; decline of, 197–200; environment and, 201, 266–269; movements, 298; youth movement and, 199–200

Repression, subculture and, 105

Reston, James, 164

Retreatist social movements, 295

Reuss, Henry S., 254

Revolution, sociology and, 112–113

Revolutionary movements, 295

Riessman, Frank, 151–152

Rightist, defined, 225

Rioting, 292–293

Rising expectations, concept of, 250–251

Roles, status and, 131–132

Roman Catholicism, 161, 192, 193–194

Rose, Arnold, 223

Roszak, Theodore, 244

Roy, Jules, 297

Rustin, Bayard, 150

Sanctions, 22

Saposs, David, 227

Schneider, Michael, 252

Schools: in crisis, 209–210; de-schooled society and, 210–212; inner city, 209; prisonization of, 212

Schrag, Peter, 161

Scientific method: controlling variables, 88–91; empiricism and, 90–91; sociology and, 87–88; usefulness of, 83, 84. See also Scientific sociology

Scientific sociology: controlling variables in, 88–91; objectivity in, 84–87

Secondary groups, 102–103; relationships in, 103

Secular society, 100

Segal, Ronald, 101

Self: defined, 45; growth of, 45–47

Self-fulfilling prophecy, 38–40

Sensate systems, 301, 321

Sex education, 40–41

Sexual orientation, sociological interpretation of, 40–42

Sheriff, Muzafer, 68

Shockley, William, 14–15, 25

Sibley, Eldridge, 69–70, 81–82

Simpson, George, 65, 72

Simultaneous inventions, 106

Sjoberg, Gideon, 157

Skeels, Harold, 17

Skinner, B. F., 42, 82

Skodak, Marie, 17

Social contagion, collective behavior and, 291–292

Social control, defined, 103

Social differentiation, 121–141; defined, 121; dimensions of, 122–124; life and death aspects of, 124–128; malnutrition and, 125–127; status and, 128–129

Social disorganization, theory of, 300

Social interaction, 61; classification of types, 98; defined, 97–98

Social movements, 295–298; collective behavior and, 290; esprit de corps and, 295, 296–297; ideology and, 295, 297–298; types of, 295

Social order, 97–103; communities and, 98–100; groups and, 98–100; ideal type societies and, 101–102; just and unjust societies and, 100–101; primary and secondary groups and, 102–103; social interaction and, 97–98; society and, 98–100

Social organizations: change and challenges and, 240. See also Social order

Social phenomena, approaches to, 86–87

Social problems, educational cures of, 209

Social processes, interaction and, 98

Social relationships, sociology and, 60–61. See also Social interaction

Social science, two schools in, 73–74

Social status, social stratification and, 133–134

Social stratification, 133–141; caste and, 134–136; challenges to, 160–163; class system of, 137–140; classless society and, 140–141; estate system of, 136–137; hierarchical principle in, 160; humanism and, 163–165; lower classes, 151–152; major trends in, 160–163; middle classes, 152–155; in United States, 147–165; United States' caste system, 148–150; upper classes, 155–156

Social systems, bureaucracy as, 132–133. See also Social order

Social work, sociology and, 69

Socialists, 229

Socialization, in societies, 178

Societies: associational, 100; communal, 100; culture and, 9; folk, 99; functional prerequisites of, 178; ideal type, 101–102; just, 100–101; mass, 222–223; paramarriage and, 204; personality and, 9; primary groups in, 102–

103; religion and, 195–197; secondary groups in, 102–103; secular, 100; sociological concept of, 99; unjust, 100–101; vertical mobility and, 157

Sociocultural anthropology, defined, 66–67

Sociocultural change, 299–307; induced, 301–307; inventions and, 106; organization and, 302–304; theories of, 299–301

Sociocultural compatibility, 191–192; education and, 205; religion and, 192–201

Sociocultural order: basic concepts, 97–115; collective behavior and, 290; freedom and, 112–115

Sociology: anthropology and, 65, 66–67; biology and, 12–14; conservatism of, 114–115; counterrevolution and, 113–115; culture and, 104; defined, 59–61; economics and, 64–65; experimental psychology and, 68–69; extremism in, 81–82; historical development of, 61–64; human ecology and, 265; humanistic, 3–5, 74–76; mongolism and, 37–40; political science and, 64–65; psychology and, 67–69; as pure science, 69–70; revolution and, 112–113; scientific method in, 81–88; social factors and, 9; social work and, 69; structural functional, 70–71; talent and, 19–25; terms in, 97; value-free position, 70–74. See also Scientific sociology

Sorokin, Pitirim, 300–301

Specific social movements, 295

Spencer, Herbert, 64

Stabilization, institutions and, 173–177

Stanford–Binet I.Q. test, 16, 17

Statuses: achieved, 129–130; ascribed, 129–131; basic forms of, 129–113; social differentiation and, 128–129

Stereotypes, 111–112

Structural–functionalists, 70–71

Subculture, repression and, 105

Subsidies, in American tax system, 252–253

Sumner, William Graham, 64, 107, 171–172

Supernaturalism, decline of, 197–201

Symbolic interactionism, defined, 87

Systematization: bureaucracy and, 177; humanistic values and, 185–186; institutions and, 173–177

Talent, sociological interpretation of, 19–25

Tarter, Donald E., 82–83

Tax system, subsidies, 252–253

Teachers, militancy of, 208–209

Technicways: defined, 109, as norms, 107

Technology, ecology and, 268–269, 273–282

Testing, as culture-loaded idea, 27

They groups, 102

Thomas, W. I., 38

Thomas theorem, 38

Townsend, Robert, 185

Toynbee, Arnold, 300–301

Turkel, Henry, 39

Twins, I.Q. tests and, 18–19

Unemployment, Keynesian economics and, 247–248

United Nations Conference on the Human Environment, 282

United States: censorship in, 241–242; civil liberties in, 240–243; classes in, 151–156; communism and, 234–236; constitutional government in, 239–244; distribution of income in, 254; economic system, 244–254; élite dominance in, 230; social stratification in, 147–165; vertical mobility in, 157–160

United States Defense Department, 243

Universities: faculties and, 207–209; control of, 206–207; structure of, 206–207

University of Michigan Survey Research Center, 90

Unobtrusive measures, defined, 87

Upper classes, 155–156

Vallieres, Pierre, 241

Value-free sociology, 71–74

Values: behavior and, 106; consciousness of kind and, 110; culture and, 105–106; defined, 106; ethnocentrism and, 110–111; norms and, 107

Variables, controlling, 88–90

Veblen, Thorstein, 91

Vertical integration, free market system and, 246

Vertical mobility, 134; blacks and, 159–160; education and, 159; income and, 159; in industrial societies, 158; in United States, 157–160

Viereck, Peter, 231

Wallace, George, 228

Wallick, Henry, 279

Ward, Lester Frank, 64

Washington Post, 243

Wasps, 324

Water pollution, 274–275

Watergate, 225

We groups, 102

Weber, Max, 101–102, 138–139, 195–196

Weiner, Norbert, 21–22

Welfare, 252, 253

Wheeler, Harvey, 228, 247

White, Lynn, Jr., 269, 270

Whitman, Walt, 241

Williams, W.A., 232

Working classes, in United States, 151–152; vertical mobility and, 157–158

Youth movement, religion and, 199–201

Zero Population Growth, 268